Teaching Folklore

Revised Edition

edited by

Bruce Jackson

With Contributions by

Bruce A. Beatie, Robert H. Byington, Larry Danielson
Linda Dégh, Lydia Fish, Robert A. Georges, Thomas A. Green
Edward D. Ives, Bruce Jackson, W. F. H. Nicolaisen
W. Edson Richmond, Neil V. Rosenberg, Ellen J. Stekert
Zora Devrnja Zimmerman

A Publication of the American Folklore Society

Documentary Research, Inc.
Buffalo, New York

The 1986 printing of *Teaching Folklore* included corrections of a number of minor errors in the first printing; otherwise the contents of the two were identical. For this edition, most lists of works cited were combined into a single list at the end of the volume (lists that were part of course descriptions were not separated from the essays) and there was a small amount of editorial tinkering with some of the essays. The final essay in this edition of *Teaching Folklore* is published here for the first time.

This edition was set with *WordPerfect* 5.0 using Bitstream Charter type for the text and Broadway for the covers and title page. Master sheets were printed on a Hewlett-Packard LaserJet II.

Documentary Research, Inc.
96 Rumsey Road
Buffalo, New York 14209

All editor's and contributors' royalties from sales of *Teaching Folklore* will be donated to the American Folklore Society.

ISBN 0-939731-02-9

89 90 9 8 7 6 5 4 3

Contents

Acknowledgements

I would like to thank—

—the contributors, for baring for their colleagues matters most often kept singularly personal;

—Chris LaLonde for typing to disc most of the copy;

—Diane Christian, Kim Turnage, and Elizabeth Willis for giving the manuscript a careful reading before the last printout;

—Marta Weigle, former editor of the *Publications of the American Folklore Society*, for encouraging this experiment in micropublishing;

—Edson Richmond, who nearly twenty-five years ago helped me discover that the academic side of folklore was not without interest

—and most of all Ben Botkin, for having been a friend, for refusing to deal with folklore as if it were separable from the rest of life, for having been the best folklore teacher I ever knew.

Introduction:
One More Traditional Art

Teaching can be a risky business. There are a few bores who without interruption or a glance up at the room read superannuated lectures, there are others who seem capable of dealing with students only when they're on autopilot, but what goes on in most classrooms is a steady dynamic. Course numbers and titles may remain the same term after term, but good teachers change what they say and how they say it, they change the items or categories of things that are to be uttered and moved beyond and those that are to be discussed and dwelt upon, they reorder the segments and they rebuild the structures.

The differences occur for the same kinds of reasons differences occur in performance of oral epics or political speeches or church sermons. No group of students has the same personality or information as any other group of students. The teacher is never the same because each time he or she has the additional experience of what transpired last term and new things learned since last term and old things reevaluated since last term. Like other kinds of oral performers, teachers change what they do so they can incorporate what they know now and so they can keep the materials interesting to themselves. The acoustics and lighting of the room affect the kind of teaching that goes on, the weather affects it, the politics of the world beyond the classroom affects it. For nearly all teachers there is a continual uncertainty of outcome: some classes go wonderfully well; some classes, managed in what appears to be exactly the same way, go horridly. This uncertainty is at once the cause of teacherly terror and elation, a fact their graduate students do not learn until they find themselves managing the intellectual progress of what always begins as a roomful of mutually judgmental strangers.

Few graduate programs in the humanities teach the craft and art of teaching. Most concentrate on disciplinary substance and research methodology. The idea seems to be that if one knows how to ferret out and organize inchoate bits of information and if one knows the major texts, then one is suited to teach college or university students. Supporters of this sink-or-swim method of teacher preparation say it produces educators not locked into any mechanical (hence nearly obsolete) pedagogical model; critics say it results from a failure of imagination among those who direct graduate education. I have never seen any useful evidence on the matter one way or the other, but I do know that schools of education, where people ponder the process of teaching rather than the substance of it, have not yet been able to provide themselves or the rest of us the pedagogical millennium.

Most of us learn to teach not by taking a class in teaching or by reading a book on teaching, but by watching other teachers do it and inferring what seems to be going on; we utilize that information in real situations, and we modify the design on the basis of our own experience and need. We learn the craft of teaching exactly as other traditional craftspeople and artists learn their skills and arts. Many young teachers, who are still struggling to gain mastery of the material they profess, for several years teach the kinds of courses that seemed most useful for or pleasant to them in college and graduate school. Only gradually do they become comfortable enough with the conflation of techniques and styles to begin experimenting with their own designs.

Were teaching just a mechanical cranking out of stuff stored in the memory banks, a computer could do it as well as a person—and, for some courses, computers *do* it as well as persons. Folklore courses, humanities courses in general, however, do not seem subject to such electronic packaging. That is because humanities courses teach ideas, not items, and ideas are still best communicated by people talking to and with other people. Humanities courses that work well have a fine energy to them: we are all students in those rooms, whatever our titles and our nominal roles.

We often come to understand what works when we learn what doesn't work. An artist's preliminary sketches and early drafts can tell us more about the artistic process than the picture framed or the book printed. Sketches and drafts are personal things; few artists make them available to strangers; artists present to the world the products with which they are more or less satisfied, and it is only later, when some scholar gets to poking around, that we manage to learn how those products were achieved. For good teachers, any class is at once a draft and a product. It is a specific performance rendered for and with a specific audience, and it is a temporal conversation that will be modified before the next conversation begins. Elements of a class that work perfectly well in context may seem perfectly foolish out of context; gambits that are wonderfully instructive and stimulating one time might be useless and boring another time. Those of us who learn to teach by watching our teachers do not see the process that led to the class in its present form. We may infer the logic of the course as it is given now, but we do not know the more complex structure from which the present version of the course derives.

On several occasions in past years I have asked folklorist friends for their course syllabi; on more occasions, I had conversations with friends about texts and readings for various courses. I learned what my friends were doing and they learned what I was doing, but the conversations were, I think, only marginally useful. The limitation resulted from a kind of information seeking I had long before rejected as a research model: I was pursuing items and not seeking contexts. Items float in the world; they need the intelligence of contexts to provide the sense that makes them meaningful.

One theme was nearly a constant in those conversations, and it was iterated by younger and older folklorists alike: they all had the same curiosity I did about how other people's courses came to take the form they took, how the courses worked within the contexts in which they were given.

I suggested to Marta Weigle, then editor of the *Publications of the American Folklore Society*, a collection of essays in which working teachers discussed specific classes. Marta thought the publication would be useful, but she pointed out that the number of individuals concerned with teaching was so small it was unlikely the project would interest a commercial publisher. She was right, but I thought a simple publication format— printing from typed pages and an inexpensive binding—would make the project feasible. We could, after all, reach the likely readership easily through the American Folklore Society's publications, so we wouldn't have to commit funds to advertising, and the printing technology is such that we could begin with small press runs and reprint as the need arose. Even though the distribution would be small, the book had the promise of serving a real need. Marta authorized the project.

So I asked several colleagues if they would write brief articles describing a single recent class they had taught. The only requirement was that it be a class they enjoyed teaching. I asked them to locate the course in the curriculum, describe the students, detail what worked and what seemed problematic, discuss the actual teaching materials used and evaluate those materials. I asked contributors to provide course reading lists if such lists were given to students. (When these were included as part of the articles, I kept the authors' formats. I took the liberty of converting other references to a consistent style.)

The thirteen contributors to *Teaching Folklore* work in different parts of the country; they work in institutions of different sizes and personalities; their personal situations within those institutions vary. Seven received their doctorates in fields other than folklore, though several of those did extensive folklore graduate work within other departments (two, for example, took their degrees in comparative literature—Beatie at Harvard and Zimmerman at Buffalo; both did folklore-centered theses and both subsequently took part in NEH Summer Seminars for College Teachers in folklore). Two contributors—Dégh and Richmond—are from one university, but Richmond teaches his graduate seminar in ballad from a literary base, while Dégh teaches her legend seminar within the context of the Folklore Institute. Six contributors are based in English departments, two are in anthropology, one is in comparative literature and German, four are in graduate folklore programs. All teach at public institutions. That wasn't planned, but three of the four individuals invited to contribute who declined teach at private colleges, and so did one individual who became so fearful of displeasing other teachers on his campus he withdrew his contribution just before *Teaching Folklore* went to press. I do not think the exigencies of teaching folklore vary so much in public and private institutions for the absence of private college teachers to matter significantly. More important are the differences between large schools and small schools, between schools without graduate folklore programs and schools with folklore programs, between undergraduate introductions to folklore and graduate seminars in specific aspects of folklore studies—and that range is well represented here.

Most folklore teaching in America takes place in public institutions with no formal graduate program and no undergraduate major in folklore; the course taught most frequently is an introductory survey. Nine of the articles in *Teaching Folklore* deal with undergraduate courses, and eight of these are some form of general introduction. Introductory courses are the bread-and-butter staples supporting many university departments (those large psychology, sociology, history and economics departments generate the bulk of their FTEs through the monster-introductions), but introductory courses in few fields deal with anything like the range and variety of materials and approaches and processes we find in the folklore courses detailed here. (I wrote above that I had on occasion asked folklorist friends for their syllabi; when I taught in other departments—English, Comparative Literature, Art, and Law—I never asked colleagues for their syllabi. There was no need. The boundaries in those classes were far easier to define, the subject matter was far easier to limit.)

I know of no introductory course in any other discipline that has as much potential material appropriate for inclusion as an introductory course in folklore or folklife. I know of no graduate seminar in a literature or music or philosophy or any other department that has as much potential material appropriate for inclusion as does a graduate seminar in the Folktale or Ballad or Legend. Folklorists have an extraordinary range of material at their disposal, and that is at once a delight and a burden. The authors of the articles offered here discuss how they have segmented and managed that range of material for their students, and some of them write about how they have shifted priorities over time—because of changes in their own interests, because of changing departmental needs, and because of shifting student interests.

Only a few folklorists teach in folklore Ph.D. programs. Most teach in departments or programs that permit them to offer some undergraduate courses in folklore; some teach in graduate programs (most commonly English, Anthropology, and American Studies) that may allow students to do theses in folklore so long as the other disciplinary requirements are satisfied; a few are based in other departments but have developed inter-departmental folklore graduate programs. The place of folklore in a departmental curriculum often changes with the folklore consciousness of departmental administrators. A new chair won't change the role in an English department of Shakespeare or Chaucer, but might very well change the role and function of folklore. Graduate students in English or Anthropology or American Studies departments are more likely to teach sections of the department's introductory bread and butter courses than introductory sections of folklore.

In graduate school, one doesn't only learn what is supposed to matter and how to do research, but also how and what to teach. Folklorists who do graduate work in the non-folklore Ph.D. programs may be very well educated, but they aren't exposed to many models of teaching folklore. Graduates of folklore Ph.D. programs are rarely prepared for what they are most likely to find once they start teaching, for few of them find employment in the handful of universities with undergraduate or graduate folklore majors. While they are teaching assistants or assistant instructors, they belong to a distinct group from which they can draw practical information and to which they may go for aid at times of confusion; the folklore class they teach is part of a group of folklore classes taught by other graduate students like them and those other graduate students provide a continuing community of folk information central to the kind of work being done. There might even be a senior faculty person who meets regularly with the teaching graduate students to discuss with them pedagogical problems. When they leave graduate school and take a teaching job, things change.

As almost every teacher in this volume who received a Ph.D. in folklore points out, nothing in the Ph.D. training prepared them for the teaching situations in which they actually wound up. Nothing surprising in that. No one is so rigidly and specifically prepared. I suspect one would find few new assistant professors in English or history who are specifically prepared for the work which will occupy most of their time. But new English teachers have other English teachers with whom to discuss their problems; most folklorists are the only folklorist on their campuses and they are very much on their own.

Teaching is a craft, like any other, and it is learned, like any other: by watching, listening, reading, and practicing. The most important parts one works out for oneself—just as the journeyman carpenter decides what will be made with the skills learned as an apprentice and the tools presently available. Techniques developed by others often find application or adaptation in one's own work, and that is the reason for the present collection of essays. "Teachers learn as much in the classroom as students," writes Larry Danielson. In *Teaching Folklore*, some of our colleagues describe how they presently apply what they have learned. They tell us what has worked and what hasn't, what texts have been useful in what kinds of courses and what texts have been cumbersome impediments to conversation and learning. They discuss kinds of teaching problems we all share and problems specific to a particular place or person.

I was impressed by (and pleased to learn about) how many of the contributors are not comfortable with the current versions of their courses: almost all see their courses in flux, in motion, in a state of change. Several report abandoning early notions of what *had* to be included: the motif indexes, the type numbers, the things professional folklorists are supposed to cherish are often dropped or glossed over in exchange for devices and subjects that better help students understand what folklore is and how it works.

The essays in *Teaching Folklore* should be read as drafts, as statements about works in progress, as attempts by some of our colleagues to describe how they presently manage the single enterprise we all share: helping others understand what folklore is really about. As anyone who tries to keep up with the wide range of published research in the field knows full well, the definitions themselves are in flux, so it should be no surprise that most of these courses have a parallel vitality.

1984

Foreword to the Second Revised Edition

Shortly after publication of the first edition of *Teaching Folklore* one of the contributors send me a letter articulating the conditional tense in which all contributors to this collection wrote:

> I was more than a little nervous about displaying the design and theory of my class for an anonymous world to consider and evaluate. Teaching is for me a continuing process of approximation. I've never felt I've had it perfectly right (each semester teaches me something I incorporate in subsequent semesters) and each class is unique anyway (whatever design I begin the term with is modulated by the people waiting for me in the room on that first day). I was happy, therefore, to see that most of the other contributors saw their teaching work as being a process rather than a steady state, that they saw themselves still very much as learners. I hope people reading the book don't think we're out here smug about pedagogy. Some of us have been teaching a while, but that doesn't mean we think we've got the basic questions about why we're here and what we're doing all in a neat box.

Another contributor wrote:

> I've been thinking about you lurking on the perimeter of all of this. It's one thing to organize this project and edit our essays and write an

introduction, but if there's another edition I think you owe it to the 13 of us to jump into the pool. Right now, it's like we've all gone skinny-dipping at the home of a shared pal and there he is on the deck commenting on our swimming style. To quote the title of one of your own books, get your ass in the water and swim like me.

Fair enough: this edition of *Teaching Folklore* contains two more essays than its predecessor. All the essays in the previous edition dealt with courses that were wholly folkloric in content, and all but one of the graduate descriptions were about courses given in graduate folklore programs. But a good deal of folklore teaching takes place in courses more humanistically defined, and they serve a broader range of student interests and needs. We had no representation of that kind of course in the book, so I decided to write about my *Epic* seminar, in which folk or traditional epic is seen as part of a complex narrative continuum. Then one of the proofreaders pointed out that fieldwork, an activity central to all folklore scholarship, was mentioned in these essays only in passing, and mostly in discussions of undergraduate classes. So I wrote a brief second essay, this one describing my *Fieldwork* seminar, which is also designed for an interdisciplinary mixture of students.

With the addition of those two essays, this collection now contains a three-generation line. After I wrote my essays I reread Edson Richmond's chapter and I realized that several techniques I'd thought I'd invented had instead been lifted directly or modified slightly from the *Ballad* and *Medieval Romance* seminars I took with him 25 years ago. And when I reread Zora Zimmerman's essay I suspected that some of the techniques she writes about may have been adopted from the *Traditional Narrative* seminar she did with me 15 years ago. Robert Fitzgerald was my teacher for Homer and I've always used his translation of the *Odyssey* in my seminars; I was pleased to read that Zora insists her students use the same translation.

I've been friends with most of the contributors to this volume for a long time, but now that I'm a participant rather than just the organizer I am aware of a resonance across time that is central to the profession of teaching. Many folklorists still talk about folklore as being the kind of thing you learn outside formal channels of instruction, outside the classroom especially. What a silly notion that turns out to be.

1989

Edward D. Ives

University of Maine at Orono

Introduction to Folklore at Maine

"Whenever anyone asks me what it is I teach, I always say 'Shakespeare,'" Mark Van Doren said in lecture one day, "because no matter what the class may be, that's the way it always turns out."

I wasn't entirely sure what he meant thirty-five years ago when I heard him say it, but I've had leisure to see how right he was. Whatever I've taught over the years—whatever the courses have been called—there always seems to be a hidden agenda, and for each course that hidden agenda turns out to be remarkably the same. Unfortunately I have no single word or phrase like "Shakespeare" that will cover it, but it is generated by two rather simplistic statements: Wherever and whenever we have found groups of human beings we have found (1) that music and storytelling play an important part in their lives and (2) that they have developed systems of environmental prediction and control.

The first statement is fascinating enough in itself—I know of no satisfactory explanation for the amount of energy we humans devote to such pragmatically unproductive pursuits as music and storytelling, to begin with—but it is no more fascinating than a number of distinctions (many of them polarities) that its exploration calls on us to develop. In order, for example, for us even to begin discussing the universality of music, we have to establish just what music is. How does it differ from mere noise? How do we distinguish between singing and speaking? Between a song and something sung that is not a song? And so on. As for storytelling, what is a story, and how is it different from any other communicative event that is not a story? How are truth and fiction different, and what is the nature of history? What makes some stories "funny," others "sad" (more universal terms than "comedy" and "tragedy," which are essentially in-house problems for Western high culture)? The second statement is less interesting in itself, but it generates its own set of thought-provoking polarities. What is the distinction between what we call "science" and what we call "superstition?" Between "natural" and "supernatural?" And what are the relationships between observation and theory?

Both statements, the expressive and the practical, can be seen in two larger contexts: first, that of the constant tension—and its continuing resolution— between tradition and invention; second, that of the effects of transmission, specifically oral vis-á-vis written traditions. All of these questions go far beyond folklore, but I know of no better way to begin exploring than through folklore. It is, of course, impossible to cover them all in any one-semester course, and it would be presumptuous of me to claim that I can satisfactorily answer *any* of them in that time. Nonetheless they form my hidden agenda. I would prefer students leave my classes aware of the questions (though I will certainly provide them with some materials toward their answers) than knowing what a Child ballad or a Märchen is (though I hope they will know those things too).

There are real dangers in this approach to teaching. For one thing, the teacher may become so astonished at his own profundity in merely raising such issues that he mesmerizes himself into believing his ignorance is some sort of wisdom, much in the manner of Emily Dickinson's preacher who "preached upon 'Breadth' till it argued him narrow" (1955:839). For another, it is apt to lead students (and their professor) away from content, from things which are, into an intellectual stratosphere where all is some modality of being, if even that. In other words, it all gets pretty rarified and conceptual, suggesting that the knowledge that matters is knowledge *about* not knowledge *of.* As an antidote, I never let myself forget how much Shakespeare I learned from a professor who all but made us memorize the plays, his tests consisting of maybe twenty short quotations for which we had to tell who spoke the lines, to whom, and on what occasion. Vastitude is splendid, but it must never lose touch with specific content. As a final point here, I find that introductory students have only limited tolerance for such thin conceptual stuff. They take my course to learn something of folklore, and if they find the professor is constantly bombinating about in the circumambient gas they quickly lose interest. The questions are important, and I want the students to think about them, but their asking must grow out of a solid content from which they never get too far removed.

It is perhaps time that I myself came down out of the stratosphere, stopped preambling around, and started dealing with the way I teach my *Introduction to Folklore.* It is a three-credit course (two seventy-minute meetings a week) taught every fall in the Anthropology Department, has no prerequisites, and is open to all classes and colleges. As a result it gets a sizeable—somewhere around a hundred—and varied enrollment. Students take the course for many reasons—some to fulfill various social science requirements (interestingly, in the College of Education it can also be used to fulfill a humanities requirement), some out of curiosity (the course has a generally good reputation as an elective), and some (though these are not many) because they are already interested in folklore (I should also add that it is one of a group of three courses from which all Anthropology majors have to choose two). Consequently, *Introduction to Folklore* must cater to a broad student spectrum, from the casual and occasional forester or engineer (frequently neither that casual—nor that occasional) to the already committed anthropology major.

Since obviously I cast a wide net and welcome freshmen and sophomores, this course is one of those through which the Department hopes to attract new anthropology majors, while at the same time it serves to acquaint our present majors with a related if not ancillary discipline. All of which means that the course is yanked a number of different ways by trying to be all things to all students, and I'm not entirely happy with the results. Majors, for example, many of whom come to the course in their junior and senior years, often find themselves bored by going over ground they've already covered pretty well in other courses. One of the first moves I will make in the coming year is to eliminate this course as a major requirement, substituting for it one of three upper-level folklore courses (*Folksong, Narrative,* or *Oral History and Folklore Field Work*), thus freeing the introductory course to be what it really should be.

The course develops along two lines, the lectures and the readings, and I make only minimal efforts to coordinate them. Of course, if I am using an anthology of articles containing an essay on traditional medicine I will try to have the students read that essay at the same time I am lecturing on that subject, but in general I let the readings go their way while I go mine. If I were to try to coordinate, say, Barre Toelken's *The Dynamics of Folklore* (1979) or Dorson's *Buying the Wind* (1964) with my lectures, I would have to skip around so wildly in them as to leave them emasculate (both, after all, have their own programs), and, since I like my lecture schedule, I don't want to tailor my lectures to the text. The best compromise seems to be to leave well enough alone. I always explain this matter of non- coordination to my classes at the outset, and while once in a while a student will complain about it, for the most part it allows for variety it would be hard to achieve in any other way.

At present I am using two texts: Barre Toelken's *The Dynamics of Folklore* and Jan Brunvand's *Readings in American Folklore* (1979). Toelken's text is almost perfect for my approach, since he develops a set of ideas that are far from at odds with my own in a way that differs from mine, and—better yet—he develops at length some matters I do no more than suggest, such as his chapter on world-view (Toelken 1979:225-260). The Brunvand book offers a collection of essays—not all of them first-rate but only a couple of them so bad I won't assign them—that gives students a rather representative sampling of how folklorists go about their trade. These essays I back up with selections from Alan Dundes's *The Study of Folklore* (1965) and Dorson's *Folklore and Folklife* (1972), both of which I have on reserve in the library in multiple copies, making it very easy for the students to get at them. In the past I have used Dorson's *Buying the Wind* (which I will use again from time to time) and Brunvand's *The Study of American Folklore* (1978), although I've always had it on reserve, never as a text. In sum, given my particular approach of letting the text go its own way, I've never had much trouble finding adequate ones. I always reserve the opening of each class for questions on the readings, and I occasionally use this time to make a few comments of my own. But on the whole a philosophic anarchy prevails, and that's fine by me.

Not that there aren't some problems with this system, and anyone who has taught introductory courses should be able to recognize the chief one. It is all very well to "allow time for questions," but in a large and amorphous class in which something like half the students are freshmen and sophomores, those questions are not often forthcoming. I have suggested that students write out their questions and leave them on the podium before class, but they very seldom do, even though there are difficult patches in the reading that I'm sure many of them could use help with. Of course, nothing stops me, I suppose, from elucidating such passages for them on my own, but I have chosen not to, preferring to make the students responsible for their own enlightenment, even though I know many of them will not shoulder that responsibility. Perhaps that's a cop-out, but I've decided to risk it.

And now to my lectures. Since I'm in an anthropology department, I always begin with a fairly old-fashioned attempt to define culture, using as my starting point Melville Herskovits's three cultural paradoxes and a discussion of universal aspects of culture (food-getting, shelter, training the young, social and political organization, etc.) (Herskovits 1956:18-21, 229-457). This beginning allows me to move easily into showing how what the folklorist does is different from—and overlaps with— what the anthropologist, the musicologist, and the literary scholar do (somewhere in here I always get the chance to point out that universities have entire departments to study what may be about one percent of human narrative and poetic production and experience). I usually re-create for them an interview I conducted some years ago, showing them what I was looking for (old songs), what else I found that interested me then (traditional medicine, jokes), and what else happened that *should* have interested me or that would interest me now (barn building, the structure of an "event"), all of which I can contrast with what would interest, say, a dialectician or a social anthropologist. I've never been comfortable with the definition game, and when I get through with this section of my course, I always feel that I may have either cheated the students or myself a little, but it gets us going pretty well.

What follows then is a series of five lectures on various modes of cultural transmission. Each student has filled out a form on hide-and-seek—where they learned it, when, exactly how it was played, etc.—and we spend an entire class period discussing the results of this survey (to which I need only add an historic dimension by showing that the game is at least two thousand years old). Not only does this lecture give an excellent demonstration of Herskovits's three paradoxes, it opens up such matters as variation, continuity, distribution, and function. Next we move on to oral tradition, and for this demonstration I first tell them a story called "John the Cobbler" (Type 950) which I learned from Wilmot MacDonald in 1961 up on New Brunswick's Miramichi River; then I read them Herodotus's story of the "Treasure House of Rhampsinitus," told him by the priests of Egypt almost 2500 years ago, the point being that continuity, not change, is the remarkable thing. Together with the hide-and-seek example, this helps to make the point that unwritten traditions are far more stable than our document- oriented culture gives them credit for. (For MacDonald's story, see Creighton and Ives 1962:51-60; the Heorodotus version is in book 11, chapter 121.)

Now I turn to comparison of oral and written traditions in music, pointing out that even in classical music, a predominantly written tradition, there is an oral tradition passing, for instance, from teacher to student, coach to singer, that controls "interpretation" of the written text and that the oral tradition becomes increasingly important in those aspects of musical sound where our system of notation is imprecise (dynamics and timbre). Nonetheless, a written tradition does manage to keep variations within very narrow limits, something I demonstrate by playing a Bach aria sung by two different singers forty years and two continents apart and showing them to be so nearly identical they can almost (but not quite) be perfectly superimposed. The succeeding lecture turns to folksong and demonstrates how one song (Child 4), passed from one singer to another in a very limited area (the Miramichi Valley), shows far more variation over a three-year period than the two versions of the Bach aria mentioned above, even though one singer wrote it out for the other and even though the second singer claimed he was singing it just the way the first one did. As by-products, this lecture has much to say about how one relearns a song he hasn't sung or heard for years, and about how folksong festivals—and folklorists!—affect singers' repertoires.

In a final lecture in this series on transmission, I move from a memorized tradition to the whole Parry-Lord thesis, playing some excellent selections from various *guslars* and discussing with the class those marvelous pages on occasions and learning from Lord's *The Singer of Tales* (1964:13-29). All in all, I must say I'm fairly pleased with this section of the course, though, as always happens, some years certain lectures go well, some years they don't.

At this point I make a sudden shift over to belief and superstition, a subject which will occupy the class for at least the next four weeks, and I bend every effort (and I come from a long line of effort benders) to force the students not to interpret the present material as a gallery of quaint but nugatory curiosities. I begin by demonstrating to them that both science and superstition work toward the same ends (prediction and control); that most of us accept the teachings of science on faith; that our faith in scientific authority is essentially a religion which frequently calls on us to accept things that are patently absurd to sense and logic; and that, for all its frequent irrationality, superstitious behavior often makes excellent social sense. I can't say how many of my students are convinced by my polemics, but at least they generally give the right answers on examinations (they are not fools). I group succeeding lectures around such subjects as the future (death and second sight), luck, traditional medicine and healing (including a lecture on humoral pathology), dowsing, and witchcraft. One of the themes running through these lectures is the concept—or rather the concepts—of possession and uses for good and evil of power. I also find myself introducing many of my students to the manipulation of Occam's Razor.

Somewhere after midterm I formally introduce another concept: that of the story, although obviously we have been talking about stories before this time in one way or another. Now, though, I try to get my students to define the term. This leads to a discussion of the two great orders of stories and their inter-relationships: truth (personal experience tales, legend, history, myth) and fiction (tall tale, joke, Märchen, novel, etc.). All of these things are worked out in a series of lectures on the Devil (including half a period or so on one of my favorite side-tracks: Miracles of the Virgin), ghosts (Occam's Razor again), folk-hero cycles (especially Robin Hood), tall tales (including Munchausens with just a smack at Bunyan), and jokes (which gets us into a discussion of the nature of humor). All in all, I have a lot of fun with my lectures, and I have good reason to believe my students do too.

An astute reader of these pages will have noticed that I require no writing, no essays, no term paper. Years ago I used to require some writing, but during the late sixties and early seventies the enrollment for this course climbed to as much as three hundred and I eliminated the requirement in pure self-protection. Now that the course has leveled off at somewhere between seventy-five and a hundred, I probably should require some writing. Three years ago I assigned *Huckleberry Finn* and had the students write papers analyzing it as a folklore source. It worked pretty well, but they needed more guidance than I gave them on the kinds of approaches they might take. Perhaps I'll try again. I do think a job of writing is a good thing, but it's a tradeoff between the extra work involved and the anticipated pedagogical gain.

I also used to make each student do a collection of folklore items, following some very specific guidelines I laid down, and those collections became the foundation of what is now the Northeast Archives of Folklore and Oral History. However, as the course grew I found I simply did not have the energy to read between two and three hundred of them in the final weeks of the semester and do a respectable job of it. I don't plan to bring this exercise back in its old form, but I have wondered about assigning some specific collection exercises along the line. Let's say, for example, that before the class in which I talk about the Devil I assign everyone to collect appropriate stories and beliefs and have them write a brief analysis of what they find, making it clear that finding nothing is really finding something and that *that* something needs analysis too. I may try that next year.

It remains for me to discuss how I assign grades. A student's grade is determined on the basis of four detailed objective hour-exams covering both the reading and the lectures for that particular segment of the semester. The questions are entirely content-oriented, requiring no interpretations, no comparison of what Ives said in class with what Toelken or John Messenger said in the readings. For the past several years the exams have been made up of straight true/false questions (something like 100 per exam). This year I tried an exam in which the student answered fifteen out of twenty short and very specific essays. From my point of view, this exam was both tiresome and difficult to grade, and it told me nothing I couldn't have learned from the true/false exams I had been giving. The students? They voted overwhelmingly to go back to the true/false format (and the vote was supported by the careful comments, both solicited and unsolicited, I received from about a dozen of the best students in the class). As a footnote, I'd like to add that my true/false exams always contain a "bitch-sheet," on which a student can defend an answer to any question he or she finds ambiguous. It's a device that works well, and some students raise their grades as much as ten points through their careful defenses, though I find it interesting that about eighty percent of the defenses are in defense of what would have been right answers anyway. As a second footnote, if a student feels disadvantaged by such an objective test, he or she has the privilege of designing (in consultation with me) an exam that will be more suitable. I will even agree to an oral exam, if the student prefers. Very few ever take advantage of this offer, though, and of those who do, most fare no better than they did on the objective exam, which reinforces my belief that my objective exams do a pretty good job of it.

A final word on testing. I have been teaching now for over thirty years, and I have yet to satisfy myself with any system of making official and measurable discovery of what a student has learned. For a long time I felt the essay exam was the only way, because it forced the student to "integrate," to "structure," in a word to use his knowledge effectively, but I've never been convinced it doesn't reward the glib, the professional college student who knows all too well how to play the game. For another thing, I've learned by bitter experience how subjective I can be in grading such exams, especially when I am grading sixty to one hundred of them at once. What kind of exams one gives is largely a function of what he or she wants the students to get out of the course, and I have decided that I want them to be exposed to a certain body of knowledge through my lectures and a series of readings. I hope they will think about this material, comparing what I said in class with what they read in Barre Toelken's book or Rusty Marshall's article, and I hope even more that they will use the information they have acquired to help them find answers to the questions I spoke of as my hidden agenda. Some few of them will, and I bless them. But for the purposes of this introductory course, if students can show me that they have read and listened with reasonable care, I will be satisfied. My objective exams appear to give a good indication of how reasonable that care has been, allowing me to assign grades that—so the student evaluation forms tell me—are fair. Of course, what all this fuss about tests and testing has to do with learning is problematic at best. "Real education," said Ezra Pound, "must ultimately be limited to men who INSIST on knowing, the rest is mere sheep-herding" (Pound, n.d.:84). I couldn't agree more.

Robert H. Byington

University of North Carolina at Wilmington

Introduction to Folklore

The University of North Carolina at Wilmington, "UNC By the Sea," has been expanding swiftly over the past several years, more so than any campus in the University of North Carolina system; and this rapid development has been perhaps the most significant factor in the evolution of its instructional programs. The Chancellor of the University, ignoring for rhetorical purposes the presence of the Atlantic Ocean in our backyard, attributes the phenomenal growth of the institution to "the superior quality of the faculty"; and while the faculty *is* good (as any faculty, given the current job market, should be), the possibility remains that the opportunity to surf and otherwise "beach it" all year long is at least equally attractive to prospective students.

Whatever the principal reason, the student body at UNC-W has a reputation for being fun-oriented——"laid back" is the phrase one hears most frequently—and when one couples that feature with the demographic factor that more than 60% of our students come from the seven southeastern counties of North Carolina (from the turn of the century until the recent advent of tourism the most culturally barren and educationally disadvantaged region of the state), it should not surprise anyone that what Einstein once called "the holy curiosity of inquiry" is not a salient characteristic of students at UNC By the Sea.

This condition of academic life at UNC-W has induced me to transform rather radically the presumably standard Intro course I had taught at such institutions as Lycoming College, Point Park College, The University of Pittsburgh, Carnegie-Mellon University, and Duquesne University in the 1960s and early 1970s. Although, to be sure, since my own conceptions of folklore have modified considerably since the mid-sixties, that modification is also a factor in the way I conduct my Intro course at this institution. The course (English 250: *Introduction to Folklore*) as it was proposed and introduced here, can be and is taken by any students (from freshmen to seniors) seeking to fulfill one of the Basic Humanities requirements, but its relevance to the social and behavioral sciences is stressed in the catalog description as well as in the course itself and a significant number of the students major in those disciplines. It is popular and always fills whenever it is offered (usually about once a year, since I am the only folklorist on the faculty, teach only one course a semester, and enjoy teaching an advanced course upon occasion).

The first transformation I decided upon had to do with textbooks. While I find many merits in the two introductory texts that I gather are most frequently used (Brunvand 1978 and Toelken 1979) and have used the former for years at other institutions with apparent effectiveness, I discovered in my first two years at UNC-W that the students here would accept neither: they find the Brunvand boring, irrelevant, out-of-date (particularly the appended article on Academic Folklore), and the Toelken (except for some of the social science types) pretty much beyond their comprehension. The other possibilities (e.g., Dundes's *The Study of Folklore* and Dorson's *Folklore and Folklife*) are either too sophisticated for UNC-W students or (e.g. Laubach's *Introduction to Folklore*, and the Tallmans' *Country Folks*) too simplistic and too fixated on folklore as cultural remnants to satisfy my own conception of the subject. That left me with the perennial choice of the dissatisfied folklore teacher: either write your own text, or do without one. I chose the latter.

Since folklore texts are, or should be, replete with examples of folklore as well as discussion of it, I knew I could rely upon the experience of my students for more examples of folklore than I could possibly use; and, since I felt quite competent to guide whatever discussion of that folklore was appropriate, it seemed to me a textbook in an Intro course is unnecessary; and it seems so to me still.

I do provide my students with handouts which serve certain purposes of a text: (1) A partial list of major folklore genres—verbal, partially verbal, and non-verbal, (2) A list of terms (with operational definitions) used consistently in the professional discussion of folklore, which they are expected to know as well as their own names by the end of the course, and (3) an informant's sheet, which elicits the intimate details of my students' private and public lives, and which they return to me at the conclusion of the first period (Appendices 1, 2, and 3). The last handout proves most useful in the identification of an appropriate research topic for the student, a process which invariably troubles the students at first, but with equal invariability is successfully resolved in personal conferences with the instructor in which the informant sheets are effective catalysts. Note that a syllabus is not among these handouts. Since the range of materials covered in the course is heavily dependent upon the interest and experience of the students, and since that (as well as the thoroughness and intensity with which any given subject is discussed) will vary from one aggregate of students to another, a fixed syllabus only by rare coincidence would provide a governing structure for the course as I teach it, and I dispense with one. Instead I provide the students with yet another handout specifying the requirements of the course (mid-term examination, final examination, minimum number of absences, formula for grade computation, due dates for work submitted, etc.) and the work that will be required of them, principally a major research project (upon which they will deliver a formal report to the entire class) and a maximum of interaction in class discussion.

Having done that, I devote the remainder of the first period to pointing out the following:

—That we will be studying a corpus of cultural materials, vast almost beyond comprehension, which few people ever take seriously (if they think about them at all), but which, as the course will demonstrate, are at the very center of our lives.

—That the objective of the course is not to instill in them a hazy familiarity with a fixed number of conventional folklore genres but rather to equip them with an open-ended definition of folklore which will enable them always to distinguish it from non-folklore (or vice versa) simply by the way it is processed in culture. In brief, we identify folklore not by what it is but by how it is processed.

—That in the course of their research they will be required to interact, sometimes on a highly personal level, with a number of other human beings, most of whom they will not have known beforehand, and that this work requires certain minimal people skills which, for a variety of legitimate reasons, they may not care to exercise or develop. If such is the case, they should obviously withdraw from the course (this advice is invariably acted upon by one to four students who had perceived the course heretofore as involving reading and library work almost exclusively). Nevertheless, I do tell them that in the past most students have found their collecting project the most gratifying experience of the course.

—That the name of the game in folklore is not competition (particularly a superordinate-subordinate adversary relationship between instructor and students) but, rather, collaboration, particularly collaboration among ourselves, all of whom know, use, and transmit far more folklore than we will have an opportunity to analyze in the course of one semester. After answering questions and clarifying whatever matters need it, I then dismiss the class with the assignment that each of them be prepared at the next meeting of the class to cite at least two examples of what they consider folklore and explain why.

At the next meeting of the class I provide the students with ample time to present their examples and conceptions of folklore which, with an inevitable few exceptions, consist of the following:

—Folklore is rural, old-timey stuff, such as agrarian crafts and practices (e.g., planting by the signs) associated principally with (although not exclusively practiced by) older generations.

—Folklore is stuff which, however many misguided people may believe in and practice it, is not factual, not literally true, not reliable information (e.g., belief in ghosts). Any distinction my students make between these two common conceptions of folklore is more one of emphasis than kind, and in their view one conception overlaps the other to a considerable degree.

The important thing about these conceptions, obviously, is not that they are wrong but that they are far too narrow, in certain important instances moribund, and item-focused, i.e., on knowledge, belief, or behavior whose content or form is perceived as folklore. I begin at this juncture of the course the modification and expansion of these conceptions which is the principal objective of the semester's work; and the first step in this process is my presentation of a relatively elastic definition of "folk culture," which from this point on increasingly replaces the term "folklore" in class discussion. I am aware that my open-ended operational definition is not shared by all folklorists, but, since I perceive their disagreement as aberration, I do not communicate that dysfunctional knowledge to my students. This is, after all, an introductory course. I am also aware that in strict logic any open-ended definition can hardly be considered definitive at all, but since none of my students has ever been a strict logician that has never created any difficulty.

I start with the general statement that folk culture consists of that enormous body of knowledge, belief, and behavior in any social network which has been created, exists, and persists largely in the interstices between the strands of formally organized, standardized, officially prescribed culture. It tends (a verb I use repeatedly in these definitions) to be the free-floating, non-rational, non-scientific, non-productive (in an official sense) part of the social network and is transmitted mostly by word of mouth or observation and imitation. The term "folk" in this sense, then, no longer denotes a particular kind of social grouping so much as a kind of behavior present to varying degrees in practically everyone, including, of course, all members of that present class.[1]

Since, at this point, most students have only the dimmest sense of what I am talking about, it is necessary to define further, and exemplify, exemplify, exemplify. First, I tell them, folk culture is informally transmitted (as distinct from the very formal, structured transmission of information taking place that very moment in our classroom), either by word of mouth (if it has a verbal component) and/or by demonstration/observation and imitation (if it has a non-verbal component). For example, I ask them how they learn the following: insults in various forms reflecting the rivalry between the University of North Carolina ("Carolina") and North Carolina State University ("State"); techniques of hitch-hiking; how long to wait for a tardy college instructor; how to avoid a DUI (Driving Under the Influence) arrest; how to skateboard; the tricks of the trade and jargon of any occupation; hangover remedies, hiccup cures, wart cures, etc.; how to pitch horseshoes; family holiday customs; customs accompanying attendance at the ACC (Atlantic Coast Conference) basketball tournament (for a long time the chief athletic event in North Carolina); how to play table tennis (or, for that matter) almost any other game); dirty jokes; how to ride in a rodeo; how to play and win video games; etc., etc., etc. The list is virtually limitless, and by the time one gets through a tenth of this or comparable lists, the students are adding to the list themselves and have a fairly clear idea of what informal, as distinct from formal, transmission is.

Then come the inevitable questions: What if an expression or behavior unquestionably folk in substance (e.g., a Chinese firedrill) appears on television in a teen-age movie? Is it still folklore?　The answer is unequivocally and definitively "No."　*Not* when it is thus formally/commercially transmitted. It is merely an item of popular culture, which frequently borrows such material from folk culture. The medium (formal) gives you the message, which is that anything appearing on TV by virtue of that fact, *cannot* be folk. Only human beings can transmit folk culture, and the transmission must be direct. Next question: What if someone should hear a joke, see a behavior, etc., in a movie and, finding it appealing, pass it on to a friend, who passes it on to yet another friend. Does it thus become an item of folk culture?　The answer is unequivocally and definitively "Yes."　Regardless of its origin, once an item is transmitted (or processed) as described, it becomes folk, simply by virtue of the manner of transmission. It doesn't take many questions like these to convince the students that informal

---

[1] I have a strong feeling I have read this phrasing somewhere, but I cannot for the life of me remember or locate the reference.

transmission is (at least currently) the most important feature of folk culture to keep in mind.

Next, I tell them, folk culture is traditional, by which I mean that it is passed on repeatedly in a relatively fixed form for a relatively long period of time. I stress the relativity of time here because it is important for students to realize that, while a significant, frequently inter-generational life span is not uncharacteristic of folk culture, the passage of time is not a definitive factor. Rather, it is cycles of transmission which are important here; and they must understand that items of folk culture, e.g., joke fads, which circulate widely for relatively brief periods of time, are just as "folk" as items, e.g., recipes, that have been passed down for generations. The relatively fixed framework which is at the heart of my sense of any traditional item is easier for students to apprehend since it is already a part of their prior conception (or misconception). A few examples—the fact that in all variants of the Legend of the Second Bluebook there will always be an examination situation, a trickster, and two bluebooks; the fact that all duck decoys bear some resemblance to actual ducks; etc.—suffice to demonstrate the identifiable similarity of traditional items, regardless of what variations are present. Since, given the manner of its transmission, folk culture will always show some variation, that definitive feature is the most obvious of all, at least to my students, and since it is implicit in any discussion of the relatively fixed framework of traditional items, I spend very little class time on it. I merely point out that folk culture has stability (tradition) *and* flexibility (variation), so that, say, the recognizably same jump rope rhyme will adapt to the needs of Iowa farm kids in 1984 as well as it did to those of London street kids in 1890.

I should perhaps note that, unlike many folklorists, I make no association in this course between "tradition" and the community values which may or may not have influenced it. It is interesting to explore the ways in which folk culture conforms and gives expression to shared community values, attitudes, and sense of identity; but I do not consider such an exploration important to definition. In fact, it can muddle more than it clarifies, and I invariably reserve such considerations for my advanced courses.

The last definitive feature of folk culture I emphasize in my classes is that it tends to be unreflective (or what Charles Camp in an as yet unpublished article has paraphrased as "unself-conscious"). By this I do not mean "unconscious" in a Freudian sense, but rather unquestioned, unexamined, often unrealized, not *thought* about. If, for example, you ask a dinner companion his reason for throwing a pinch of salt over his left shoulder after spilling something on the table, he'll be able to tell you. It was a deliberate act to avert bad luck. But if you ask him how it averts bad luck, he simply doesn't know. He's never thought about it one way or the other. He does it without thinking.

Then I cite another more complex example. I am presently engaged in fieldwork among tugboat crewmen in the deep sea port of Wilmington, North Carolina, located on the Cape Fear River, 23 miles from the Atlantic Ocean. The "ego ideal" of all such tugboatmen is the docking pilot (who is totally responsible for the movements of both ship and tugboats when a ship is sailing or being berthed), largely because he seems to have the easiest job, has the most status, and makes the most money. It is relatively easy to learn what a docking pilot must know to do what he does whenever he docks or sails a ship because any docking pilot can tell you. One quickly learns that the docking pilot's fixed knowledge (the capabilities of the tugs, permanent factors in river navigation, etc.) is minuscule as compared to the awesome number of interdependent, ever-changing variables he must know and control, most of which he must learn afresh every time he docks or sails a ship. Among these are the size of the ship, its draught (water and air), its "drag" (if there is more draught aft than forward) or—the opposite—how much it is "down by the bow," the ship's power, the state of its engines, the kind of propulsion (single-screw, twin-screw, variable pitch, or what), the size and make-up of the ship's crew, the stage of the tide, the velocity of the current, the velocity and direction of the wind, and a lot more. The combination is never exactly the same, and much of this information the docking pilot cannot acquire until he arrives at the ship. Moreover, he will never know it all before he begins. For example, he has to assume that all the ship's systems are working, but as that rarely proves to be the case, almost every move is an exercise in ad hoc improvisation. Docking a ship because it involves making contact rather than breaking contact, is more problematical than sailing one; and when you realize that the tolerances within which the docking pilot must position a block-long ship at the dock are at most six feet and can be as small as eight inches, you can only wonder how it's done. Because the docking pilots can't tell you.

The process of calculation and decision has become so unreflective, so unself-conscious, so internalized, that they find it almost impossible to identify the operative factors. One time I had been after Butch LeClerc—generally acknowledged the best docking pilot in the harbor—to explain the timing of certain orders I had heard him give a ship's helmsman, how he knew when to issue each one in succession. He tried hard to be of help, but obviously found it impossible to conceive the reasons let alone articulate them, and concluded in exasperation, "Christ, I don't know, Bob. You just give the order and hope for the best—and if things get fucked up, blame the quartermaster." Unreflective.

Another example I like to use is proxemic. I ask a girl in the front row of the classroom to stand up, and when she has done so, move very close to her (until our noses are almost touching) and ask her casually how she is feeling that morning. It immediately becomes apparent to the entire class how she is feeling that very moment. Uncomfortable. Invariably the subject blushes, laughs or giggles nervously, and backs hurriedly away from me. The reason, of course, is not that I have halitosis, but that I have violated our culture's conception of the appropriate proxemics for such human interaction. It takes a good bit of class discussion to bring that out, but when they realize that this cultural conception, the importance of which is indicated by the degree of personal distress its violation can induce, is one they were not even aware of and can't remember learning, they usually have a much clearer perception of what "unreflective" means and how large a sector of culture it characterizes.

We discuss briefly the anonymity of much folk culture, largely because it looms so large in their conceptions, but it does not take them long to realize that origin, known or unknown, has nothing to do with the processes that define folk culture and we pass on to more substantive matters. One of these is the relationship between folk culture and truth, i.e., literal, empirically verifiable fact. Interesting as that subject is, and however important it may be to our understanding of certain genres or sub-genres of folk culture, it still has nothing to do with the definition of folk culture itself. Folk stuff may or may not be factual, may or may not be literally true, but that does not affect the folkness of the item in any way.

I then begin the conclusion of this crucial definition phase of the course by asking each of the students to take a sheet of paper from his or her notebook and make a paper airplane. I make one, too. When we complete the airplanes, all of which are made of paper and folded to form a "fuselage" and "wings" (tradition), there are always three basic types (variation), one of which—interestingly enough, the type *I* make—is always aerodynamically superior to the others. No one can ever remember how he learned to make a paper airplane (informal transmission), and all agree that, even though many of them have not made one in years, they did it without thinking (unreflective). The paper airplane is, then, an item of folk culture not because of what it is, but because of the way it is processed. I cannot recall a student who has ever forgotten this lesson, at least within the time frame of the course itself.

The paper airplane serves another purpose, as well. When I ask my students why they made paper airplanes, where they made them, and what they did with them, originally, they always express various degrees of amusement, and confess that with few exceptions the paper airplanes were indigenous to the elementary school classroom and were useful in expressing the counter culture of the classroom, either as carriers of forbidden messages or as weapons in covert competition among the pupils or between the pupils and the teacher.

At this point I remind them that folk culture has a tendency to be interstitial, i.e., it is created and utilized to satisfy needs in areas which the net of formal, officially sanctioned culture does not reach. In this instance, of course, officially prescribed behavior for the elementary classroom does not provide mechanisms for expression of the children's inevitable discomfort with the unnatural constraints of their situation, and, among other devices, they create and utilize paper airplanes to relieve that discomfort. This example also makes amply clear that much folk culture tends to be disapproved of by its official counterparts, and therefore takes on a subversive quality, which leads at times to its legal proscription.

Almost all my students by this time have a workable idea of what folklore is and how it functions, but before moving on I always assure myself of this by giving them a quiz something like the following:

Specify which of the following are items of folk culture, which are not, and why:

Alka Seltzer/Cure for Hangover
Beethoven's *Fifth Symphony*
A snowman
The Beverly Hillbillies
Tying a shoelace
A shoelace
Giving someone "the finger"
A Currier & Ives print of a family Thanksgiving
Cockfighting
Holy Ghost People
Monopoly (the Parker Brothers game)[2]

When the returns are in (invariably reassuring, in my experience), we move on, at a significantly accelerated pace.

---

[2]Obviously the answer to this depends upon whether the item is interpreted to include the accretion of folk variations to the standard, marketed game.

The question of which genres to consider in the course now arises, and the decision usually is a combination/compromise between what I consider to have the most importance and personal relevance for my students and what they want to study. The choices more often coincide than not (although sometimes for different reasons), and we normally consider—although not necessarily in this order—folk narratives, music, art, belief, customs, humor, games, and the interaction of these genres occurring in such groups (considered ethnographically) as occupations, families, children and at least one deviant group (e.g., the gay community, bikers, drug dealers, religious cults, etc.). I, of course, tell the students that although we will be taking up the genres separately they normally occur in combination.

The next thing that occurs (concurrently with the ongoing class) is the students' selection of the subjects for their research projects. Since for a majority of them their own folk knowledge (or knowledge they have access to) is still somewhat below the level of active consciousness, the necessary raising requires a consultation with me. The two criteria of selection I insist upon are a keen, personal interest on the part of the student *and* accessibility. This means, of course, that the funeral customs of Tibetan monks, however fascinating, would not be an appropriate choice, given the roughly two months the course provides for collecting prior to the beginning of the class reports (the schedule of which is determined by lottery). Given the personal data sheets my students have provided, it normally takes us no more than fifteen minutes to decide upon a mutually satisfactory subject for their research. At the time of the consultation I also provide each student with a sheet giving them instructions about interviewing, and the specifics of organization and format I expect to govern their collecting as well as the form and substance of their final reports/papers. After about a week of such consultations the members of the class are off and running.

While I cannot conscionably exclude from class consideration the relatively static "old timey" stuff which still consumes the attention of most folklorists, my emphasis, and consequently that of my students, is consistently upon evolving, contemporary folk culture (with whatever links to the past it may have). I point out that the change or evolution of folk culture is most obvious in those genres most affected by the technologies of popular culture, and I usually consider for purposes of demonstration the genres of music, arts/crafts, and games.

As far as music is concerned, the students readily perceive by listening to a series of carefully selected tapes the evolution in form and style that has occurred in, say, white secular folk song between Almeda Riddle singing "Barbara Allen" through Jean Ritchie singing "Rosewood Casket" to the Nashville Sound, while at the same time recognizing the similarity of textual content in it all. I do the same thing with the blues, proceeding in a graduated series of tapes from field hollers through Leadbelly and Lightnin' Hopkins, Bessie Smith, etc., to B.B. King and the Rolling Stones. I demonstrate that with their utilization of available technologies these once isolated musical traditions have adapted to the demands of an ever-evolving mainstream culture, and managed not only to survive, but to dominate. The nostalgia which supports folk festivals presenting this music in its earlier stages of evolution is frequently at odds with the values of the performers themselves, many of whom for both aesthetic and financial reasons prefer the later evolved forms of music. I remind the students that Loretta Lynn learned her earliest songs by listening to the radio (a technological influence of considerable magnitude) and that Jean Ritchie's family preferred the music coming from their new radio over (to their newly educated ears) the relatively tuneless music they had known earlier.

The class then discusses the siren appeal of popular culture to isolated folk communities. We conclude that for reasons of taste, efficiency, physical convenience, and financial gain such communities will almost always abandon their previous folk culture for what they consider the clearly superior features of popular culture whenever they come into contact with it and can afford it. Hence the change in home cooking from dependence on a fireplace to the use of wood stoves, followed by gas or electric stoves, to the current microwaves. I tell my class about my excursion to a Cincinnati department store in the early fifties when color TV sets had just come on the market. The colors at that time, as some may recall, were garish, unreal, hideous in a way; and yet, surrounding these machines in the department store that day were dozens of mountain people, inhabiting some of the most glorious natural terrain in all America (Cumberland County, Kentucky, just across the river), who were awestricken by the bilious colors on the tube. I heard one old lady, shaking her head in wonder, say to another, "That's the most beautiful thing I've ever seen."

Thus has it always been, I tell my class. I ask them to imagine the situation of a Native American on the northwest coast of the continent in the late 18th century. He is on the bank of a river, laboriously chipping out the center of a cedar log with a beaver tooth chisel to make a dugout canoe. Suddenly, he looks up and sees for the first time in his life a ship under full sail gliding effortlessly up the river. I ask my class, "Is that Native American craftsman going to go back to his chipping with the same attitude? Would you?" They get the point.

Is folk culture then on its death-bed, they almost always—and, it seems to me, needlessly—ask. Only if one persists in retaining the stereotype of folk culture as *past* culture, I answer. Otherwise, it is alive, well and flourishing. In fact, contemporary communications technology speeds up the transmission of folklore through adoption by the media of folklore items themselves, or the basis for such items. We spend the rest of our class time (prior to the presentation of the first class reports) satisfying ourselves that this is indeed the case. Obviously, therefore, we tend to concentrate on the contemporary, urban-suburban scene (although not to the total exclusion of the past-oriented countryside).

What this means, practically, is that when we take up games we tend to consider card-games, drinking games, Dungeons and Dragons-type games, sex games, and the like with more seriousness than mumbly-peg and jumping rope. When we take up narratives, we discuss jokes, "urban belief" tales, and ABSM/UFO stories more thoroughly than Jack tales and folk epics, and with a heavy emphasis upon the kinds of cultural information these sub-genres contain. When we take up customs we deal with handshakes, skipping class, the students' own rites of passage (getting a driver's license, graduation, fraternity initiation, etc.) rather than conventional calendrical carryings-on. When we take up occupations, we look at the hidden culture of tool-and-die makers rather than farmers, waitresses rather than miners, office workers rather than loggers, and flyers rather than cowboys. When we take up families, we tend to stress the forms and functions of family photographs (including albums) and home movies over narratives, private language, and games. This steady focus upon the contemporary and the students' own folklore continues until the time for the students' reports approaches, and I am satisfied that by that time almost all of them understand the contemporaneity of folklore, if they understand anything about it at all. With few exceptions, the class reports reinforce this impression.

The reports themselves are scheduled to last fifteen minutes, followed by an additional five minutes to allow for questions and commentary. The reports all consist of a preliminary ethnographic sketch of the community from which the collection was elicited, the collection itself, and the collector's personal interpretation/analysis of the value and function of the material to the carriers. These reports are extremely important to the learning which takes place in the course because of the range and variety of materials covered, the opportunities they provide for covering myriad points earlier lecture/discussion could not or did not touch upon, the different methods of data collection they demonstrate, and the fact that for almost every student the collecting experience is a voyage of discovery, the enthusiasm generated by which is transmitted to the class with a pedagogical effectiveness that puts my own feeble efforts to shame. I have yet to teach such a class from which I, personally, did not emerge significantly more knowledgeable than when I entered at the beginning of the semester, and what follows is a small, representative sampling of the reports.

One student demonstrated with her collection of locally available folk art—yard decorations, mail-boxes, scarecrows, and, among other examples, snowmen—that what appears in most formal "folk art" collections across the country is pitiably meager and unrepresentative; and that the snowmen in our part of the country—which spring up by the thousands in people's yards every five or six years when there is sufficient snow to make them—represent a community-wide, folk/aesthetic response to an unusual, stimulating experience. I have a hunch one doesn't see many snowmen in Buffalo anymore.[3]

Another student, who collected from tugboatmen, demonstrated that certain folk practices resist modernization when he pointed out that the tugboat captains, with every contemporary form of maritime communication at their fingertips, still insist upon responding to a docking pilot's radio-transmitted orders by reaching up and laboriously pulling a whistle cord instead of uttering a simple "Roger" into the microphone in front of them.

Yet another student, also working with tugboatmen, showed the class how an occupational folk culture will sometimes take an item from the environing popular culture and adapt it to its own purposes. One of the customs he used to illustrate this is the tugboatmen's habit of designating a "Christmas tug" at Christmastime, mounting a steel pipe "tree" on the upper deck, festooning it with blinking lights (the captain of this tug is known on the river temporarily as "Cap'n Twinkles"), and sailing it up and down the river (eluding the Coast Guard) with speakers mounted on the main deck blaring out Christmas carols by country stars like Dolly Parton and Loretta Lynn.

One of the most electrifying reports was given by a strikingly beautiful co-ed (engaged to a cadet at the U.S. Maritime Academy) who had taped "sea story" telling sessions organized by seamen who were friends of her fiance. The "sea story," as we defined the genre, is the account of a seaman's sexual exploits while in port (which satisfies all the criteria of folklore, but—so far as I know—has never

---

[3]Not after little-bitty snowfalls under two feet. But when the stuff piles up in drifts that cover mailboxes, parked cars, and small-footed persons who failed to don snowshoes, as happens about once every five years, then the snow artists come out and perform with grace and style. Snowmen, as Prof. Byington notes, are indeed rare. Last winter's snow constructions in the vicinity of the DRI offices included R2D2, a large horse, a medium-sized gorilla, a life-sized bison, and a fair copy of the Lachaise *Standing Woman* that has for years graced the sculpture garden of New York's Museum of Modern Art. *Ed.*

been systematically collected) and goes into as much clinical detail as a XXX hard porn flick. Those tapes coupled with the co-ed's casual narration of examples not on the tapes created as much . . . shall I say, tension . . . as I have experienced in a classroom, and at the same time introduced the class to a new sub-genre of folk narrative.

The last report I shall mention here (of the hundred or more I have listened to) exemplifies how valuable folkloric information can be in an official context. The University of North Carolina system is presently under a Federal court order to increase its black student population to a certain percentage of the total by 1986. UNC-W has not been too successful in recruiting or retaining blacks. One of my black students undertook to determine exactly what the esoteric attitudes of the black student community on our campus are, and the most important data he ultimately reported to our class was (is) dismaying. For example, the blacks perceive the white students' attitudes toward them as menacing, and themselves as menaced. Given that 95% come from southeastern North Carolina, this is perhaps understandable; but, so far as I know, the administration, which is very much concerned about the problem, doesn't even know it. The black students perceive the predominantly white faculty as supercilious, disdainful and uncaring (four departments, among which, I am happy to say, was the English Department, were excluded from this characterization), and themselves as not wanted by the faculty. Whether or not these esoteric perceptions coincide with the facts is beside the point; they exist and some systematic effort should be made to change them. Since this class report and accompanying term paper came in only a week or so ago, I have not yet transmitted it to the administration, but I will.

There is simply not world enough and space here to specify the numerous categories of folkloric information presented in these reports, such as the use of questionnaires and media advertisements to elicit certain kinds of information from one's informants, but, once the students know what folklore is, the compilation and presentation of their reports is probably the most valuable thing they do in and for the course.

In fact, when the reports are completed the course is over; and although I would prefer a suitably sentimental conclusion to the experience (images of golden suns sinking beneath purple mountains, and tears streaming down the old instructor's cheeks as another English 250 class comes to an end seem not inappropriate), what actually happens is that I collect all the papers, wish the students well in their finals, and say "See ya." The world is like that.

Appendix I: SOME CATEGORIES OF FOLK EXPRESSION

Verbal
  Folk Music
  Folk Narrative
    a. Myths
    b. Legends
    c. Tales
    d. Jokes
  Folk Song
    a. Spirituals
  b. Ballads
  c. Miscellaneous
Folk Speech
  a. Dialect
  b. Argot
  c. Naming, etc.
Folk Verse
  a. Children's Verse
    (1) Jump rope rhymes

<table>
<tr><td>

   (2) Taunts
   (3) Counting Out rhymes, etc.
  b. Limericks
  c. Toasts
  d. Autograph rhymes, etc.

   Partially Verbal
Folk Belief and Superstition
Folk Medicine
Folk Drama
Folk Games
Folk Cookery
Folk Customs
  a. Calendrical
  (Christmas, birthdays, etc.)

</td><td>

  b. Ritual (Birth,
    initiation, marriage, etc.)
Folk Religion
Non-Verbal
Folk Art (Decorative)
  a. Painting
  b. Sculpture
  c. Carving
  d. Miscellaneous
Folk Crafts
  (Utilitarian)
Folk Architecture
Folk Gestures

</td></tr>
</table>

Appendix II: TERMS COMMONLY USED IN FOLKLIFE STUDIES

Folk: Any group of people whatsoever who share at least some traditions they could call their own.

Elite/Official Culture: Those cultural values, expressions and behavior supported and sometimes mandated by established institutions in government, religion, law, education and the like.

Popular Culture: Those cultural items produced and controlled by major industries and many individuals for commercial distribution to a mass audience or market.

Folk Group: Almost any group that is identifiable and set apart within or without the larger mainstream culture, retains that identity long enough for a body of folk expression and behavior to develop, and whose members express that identity through consistent interaction with other members of the group.

High Context Group: Those whose members share a significant amount of in-group knowledge, and see themselves as parts of a single community set apart that "knows." Example: Snake-handling religious sect.

Low Context Group: Those more like the larger society, whose members have a lot of folklore, but who do not see themselves as set apart and closely related. Example: College students.

Variant: A single variation of a clearly identifiable folk item that may occur in many such variations, each distinguishable from the others.

Diffusion: The theory that a particular folk item found in possibly hundreds of variants must have originated in one time and place by an act of conscious invention, and then traveled in ever-widening arcs from its point of origin.

Polygenesis: The theory that those hundreds of variants of a particular folk item originated separately and independently of each other as products of similar cultural circumstances in different times and places.

Esoteric: What one group thinks of itself, and what it supposes others think of it.

Exoteric: What one group thinks of another group.

Appendix III: ENGLISH 250 PARTICIPANT BACKGROUND SHEET

Name:

University Class-level: Major:

Home town and other places you have resided for any length of time:

Occupations (other than student) in which you have been employed:

Hobbies:

Recreational Activities

Notes

Thomas A. Green

Texas A&M University

Teaching *Introduction to Folklore* at Texas A&M

For the past five years I have taught *Introduction to Folklore* at Texas A&M University. A&M's enrollment figures of well over 30,000 suggest ample room for academic diversity, but the technological orientation of the institution and the restrictions imposed within most degree plans inevitably, though inadvertently, impede growth in the liberal arts. Administrators charged with establishing degree requirements do not regard a folklore course as essential to nor practical for the engineering, agricultural, or mathematics student, and they allot only a limited number of elective hours of *any* sort within the curricula of these programs. Such electives must be selected from a list of approved offerings. Engineering, for example, does not include folklore courses among its alternatives.

Despite this benignly indifferent intellectual climate, the course does well. I think some of the reasons for this success are suspect, however. Folklorists scarcely need to be reminded that far too many people associate what we do only with children's fairy tales and the quaint customs of "backward" communities. (If you aren't aware of that you probably haven't been to a cocktail party or a family reunion since you entered the profession.) This misconception leads some students, and even some of their advisors, to turn to a folklore course as a means of bolstering faltering grade point averages. When this is the motive, students choose the introductory course; significantly higher enrollments than in the other two courses attest to that. They do so, I assume, because *Introduction to Folklore* is assigned a lower number in our listing of folklore courses (329, as opposed to 331 and 489) and because its catalogue description seems less specialized than the other two courses'. The prerequisites for all three courses are the same, however. Beyond high enrollment figures, I have more substantial evidence for my belief that some students regard 329 as "three easy credits." Some students register dismay at making less than an A or B on early assignments and rush to drop the course. One student summed up the attitude of this faction by asking me, "How am I going to explain to my father that I'm failing FOLKLORE?" As opposed to a real course such as math, physics, or marketing, I suppose.

I must sound terribly cynical at this point. That is not my intention, but it is a fact that some students are more concerned with their transcripts than their educations. Fortunately, not all students enroll because they believe folklore will boost their averages or serve as a painless alternative to the standard literature course. Many have a genuine interest in (though only rarely any genuine sense of) the field. In fact, within certain programs (education, anthropology, and English, for example) advisors recommend the course; Parks and Recreation even requires *Introduction to Folklore* for certain concentrations. This variety of perceptions of the course and motives for enrolling yields class sizes which range from sixty to over one hundred per section, and we generally offer two sections every semester.

The large enrollments, in turn, make the course popular, if only for financial reasons, with the administration of the English Department. These figures encouraged the department to allow my two colleagues to introduce two additional courses in Folklore during the last three years: English 331 (*Ballad and Folksong*) and English 489 (*Mexican-American Folklore*).

Unfortunately, these offerings have not achieved similar success; their enrollments have attained only the minimum, or slightly above the minimum, limits. This lackluster showing cannot be explained by instructor charisma, since the same teachers regularly fill the *Introduction to Folklore* to the bursting point. Some of the factors which control enrollments, beyond those already mentioned, seem to be gossip (the students who stick with the introduction enjoy the course) and longevity (*Introduction to Folklore* has been taught here for decades). Other factors must exist, but we have not been able to ascertain them yet. The effect of these various elements is clear, however. Although the prerequisites for these courses are the same, and students can enroll in any of the three courses first, the introductory course is the overwhelming favorite.

As a result, I have to go about teaching the course keeping certain facts in mind. There is no cadre of students devoted to the discipline; no mechanism exists for majoring in the field, and diverse factors draw students to my classes. I cannot deal with my students as if I am establishing a foundation for subsequent study. A student's taking another folklore course after having had my introductory course is extraordinary. Nevertheless, I do hope to offer knowledge which will be of value to anyone beyond the single semester's exposure to the field. Without misrepresenting my discipline or slighting the 20% of the students in the class whose advisors recommend a solid background in folklore, I try to influence my students' attitudes about culture—their own and others'. I believe that some sense of cultural relativism and an appreciation of the ways groups understand themselves and express that understanding in traditional art will remain with students longer (and do them more good) than memorizing the distinction between Tale Types 510A and 510B.

Choosing texts for the course always presents me with several problems. I prefer an approach which allows students to examine folklore in specific cultural contexts. If they read several book-length studies of folklore in specific settings, as opposed, for example, to simply learning the general features of legends cross-culturally, I have found that they come away from the course with a better understanding of what expressive culture does for the folk group.

This is one reason I opt for a set of short readings on folklore in combination with several extended studies of particular forms in specific settings instead of a more general introductory text. I have tried using introductory texts, Barre Toelken's *The Dynamics of Folklore* and Jan Brunvand's *The Study of American Folklore*, along with the ethnographic works, but the reading load overwhelmed even the best students. I seem to accomplish the task of defining the field and setting up analytical frameworks with my present system as well as I did with the heavier reading load, and students also have the time to read the material more closely and, more importantly, to mull over the arguments they contain.

Selecting a set of texts which presents folklore in context gives me a bigger headache. Finding studies which are appropriate for novices who are beginning to develop some sense of the discipline is often difficult. Most available books posit a general audience with no knowledge of folklore, or they are written with the specialist in mind. I also want to cover a fairly wide range of genres in the course, but most studies restrict themselves to a narrow spectrum of forms, frequently only a single type. Of the texts I now use, only Zora Neale Hurston's *Mules and Men* cuts a wide swath. I wish I could deal with material culture in greater depth, but I am still searching for a suitable text. For now, I lecture on these genres when we discuss cultural backgrounds of the American Indian and Afro-Americans.

Although I choose not to use a general introductory text, I begin the course in much the same fashion as do the authors of folklore texts, by establishing the nature of the discipline. While doing this, I also present the concept of cultural conditioning. I introduce this notion as early as possible in order to help them overcome perceptions of the behavior of other groups as merely curious or quaint. I have found that tendencies toward ethnocentrism are weakened once students come to terms with the structured nature of their own actions, that is, once they recognize the cultural conditioning which makes them act, in most cases, not as they will but as they must.   Before suggesting to them that their wills may be far from free, it is easier to get them to begin examining their cultural conditioning by considering the preconceptions which influence judgments. Because they begin the semester with some definite preconceptions about folklore, we start there. We discuss such beliefs as: "folklore is untrue," "folklore is dying out," "folklore is the exclusive property of the illiterate," etc. With a little coaxing and playing the Devil's advocate, I am able to tease out many of the students' popular misconceptions surrounding folklore. I then attempt to point out the ways in which such misconceptions may have developed and the fact that some may not be entirely groundless. For example, "Folklore is false," but in a sense so are all of our art forms: elite, popular and folk; they are artifice, constructs, products of the human imagination. Thus, some assumptions about folklore are rehabilitated, some are discarded, but all, I believe, are understood a little better, as is the general notion of preconception.

Students read the "Preface" and "Introduction: Into Folkloristics with Gun and Camera" to Barre Toelken's *The Dynamics of Folklore* while we are engaged in this discussion. These selections are useful for developing a definition of folklore, because in them Toelken covers basic approaches, central terms, and common misconceptions of the field. Although he advocates focusing on folklore as a dynamic process (an approach consistent with mine), his treatment of the discipline does not neglect other strategies for the study of traditional art.

After establishing what folklorists consider to be a useful definition of the discipline and introducing concepts such as text, genre, and folk group, I lead the class into a discussion of cultural difference and the preconceptions arising from these differences. Racial stereotypes provide the most vivid examples because most students are aware of having them and ultimately most are willing to identify them as products of cultural conditioning rather than as products of empirical investigation. As we grapple with this problem, we consider esoteric-exoteric elements in folklore and consider the general functions of expressive culture within the students' own groups: ethnic, religious, and special interest. The class reads Laura Bohannan's "Shakespeare in the Bush" which describes the author's failure to translate the plot of *Hamlet* to a group of Tiv storytellers. Bohannan's failure was due to cultural disparities ranging from the linguistic through the social to the aesthetic. Her point that there is an intimate relationship between culture and art makes immediate sense to students, many of whom offer their own examples of things which "don't translate" from one context to another.

By this point, usually one and a half to two weeks into the semester, the class realizes that the study of traditional expressive culture embraces far more sophisticated issues than most of them suspected. Play can be serious business. Jokes not only have a punchline, they have a point. Perceptions of reality are influenced by one's cultural background. These are a few of the notions with which I have confronted them. They begin to realize that they possess information concerning these issues that they have derived from their own experiences as folk. All they lack is a systematic means of exploring that information.

In order to supply such a framework, I assign Richard Dorson's "Introduction" to *Folklore and Folklife: An Introduction*, which provides for students the most comprehensive brief overview of the approaches to the study of folklore that I have discovered. This selection presents some serious problems, however. I believe it is more appropriate for graduate than for undergraduate classes. Many of his points (e.g., *Urformen* vs. *Normalformen*) whiz over the heads of my students, and many members of the class lose sight of the basic arguments which lurk among his copious bibliographical references. I find that many students at this level cower in the presence of naked theory anyway. I devote my efforts during the week we consider this section to reducing Dorson's prose to the basic elements of each theory: the intellectual climate which encouraged its formulation, the fundamental premises of the theory, its basic methods and goals. I also give examples of how the theories are used and point out how they can serve as means to develop answers to some of the questions we discussed earlier in the semester.

Most students claim that this is the most painful segment of the semester. Despite the pain, I believe it not only prepares them for writing their own analyses of folklore later in the semester, but the experience serves them well in any course in which they must wrestle with theory.

The next discussion of the semester is based on the first chapter of Peter Farb's *Word Play*. This assignment deals with language and speech structures and the ways in which they can be manipulated to produce verbal art. After the comparatively arid theoretical terrain we have just traversed, students are eager for a discussion, so I can count on them to provide examples of the ways in which our rules for speaking are slavishly followed or violated in play. During this session, I introduce them to the principles of intensification and inversion which are central to the arguments in the next reading assignment.

This assignment, Roger Abrahams's "Toward an Enactment-Centered Theory of Folklore," proves at least as difficult for the majority of students as Dorson. I include it in the readings because in it Abrahams' typology of enactments—performances, games/sports, festivities/celebrations, and rituals—provides an efficient way for me to make general distinctions among the genres we cover in the course. Since the essay focusses on mode of enactment rather than on the text which is enacted, the framework is consistent with the performance-centered approach I present. By this, the fourth week of the semester, I have introduced the basic concepts we use for the remainder of the course.

For the next two weeks I go back to Farb in order to discuss, in turn, folk speech, proverb, riddle, and the verbal duel. I do this for two reasons. The readings which follow, with the exception of Hurston's *Mules and Men* which includes a few examples of verbal duelling, don't provide easy entry into the discussion of these genres. Also, the consideration of these genres draws us into a less abstract and more extended discussion of matter introduced earlier: inversion, intensification, framing, and function, for example. I allot approximately one class period to the examination of each of these forms, and although Farb's primary concern is language in general rather than folklore specifically, I have been able to make appropriate reading assignments in *Word Play*. I try to rely on class discussion as much as possible during these sessions. The readings and their own experiences with these genres allow students to carry their own weight, and encouraging them to grapple with the data on their own prepares them for their first major examination.

Before the first exam, I generally give at least two of the five or six reading quizzes students take during the semester. These unannounced quizzes consist of four or five questions assigned for the class meeting on which the test is administered. Most of the questions can be answered by means of a short phrase or a single word. These quizzes serve four purposes for me. They allow me to discover as early as possible those areas of the readings that students fail to comprehend. They indicate to students those points which I consider important. They encourage class members to read the material upon which the day's lecture and discussion will be based; therefore, they make for more energetic and fruitful class sessions.

The first major examination focusses on the basic methods and concepts of folklore: genres, theories, key terms, central issues, etc. Fifty percent of the test is devoted to definitions and short answers, customarily five of each. The remainder of the exam consists of two or three discussion questions. In order to respond to the essay questions, students must apply basic notions to their own lore or cultural patterns. Most often I ask them to choose traditional items from their own experience, the ways in which ordinary behaviors are intensified or inverted during a festival or celebration, for example, or I describe a familiar situation and ask them how a knowledge of folklore would help them understand what is going on. In these essay questions, then, I continue badgering them about the structured nature of their own behavior and the emergence of that structure in expressive culture.

In the seventh week of the semester we turn to more extensive studies of folklore in context (urban Euro-American, Native American, and Afro-American). Although the abstractions of the first few weeks of class leave many students cold (in fact, I can expect a 10% drop rate during the period in which the lectures and readings deal exclusively with theory), I feel that students need to develop some framework for analyzing the materials before they can make interesting and informed comments on folklore—their own and others'. I have tried jumping right into what a member of last semester's class characterized as "the real stuff" rather than (his label again) "this theory crap," but I have found that I constantly need to backtrack in order to explain why and how it was possible to interpret a particular custom or enactment in a particular fashion. By beginning with analytical frameworks, I can let the students discover meaning for themselves. As a result, I find myself talking less; I find them taking fewer notes (and thinking more), and

I find all of us enjoying our time together more as the semester progresses.

In the seventh and eighth weeks of the semester, the class reads Jan Brunvand's *The Vanishing Hitchhiker*. I choose to begin the readings on folklore in specific contexts with this because the book examines the urban legends which invariably comprise a major portion of the students' active repertoires. The class responds enthusiastically, and my role is generally limited to keeping discussions on track and making sure that we finish this unit in two (rather than three or four) weeks. On the first day of our discussion, I assign the term project, the collection and analysis of folk performance (see appendix for details). After reading Brunvand, the members of the class realize that traditional performances are accessible to them, and most are eager to examine their own traditions from the new perspectives offered in the book. The author includes a section on collecting and analyzing urban legends as well as providing cultural interpretations for the texts in his collection. These features simplify matters for me, but I also lecture on fieldwork and provide them with a list of journal articles to serve as models for their own analyses. Although I suggest that they might want to work with legends, I do not limit their projects to that specific genre. Most do choose to analyze items similar to those in the book, but some have completed successful projects on riddles, jokes, anecdotes, and tall tales in the two semesters that I have used *Vanishing Hitchhiker*. While Brunvand's historic-geographic concerns diverge from my emphasis on performance, he does argue for the importance of remaining aware of cultural and performance contexts, and he includes examples of symbolic analyses in his glosses of the texts.

During the next two and a half weeks we study American Indian mythology. The text I adopted for this component this semester, Tristram Coffin's *Indian Tales of North America*, is unsatisfactory for use in the course. I am dissatisfied with this anthology primarily because it provides no real sense of cultural context; the book is designed for a general audience. I had hoped it might provide a suitable alternative to Jerome Rothenberg's *Shaking the Pumpkin* (an anthology which does provide information on cultural contexts, but in a format which strives for a total translation to account for all elements of performance, a format which seems to confuse many students). The substitution did not work; I am returning to Rothenberg next semester. *Indian Tales* does include narratives from a range of Native American cultures, but I must spend an inordinate amount of class time lecturing on the cultural contexts of these narratives. Although this doesn't completely dam up the flood of class comment which began with the discussion of urban legend, it does slow it to a trickle. Some good does come of this problem, however. It reinforces my arguments to students that they must provide adequate background on cultural and performance contexts for the material they collect.

As well as lecturing on the setting and function of the myth in Coffin's collection, I cover mythological systems in general, with an emphasis on the classical and Judaeo-Christian. Beyond allowing us to develop a sense of the generic qualities of myth, I find that juxtaposing American Indian texts with the other traditions erodes many prejudices about "those primitives" as opposed to "civilized" cultures such as ours. If the discussion of Euro-American traditions initiated in conjunction with *The Vanishing Hitchhiker* can be considered as rendering the familiar "strange," Then this set of classes has as one of its goals the making of the strange "familiar."

At this point, it is the eleventh week of a fourteen-week semester, and the class has worked on the term project for at least five weeks. I emphasize at least five weeks, because I discuss the general guidelines for the project during the first session of the semester, and many of the more compulsive members of the class began casting about for a topic shortly thereafter. Students turn in their essays now, and we begin our discussion of Afro-American folklore.

This final section of the course presents yet another way to juxtapose cultures. Students had an intimate knowledge of Euro-Americans and their urban legends. My primary role was to suggest means for analyzing the data, to provide novel perspectives for exploring familiar terrain. Native American culture, despite student stereotypes, was terra incognita. Once we addressed initial assumptions (the monolithic nature of "Indian culture," for example), students rarely felt the need to question the basic premises I suggested. In contrast, virtually all my students have had varying degrees of exposure to Black culture, but since the overwhelming majority of students in the typical class are middle class Whites (this semester I have one Black class member), their contact has been superficial. Although students believe they know a great deal about Afro-Americans, their perceptions, though rarely malicious, invariably are skewed. As a result, I feel compelled to readjust some cultural perspectives without losing my own and indulging in glorifying or condemning either the perceived or the perceivers.

I have chosen Zora Neale Hurston's *Mules and Men* for this segment of the course for several reasons. It unfolds in narrative fashion with traditional performances embedded in larger contexts. This format provides some sense of performance settings for the class. Also, it offers a wider range of genres than do the Brunvand or Coffin books: folktale, tall tale, folksong, belief, religion, magic, and healing are presented in context, often as interrelated forms. Overall, *Mules and Men* reveals more dimensions of folklore than the other works we read.

The primary reason I reserve discussion of this book for the end of the semester is to allow the students to complete their own collection projects. After this experience, most members of the class are eager to compare the ways in which their own discoveries and field methods corresponded to or diverged from Hurston's. They always question the author's ability to remember intricate contextual details or to take rapid dictation while dancing, fishing, or eating. At least part of the explanation is that Hurston actually violated one of the major ground rules I establish for my students. Her contextual materials were rearranged, condensed, and reconstructed, although she maintained that none of these events were fabricated. My classes are both disappointed and relieved by this revelation. They are let down that this, in a sense, is not the genuine article, but they are pleased to find that their informants are not as dull as the initial comparison to Hurston's would indicate. Hurston's reworking of her collection notwithstanding, students at this level still seem to achieve a solid sense of the milieux of folk performance and the nature of field work from the book. Certainly no other reading I have ever used inspires such a spontaneous, heated, and productive discussion of field techniques as this one. If that were the only end it accomplished it would be worth using.

A couple of potential problems that might arise from using this book are worth mentioning. *Mules and Men* documents Hurston's experience in several Afro-American communities in the southern United States during the 1920s. Black culture and the response to it by scholars and lay-persons alike bear the marks of the fifty years which have elapsed since the publication of this work. Although Robert Hemenway's introduction to the edition we use addresses some of these factors, I feel that time should be devoted to contextualizing this work. I tend to forget that my students are willing to regard any ethnography as the definitive statement on the subject. This has returned to haunt me not only in statements by White students about "the Blacks" (or "the Indians" or "the Mexican-Americans"), but in this case by Black students asserting that, "We never did anything like that." The dialect in which Hurston transcribes most of her material entails a related problem. Since I think one of the reasonable goals I can set for the class is to help the members attain greater respect for the traditions studied and for the bearers of those traditions, I am wary of reinforcing any stereotypes they might have regarding Black speakers of English. To mitigate this danger, we approach Hurston's handling of her informants' dialect through a discussion (actually a review of a discussion held in the opening weeks of the term while reading Farb) of dialect in general, the features of stereotype, and related matters.

In the closing sessions of the semester, *Mules and Men* facilitates discussions of folktales, tall tales, folksong, belief, folk medicine, magic, and religion in turn. I remain dissatisfied with treating so many genres in such a short span, but Hurston's presentation ties these forms together and binds them to their cultural context. Thus, while I regret covering this number of major types in only five or six sessions, I believe that a more important goal is attained—establishing the interrelatedness of various elements of traditional life in a particular cultural context.

Introduction to Folklore concludes with a final exam. This examination adheres to the format described for the earlier major test, but the questions focus on the cultures and forms considered since the sixth week of the semester. Obviously there is some overlap. The techniques for analysis have been developed throughout the semester, but the data examined is restricted to the material discussed in class from the seventh through the fourteenth weeks. Also, I generally include a question which allows students to utilize knowledge gained in the course of their analysis of a folk performance. This question is phrased something like:

> *What theoretical framework did you use for your term project? In the light of this experience, what are the strengths, weaknesses, problems inherent in the approach? Given a similar assignment, would you use this method again? If so, why? If not, what alternative would you consider and why?*

In general, I am satisfied with the preceding approach to teaching *Introduction to Folklore*. I think it supplies my classes with insights they can use—both as people and as students. In the latter area, former students have gone on to complete additional course work in folklore; one has begun the process of applying to a graduate program. Many have returned later in their undergraduate careers for help in applying their knowledge of folklore to projects assigned in education, sociology, anthropology, and English courses. All this makes me conclude that, although few students see the academic relevance of the course at the outset, such an awareness develops.

As far as inculcating a sense of cultural relativism and tolerance is concerned, it takes more than one course to complete that process. But 329 may be a place to begin. This comment written at the end of a final exam last semester suggests that something clicked for one student: "I had to smile when I wrote it [the answer to an essay question], because sometimes it made me sound like a racist, and I was getting embarrassed."

Appendix

Course Content:

English 329 offers an intensive, though selective, introduction to traditional art forms and their relationships to the cultures in which they arise. Materials ranging from proverb, riddle, legend, and folksong to ritual, witchcraft, and folk medicine will be analyzed by means of theory drawn from literary criticism, linguistics, anthropology, psychology, and other fields. Individual forms of folklore and the interrelationships between these forms will be examined in order to answer questions concerning structure, content, and social function.

In general, class will consist of a combination of lecture and discussion geared to the readings.

Grading:

> 50% Two exams
> 25% Quiz average
> 25% Term Project

Other Matters:

1. All work is due on the date designated on the syllabus. If you have a valid reason for missing an assignment (illness, court appearance, etc.), you will be allowed to make up the work if you can provide written verification. Please bring this verification when you return to class. If you have a valid excuse for missing a quiz, you will not be required to make it up. Your average will be based only on those you have taken.

2. Consistent, relevant class participation will have a positive effect on your final grade, and you can count on being asked to comment on reading assignments during class discussions. Therefore, you should always study the readings carefully and bring the appropriate text to class.

3. Remember that this is an English course. Therefore, points will be deducted for excessive spelling and grammatical errors.

4. Above all, don't simply read or attempt to mindlessly memorize the assigned material. Think about it! Many exam questions will ask you to apply and analyze what you have read, what we have discussed, and what you have experienced as a member of your own folk group. The best way to understand the concepts that are introduced in this course is to relate them to your unique folk experience.

Assignments

[For the purpose of this article, assignments are listed by class number rather than by dates. The class meets twice a week for 75 minutes, which translates to twenty-seven times during a fourteen-week semester. The Dorson, Toelken, Bohannan and Abrahams materials are on Reserve; the other texts are ordered.]

1-3: Introduction to Folklore: Methods, materials, concepts (Toelken, ix-xiii, 3-21; Bohannan)
4-5: Theoretical Perspectives (Dorson 1-51)
6: Language, Speech, and Verbal Art (Farb 1-13)
7: Modes of Behavior and Performance (Abrahams)
8: Folk Speech and Gesture (Farb 17-63, 231-247)
9: Proverb (Farb 107-127)
10: Riddle (Farb 107-127)
11: Verbal Duel (Farb 107-127)
12: First Exam
13: Introduction to the Urban Legend; Discussion of Term Project (Brunvand xi-xiv, 197-202; "Term Project" handout
14: Automobile Motifs (Brunvand 1-46)
15: Murder, Contamination, and Fear of the Dead (Brunvand 47-123)
16: Exposure, Rip-off, and Rumors (Brunvand 125-191)
17: Introduction to American Indian Folklore and Culture (Coffin ix-xviii)
18: Creation Myths (Coffin 5-11)
19: Tricksters, Culture Heroes, and the Taming of the Universe (Coffin 21-22, 27-33, 40-48, 50-51)
20: The Trickster-Culture Hero Cycle (Coffin 63-74)
21: Deviance and Models for Avoidance (Coffin 109-110, 127, 140-142, 146-151); Term Project Due
22: Introduction to Afro-American Culture and Folklore (Hurston x-6)
23: Folktale (Hurston 9-190)
24: Folktale; Folksong (Hurston 257-279)
25-26: Folk Belief, Folk Religion, Folk Medicine (Hurston 193-252)
27: Final Remarks

Term Project English 329

Read Brunvand's *The Vanishing Hitchhiker*, pp. 197-202. This section contains basic procedures for collecting urban legends (and narratives in general), techniques of analysis, and suggestions for organizing legend studies.

Several points are of particular importance. Legends should be recorded (either taped or written) exactly as they are performed; do not edit or rewrite them in order to "improve" the text. Make notes on the gestures, movements, tone of voice, etc., used during performances. Make notes on audience reactions and interactions. Try to determine the performer's feelings about the narrative. Essential facts (Brunvand discusses these facts on p. 198) about performers should be obtained.

Brunvand's primary interest is in the text of legends. Green is interested in the performance of legends, also. Both of us are interested in the relationship between narratives and the sociocultural system of the folk group. Make sure both of us would be satisfied with your paper.

Your paper should provide as complete a transcription of a performance as you can develop. In addition, you should analyze the legend in an essay of 1000-1250 words (4-5 typed pages). Develop a particular thesis, and it probably would be useful to take a particular theoretical perspective. You should not need to do library research. The information obtained through class readings and lectures should have provided you with everything you need to know in order to complete this project.

   If you prefer to work with some other type of performance (a joke, for example), discuss this with me. Also, I would strongly urge you to discuss your legend project with me. Let's hold this discussion in my office. Don't try to talk about a project as complex and important as this one in the few minutes preceding or following class.

   Good luck!

I would like to thank Sylvia Grider for her close reading of and valuable comments on an earlier version of this essay.

Lydia Fish

State University of New York College at Buffalo

Introduction to Folklore and Folklife

I teach at State University College at Buffalo (enrollment 11,662), a former teachers' college which became a liberal arts school (at least officially) only a few years before I arrived in 1967. I was originally hired in the English department, but, after many years of explaining to my colleagues that my field was not a branch of children's literature, I took advantage of a general administrative reorganization and transferred, with deep thankfulness, to the Anthropology department. Although I taught the usual literature-related courses in my English department days (ballad, folktale, etc.) and have done some interdepartmental courses (folklore and history, a class on Buffalo churches for the religious studies program, and one on ethnic neighborhoods in Buffalo for the Geography department), my first love has always been the introductory course. (*Introduction to Folklore and Folklife*, Anthropology 144) Because of its numbering it is technically a freshman course, although many of my students are upperclassmen.

I occasionally teach an upper-level course in urban folklore and supervise quite a few independent studies in folklore every year. There are also some folklore courses in other departments—the English department offers an introductory course and one in American folklore, plus a few genre courses on the graduate level, and the Music department has an ethnomusicologist and a popular music specialist who teach courses in folk music, blues, and country music. I do a bit of lecturing in other departments from time to time—folklore in the media for the journalism students and folklore of death and dying for a class in human development.

Introduction to Folklore and Folklife is taken as an optional ethnography course by anthropology majors, as an all-college elective by anyone who is interested, and has been tentatively approved as one of the social science courses in the proposed liberal arts core curriculum. (Since a large percentage of our students are still registered in B.S. rather than B.A. programs, more than half of my students are majoring in criminal justice, broadcasting and journalism, business, or dietetics rather than the traditional liberal arts and social science departments.) It is also offered for continuing education credit, so it can be taken by non-matriculated students. I have taught it as an evening course and as a weekend course, as well as in summer school. When it is taught as a module course during the summer and the class meets for three hours each day it often turns into a sort of neighborhood walking tour, with visits to ethnic markets and bakeries, old cemeteries and churches, and street fairs and festivals. I teach at least one section each semester and have taught as many as three. My colleagues are immensely supportive—a generous chunk of department film, instructional, supply, and library budgets is at my disposal and the school gives me an extra office to house my current research project and the file cabinets containing the S.U.C.A.B. Folklore Archives. (In the most recent version of the class we screened and discussed *The Popovich Brothers of South Chicago, One Generation is Not Enough, In the Rapture, Palio,* and *Always for Pleasure.*)

Buffalo is a multi-ethnic, heavily Roman Catholic, industrial city with a population of about 357,000. Most of them are second or third generation immigrants. (Once I had a class which included students from thirteen ethnic backgrounds.) Many of my students are older—particularly in my evening classes, which have the heaviest concentration of continuing education students, I often have mothers and grandmothers who have returned to school after raising their families; veterans; and men and women who are working at fulltime jobs but who have decided that they also want a college degree. One summer I had most of the Hamburg Fire Department. Most of the kids are bright and street-wise and the older students, especially, are very well-motivated.

The first problem I had to solve was the text—because most of my students are not well off (in fact, most of them have part-time jobs) I couldn't take the ideal solution of having them buy several books and use part of each. I tried several unsatisfactory compromises and, like many other folklorists, blessed the names of Brunvand and Norton when *The Study of American Folklore* first appeared in 1968. I have used this book ever since, sometimes with an additional book on a special topic or a reader. (The book has certain problems, as anyone who has ever tried to use it knows. However, the students find the definitions and the bibliography very helpful and the other two available texts would not be suitable for my classes—Dorson's *Folklore and Folklife* is too advanced and Barre Toelken's fine *Dynamics of Folklore* is very idiosyncratic. I have never figured out how anyone except Barre does use it as a text, although I have been telling the publisher's rep from Houghton Mifflin for years that if they would bring out a paperback edition I would definitely use it as a second book.) Bert Wilson's *On Being Human*—the best introduction I have ever found to the functional approach—is also now on the required list. Bruce Jackson's *Fieldwork* is indispensible—it is at once a lucid practical manual on the social and technical aspects of fieldwork and a fine examination of the theoretical and ethical questions involved in any field project.

I have a large reserve list in the library, which saves the students' having to buy extra books; if they are feeling flush they can always copy the assigned articles and read them at home. This list changes from time to time, but I usually assign articles from Dundes' *Study of Folklore* and *Interpreting Folklore,* Clarke and Clarke's *Folklore Reader,* Brunvand's *Readings in American Folklore,* Coffin's *Our Living Traditions,* and Dorson's *Folklore and Folklife.* There is also an ever-changing list of xeroxed journal articles. Recently I have been experimenting with putting audio-cassettes on reserve—I have found that many of my students would rather listen to something than read it. The *American Folklore* series which Everett Edwards put out several years ago is an extremely mixed bag, but it contains a couple of real gems: Larry Danielson on immigrant folklore, Dave Hufford on hospital folk speech, and Jane Beck on preppie folklore. Other folklore lectures are available from National Public Radio (Bettelheim, Dundes, and Toelken) and I tape visiting folklore lecturers on campus. Now that I have a very portable tape recorder I have thought of taping some of the more interesting papers at folklore meetings for this purpose. The commuting students listen to these on buses with their Walkman recorders or play them on their car stereos. I have also been thinking about the possibility of putting videocassettes on reserve. (I tend to use a good deal of audio-visual material in the classroom as well—film, videotapes, audio tape, and lots and lots of slides from my own fieldwork.)

I think that the hardest lesson for any eager young Ph.D. in folklore to learn is that a large part of the stuff he just got through memorizing for his prelims is of no real help in the classroom. Usually the neophyte folklorist has no teaching experience (most folklore students seem to work as graduate research and editorial assistants rather than as T.A.'s) and the last time he (or she) had much contact with undergraduates was when he was one himself. Decompressing from the higher altitudes of theory can be a traumatic experience for both teacher and students. As a true product of Indiana, I spent several years boring my students silly with type and motif numbers before I realized that this was probably the only time they would ever take a folklore course and that they really did not need to have all that information. I have learned over the years that my students already know a tremendous amount of folklore and that if I just shut up occasionally they will tell me about it. I have only to start a discussion of games to be overwhelmed by a very technical debate over the relative merits of street hockey (Buffalo) and stickball (Brooklyn). On ethnic calendar custom and rites of passage my students are a perfect gold mine of information and they pick up each new urban legend as soon as it surfaces. (The alligators from the New York sewers are currently appearing in the new Buffalo metro tunnels.) Occupational folklore runs the gamut from steelworker and postal inspector to Vietnam veteran, and I have yet to teach a class in which there is not at least one student whose grandmother can take off the evil eye. I sometimes think that my course should be called *Folklore Appreciation*—what I really try to do is teach them to recognize and analyze their own traditions. Like the character in *Le Bourgeois Gentilhomme* who is surprised to learn that he has always spoken in prose, my students are fascinated by the discovery that "all these things I've been doing all my life" are really folklore.

Originally I organized the course pretty much on a genre basis—I gave a brief introduction and then more or less used Brunvand as an outline. I now find that I spend about half the semester on discussions about who the folk are, and how and why they transmit folklore. (My theoretical approach tends to be heavily functional, with slight Freudian overtones.) I am becoming more and more fascinated by the relationship between folklore and the media, so these days we are talking a lot about that. We spend some time on fieldwork and library technique, since each student does an annotated field collection. I then do a survey of genres, placing less emphasis on the "oral literature" ones like riddle, proverb, ballad and folktale (which I think their text handles quite well) and more on folk belief, rites of passage (including occupational folklore), calendar custom, festivals, and celebrations, which are my own areas of specialization.

The course varies greatly in emphasis from semester to semester—it has to, if I am not going to get stale teaching it at least four times a year. I usually draw heavily on my own current research—after I spent a summer in Siena two years ago I assigned *La Terra in Piazza*, showed lots of slides which I had taken, and we used the palio as an example in discussions of community, esoteric and exoteric factors, function, and festivals. Last year I was doing fieldwork with Vietnam veterans and most of my students were watching the PBS series on the history of the Vietnam War, so we talked about folklore as a strategy for survival under combat conditions and in the veteran community. A great deal also depends on the makeup of the class. One semester several years ago I had a class composed almost entirely of kids from one small area of Long Island; they had all attended each other's bar mitzvahs and sweet sixteen parties. That semester was heavy on Jewish folklore. Some years I have classes which are primarily from the west side (Italian) or the east side (Polish) of Buffalo. Often one student who is willing to talk will make a difference in the direction of a class—if someone starts a discussion the rest will usually join in. This semester I have an older man in one class who is fascinating my little urbanites with stories about hunting, fishing, and maple-sugaring in his rural New York boyhood. The best class I ever had included one extremely articulate Vietnam veteran, a recent grandmother who loved to talk about her Italian background, and an enchanting little blonde airhead who was a real expert on high school customs like senior prom garter ceremonies. Every so often I get a real folkie in class and the whole class gets plugged into the Buffalo folksong scene.

Each student is expected to make an annotated field collection. This collection may be based on interviews or (in the case of barns or grave-markers) photographs or sketches. Occasionally someone becomes really ambitious and uses super-8mm film or videotape. I give several lectures on basic fieldwork techniques ("Make appointments with your informants in advance. Make sure you know how to operate your tape recorder and/or camera before you go into the field. . . .") and stress the importance of making careful and complete documentation. They are instructed to transcribe their tapes and catalog their slides and then to go to the library and try to annotate what they have collected. The annotation can serve both as identification and as a basis for comparative analysis. They are told that they are to make some sort of analysis of their material—I don't really care whether it is structural, comparative, or functional, but I do want them to think a little about what all that stuff they have collected means. Except for very mechanical directions ("put your name on every page of your collection, label slides, type") I leave the form of the paper up to them. They are to include a bibliography of works consulted. Grading collection projects tends to be very subjective: given the topic, the difficulty of collecting material on that topic in Buffalo, and the amount of scholarship available for annotation, how good a job has this student done? Sometimes a new book comes along that makes all the difference. Steve Zeitlin, Amy Kotkin, and Holly Cutting Baker's *A Celebration of American Family Folklore* is an excellent example of this—it established some workable categories of this extremely amorphous topic and provides an excellent bibliography.

I ask my students to check out their collection topics with me so they don't get started on something more suitable for a dissertation topic, but otherwise it is up to them. The range of topics they come up with is absolutely staggering—coon-dog trials, customs of Grateful Dead fans, folklore of blind students ("the most embarrassing thing my guide dog ever did. . . ."), car jewelry (things you hang on the rear-view mirror of your car), St. Joseph tables, water witching in the family, and folklore among members of the Society for Creative Anachronisms and Dungeon and Dragon players. The enthusiasm and ingenuity with which they pursue these topics are also amazing—one of my students who was working on military funeral customs struck up a quite chummy long-distance relationship with the director of protocol at Arlington and I will never forget being awakened in the small hours by a call from a student who had just been picked up (undeservedly, as it turned out) in a campus drug bust. He foresaw that he would be spending some time in the Erie County holding center and would it be all right if he did his collection project on jailhouse folklore? Also, since he just had one telephone call, would I please be kind enough to call his lawyer?

The students also learn to use the library to annotate their collections and are expected to write a concluding essay about their collecting experiences and what they think the material they have collected means. The reference librarians have been wonderful—one of them has worked out a special lecture in folklore bibliography, complete with slides, which she gives to all my classes. They are also getting very good at finding the proper terms to do computer searches for my students (it is a nuisance working in a field which doesn't have its own data base) and showing them how to use the University Microfilm catalogs. (Most students are very surprised to find out how cheap and easy it is to buy dissertations on microfilm.) I believe that both the fieldwork and the library experience are crucial to a student's understanding of folklore—if for no other reason than at least raising the question of "how is this discipline different from all others?" I also feel that the essay gives the students a chance to sort out their fieldwork experiences in their own minds and to make some analyses of their data. My tests tend to be pretty much a matter of facts and definitions. I tell my students that the tests only tell me if they have come to class and done their homework—their collection project (which counts for more than half of their grade) will tell me if they understood any of it.

Like many folklorists who do fieldwork in their own communities, I am often used as a resource person by the groups I study. This contributes immeasurably to my classroom teaching and also means that I do a lot of teaching outside the classroom. For example, several years ago, when I was doing fieldwork at our local Greek Orthodox church, the priest asked me to prepare a slide and tape presentation on Orthodox domestic religious custom for the annual Hellenic Festival. Also, several of my students have worked at the festival as office help, photographers, and general volunteers—thus learning more about ethnic tradition in Buffalo than they could have picked up in a classroom.

Sometimes this community participation has unexpected ramifications. This spring I am offering a course in the Vietnam veteran subculture which I have been studying for the past year and have asked members of that community to share their stories with the class. What started as an attempt to show how the shared traditions of these men and women had enabled them to survive the experiences of a particularly dreadful war and of the almost equally traumatic period which followed it turned rapidly into something much more intense. Veterans who found that being able to tell their stories to a fascinated and empathetic class served as a sort of validation of their experiences started to bring their friends. One man who has been attending regularly has been sitting in his living room for ten years. He says that this is the first time he has been able to talk about his war and has started bringing his sons and mother so they can understand what happened to him. The students have become equally involved—two of them spent their spring break at the vigil held for the POW/MIAs at the Vietnam Veterans Memorial in Washington. It had never occurred to me before that social action might be a form of applied folklore. (Nancy Groce refers to this as "guerilla academics.")

During the years I've been in Buffalo I have often run across students of Harold Thompson, who taught an introductory folklore course at Cornell in the forties and fifties which absolutely everyone who went to college there seems to have taken. Upon learning that I am a folklorist these people (usually professional types in three-piece suits) will say something like, "I took Dr. Tommy's course when I was an undergraduate at Cornell and I loved it. Do you know, ever since then I've really *noticed* folklore." If someone is saying this about me in 30 years, I shall be very happy.

Ellen J. Stekert

University of Minnesota

An *Introduction to Folklore* (In Context)

History of the Teacher and the Course

I arrived in the Department of English at the University of Minnesota in 1973, having taught nine years in the English Department at Wayne State University in Detroit and one year as a visiting professor of Anthropology at the University of California, Berkeley. The University of Minnesota presently has a student body of 45,000. The undergraduates represent a wide range of middle America, while the graduate students represent a wide range of both the United States and foreign countries. The University students are from rural and urban areas; their value systems run the gamut from avant garde to blatant reactionary; they are urbane and mundane. In general, the majority (who are from the Upper Midwest) give me the impression that they feel they exist in the center of things: East is "out east" and West is "out west" in local folk speech. If a student is from "The Cities" (Minneapolis and Saint Paul—an important distinction to learn quickly) the rest of the state is simply "out state." I have yet to meet a rural Minnesotan who welcomed that description; it has strong implications of being "out of it"—and "it" is generally held to be "The Cities." But even with this feeling of certainty that Minnesota is the center, most students from Minnesota wish to leave the state eventually; leave it for "real life" elsewhere.

When I arrived at the University of Minnesota, I was already a full professor. My rank, plus the fact that a nation-wide search for a folklorist had been made by my department as a top priority, strengthened my case during initial negotiations. I realized being the only folklorist in the department and at the University would make future bargaining for courses or other options difficult. The outcome of my initial negotiations with the English Department was that I taught a normal load (now five courses in three quarters), was given adequate audio-visual equipment, had graduate faculty status, and taught only folklore. I developed a series of three successive courses in Introduction to Folklore, all on the 5-XXX level (upper class and graduate students). The last of the three courses is a collecting course and at least one of the initial courses has to be taken in order for a student to enroll in it. I also developed a series of two Anglo- and Afro-American folksong courses on the 5-XXX level, and one graduate folklore seminar with an open title.

I was determined not to begin with a huge lower level introductory course and attempt to work "up" from there. Making folklore available to the more advanced students first actually made it easier to introduce additional lower level courses.

(Unfortunately I could not do away with the quarter system.) Ten years after arriving at Minnesota, I now have proposed a 1-XXX level introductory course, and four years ago I introduced a 3-XXX level course in American Folklore. In short, I was hired to teach folklore and nothing else, and I have been able to develop an interesting and full series of courses within the Department of English. All of these courses are listed under English and may be taken by any student. They fulfill some requirements for both graduate and undergraduate English majors, and also fulfill the English distribution requirements in the College of Liberal Arts or can be taken as an elective. If I ever decide to teach a course not listed, I always have the opportunity to teach under one of the "open" listings the Department keeps at either graduate or undergraduate level. I also have taken advantage of teaching "open" courses in other Departments and Programs, such as Humanities and American Studies.

Cross-listing of courses was difficult when I first arrived, but now it is encouraged, and I am in the process of exploring the potential with American Studies, Anthropology, and Music. In 1983-84 a new administration began its term in the English Department; with their encouragement I am presently restructuring the folklore offerings, integrating them with other groups of courses in the department, and generally making folklore more visible and more a part of existing programs and concentrations in both the Department of English and other units of the University.

The three courses which constitute an introduction to the field of folklore are an introduction to genre, complete with discussion of the problems therein (English 5481); an introduction to folk belief systems and folk behaviors, complete with a discussion of how the "item" is necessarily related to context and world-view, and thus genre of some sort must be taken into account (English 5482); and a field work course (at least one of the other courses is prerequisite) in which each student does a pilot field project under weekly supervision of the Instructor (English 5483).

Because I was going to be on leave in the Winter 1983 quarter, I chose to condense the two initial introductory courses into one single course for the Fall quarter. The combined course was thus an introduction to Folklore by both genre and by belief and behavior systems. In teaching it I attempted to cover the basic material in folklore which a student should have before being let loose to do fieldwork and which any student should have to claim a sound beginning knowledge of the discipline.

Course Objectives and Related Requirements

My goal in teaching folklore is to communicate the meaning of the field, in part, by the manner in which I teach the course. I try to show that the classroom is a folklore context in itself, and I attempt to relate my behavior as a teacher to the class's behavior as students. On occasion I purposefully break with traditional teacher role behavior. For example, on the first day of classes I request that each student (if willing) fill out a card which gives name, class year, college, major, previous folklore or related courses (such as cultural anthropology or mythology), place of birth and places lived, reasons for taking the course (distribution requirement, interest, helpful to major field, etc.; "nice words" are specifically discouraged). When these are handed in I give a brief biography of myself and then ask the class to address any question to me that they wish. This soon turns into an exercise in the folklore of academe; often what is not asked is more important to the students than what is asked. So what is proper to ask the teacher? Where are the boundaries? This class session usually results in a clear understanding that we all function in everyday settings according to unwritten yet stringent and unvoiced rules—part of our folklore.

Another of my basic goals in teaching an introductory folklore course is to help the student feel at ease working in the discipline. Most students arrive in the course with widely diverse ideas of the field; the initial classes are directed toward a general understanding of the subject matter and a discussion of the "folklore of folklore" (or to be precise, the "metafolklore" they have learned in their everyday lives). Another goal is to show them, and have them see for themselves, that good scholarship is an exciting endeavor and that the materials of the field of folklore can be studied carefully and fully and yield both important insights and gratifying intellectual and creative results. I require a paper and examinations since I find these help students learn to communicate their findings.

I do not slight the profound joy of good academic investigation, but I insist that each student relate the subject-matter of the course to her or his life, so that once through the course that student will walk through the world with greater understanding. One way I attempt this is to assign projects which require students to set down in rigorous fashion some traditional event they have experienced during the quarter. It is my hope that by the end of the quarter each student will have developed a consciousness that all human beings necessarily have a set of assumptions about life that result in a myriad of ideas and behaviors some of which are often "taken for granted" by the person who lives in accordance with them, but which can be seen as strange and bizarre by anyone with another world-view. In other words, I hope that by the time my students have finished this introduction to folklore they will recognize both the necessity and the arbitrary quality of many of their mute assumptions.

In teaching the introduction to folklore, I attempt to give my students a diachronic view of both the field itself (the history of folklore scholarship) and of its subject matter (how did "Cinderella" or "The Daemon Lover" change through time, and why?). This is balanced with a synchronic view of the field as it is today and how folklore affects and is used by people in the present.

Because of the persistent influence of Social Darwinism on the general public's attitude toward folklore, it is important that students realize that folklore is not a deterrent to creativity, but rather is a means by which one may be creative. The use of folklore in context, the choice of material, the changes made within the unspoken norms—even pushing the boundaries of those norms—are all part of the folk process. Somewhere within the confines of my own syllabus, I make certain that I offer a fairly complex lecture on "creativity" within "high" culture (say opera), and "folk" culture (say folksong), showing which elements must be examined and what questions can be asked: the conclusion is that both "high" art and "folk" art have equal potential for creativity (and in some cases the potential is greater for the folk artist). When using Toelken's text, I like to include his descriptions of Japanese-American foodways, and then show how "creativity" and change actually occurred in this area by referring to D. Mas Masumoto's good-natured note on brown rice sushi (1983).

The Mechanics of the Course and Their Purpose

What texts to use? Until the publication of Barre Toelken's *The Dynamics of Folklore* most texts were either too limited or too encased in past "item-oriented" studies for me to use as more than historical examples and contrasts to what is currently being done by others. Toelken has gracefully summarized one of the recent major recognitions of folklorists: that the process which in part defines the subject matter of the field must be presented. But Toelken's work needs strong supplementary texts and assignments to give students a feeling of security. "Process" is an abstract concept, no matter how well Toelken illustrates it, and this makes his text difficult to use in an introductory class. I feel that some more genre-oriented texts are needed to put the class at ease so that they can understand the very point of Toelken's text. At times I have used as a supplementary text Dorson's *Folklore and Folklife* and at others I have used his *Buying the Wind* (despite its concentration on American materials) or Dundes's *The Study of Folklore*. This particular year I tried Brunvand's *Readings in American Folklore* (again, despite the American emphasis) to help "ground" the class in specific investigations and in some genre-oriented studies. I also used Dundes's *Interpreting Folklore* to show the class how to critique studies—and to help them see that insights can be gained as well as distorted when using concepts from other disciplines to understand folklore. For the section of the course on sexism, I found Gloria Kaufman and Mary Kay Blakely's book *Pulling Our Own Strings: Feminist Humor & Satire* (1980) an excellent example of both feminist folklore and two folk attitudes towards scholarship within the feminist movement (i.e. the two "Introductions"). The Kaufman and Blakely text provides a provocative contrast to Dundes's "The Crowing Hen and the Easter Bunny," and "Into the Endzone for a Touchdown" (both in *Interpreting Folklore*). It is interesting that many students view both supplementary texts as politically motivated, or, generally lacking objectivity and balancing data. I seriously doubt that Kaufman and Blakely would argue with this observation of their work—which is exactly why I like to use it.

Apart from a few outside assignments, the basic requirements for the course are a research paper, a midquarter, and a final. The paper is tailored to each student's interest or major. This necessitates many contact hours per student for the instructor, but it serves as a powerful incentive for the student to become deeply involved in the research. It is also one of the most interesting aspects of the course for the instructor, for it allows me to learn constantly, not only during class discussions but also during the period in which I counsel the student on the project. Each student is given a list of periodicals and research tools at the beginning of the quarter and then is required to present by the middle of the quarter a preliminary outline of the projected paper, complete with a preliminary annotated bibliography (indicating how each item relates to the project). This requirement moves students into the library early and prevents last minute panic. It also allows me to post outside my office door a list of student projects and lists of additional bibliography; I update the lists every week or three weeks, and encourage students to see if they can help others in the class with items discovered during library research. The posting of the topics and bibliography tends to unite the class, and often two or more students with similar topics work together. It also helps keep me updated on bibliography and encourages useful excursions through past bibliography.

I always give the "midquarter" exam in the seventh week. Since the material and the approach to it is usually totally new to most students, I find the "late-quarter" rather the "midquarter" timing relieves anxiety. The exam almost always requires essay answers, with a few short-answer questions thrown in to allay anxiety and to benefit those students who have been attending class. Depending on how the class progresses, the final is either a take-home examination or an in-class written exam with one take-home question brought in at the time the rest of the exam is taken.

The class size is controlled at 40 students. I find it best to give out the complex introductory sheet on the first day of class. It clearly outlines what is expected of the student and therefore weeds out those students who have come to the course with less than honorable academic intent, i.e., those who have taken the course because of their folklore about folklore. There is normal "shrinkage" during the quarter: some students find the work too burdensome, the subject not what they want, the academic standards too stringent, or the instructor unbearable. In addition, I have recently chosen to teach my course on the Tuesday-Thursday schedule (one hour and fifteen minutes per session twice a week), and prefer to start at an early hour: 8:15 a.m. To accommodate students who work, I arrive at school by seven so that it is possible to have some office hours before class. Partly as a result of our shared experience of making it to school in the dark and frozen winter mornings, the class becomes closely knit as the quarter progresses. In fact, the meeting hour serves to start the class on subject matter: how many students are "day people" and how many are "night people"? By what folk means, large or small, do we identify and label people? (I am always surprised when, invariably, most of the class identify themselves as "night people.")

The class is composed of both undergraduate and graduate students. I give an additional assignment to graduate students and carefully explain to the entire class that my system of marking is not determined by a predestined curve or by my staircase, but rather by the quality of work they do. I make it clear from the beginning that "C" is adequate, "B" is very good, and "A" is exceptional if not inspired—no matter class status.

There are usually about five to ten graduate students in the course, and I require that they give an oral report (also submitted in written form the day it is given) on an article that they and the instructor choose. The reports are scheduled for ten minutes with a short time set aside after for class discussion (if wished). I always plan these reports for the day in the Fall when I will be at the AFS meetings plus part of the following class period, and I assign one student the task of running the class and of recording the session on tape. This arrangement invariably generates discussion. Articles are picked on the basis of what interests each student, and what the class can benefit from most. I have used such articles as Kay Stone's "Märchen to Fairy Tale: An Unmagical Transformation," or Stone's other articles which deal with the interaction of folk and popular culture; Barbara Kirshenblatt-Gimblett's "A Parable in Context: A Social Interactional Analysis of Storytelling Performance" (I suggest that the class discuss this in contrast with Toelken's presentation of "Tina's Proverb"); and William Hugh Jansen's now famous "esoteric/exoteric" article (I like to ask students, after they hear the report, to draw a representation of this concept of how folklore "works"). Such articles generate discussion and allow the students to become familiar with ideas they otherwise would not meet in an already heavy reading schedule.

The Content of the Course and the Hidden Agenda

In each of the introductory courses I find it necessary to confront the metafolklore (the folklore about folklore) of the culture(s) from which the students come. I ask them to "collect" from each other, or think of how people generally use the term; the concepts of "unscientific," "the old days," "unimportant and trivial," "childlike and innocent," and more, surface at once. After a thorough discussion of positive, negative, and neutral aspects of the use of the term, I give the class my definition of folklore, which I tell them will serve as a working definition and that I welcome questions, modifications, and discussion at any time during the course.

My definition of folklore, in a truncated form, is this: Folklore is the study of learned traditions of behavior and belief which have been passed within and amongst groups through human communication and which do not have a fixed source from which the behavior or belief is consistently corrected; essentially, folklore is the study of change in certain elements of culture. Thus, "folklore" is a descriptive and not a normative word. I encourage the class to think of a spectrum, one end of which is popular culture (material which reflects important aspects of a society but which does not endure temporally although it might spread spatially) and the other end of which is folklore (such as the "Cinderella" tale, which has lived and changed through centuries and multiple cultures, reflecting the values of the various groups in which it was perpetuated). I emphasize that the two types of material mix in a grey area, the kind of area humanist scholars find at once the most frustrating and the most rewarding. The material of popular culture can be studied in much the same manner and have much the same questions asked of it as the material of folklore. And as with any study of human activity, careful delineations and descriptions must be taken into account before conclusions may be drawn.

After the definition of folklore, someone inevitably asks: "What isn't folklore"? Answer: not much, just as "What isn't history, literature, philosophy, art and so forth?" It is too easy to spend a great deal of time defining folklore, and I believe it is best to take the necessary (defensive) stance of asking anyone in the class to define his or her field. This usually returns the class to a sense of proportion.

I ask that students rid themselves of the habit (if they have it) of using the term "folklore" as a value word in class. The term is meant to describe, not to judge. Thus I do not use the pop term "fakelore" in class, since it lacks any clear, non-judgmental definition. If students feel the term has merit, then I encourage them to explore its history and I welcome for scrutiny any new definition they might develop.

The definition of folklore which I give is one of process, and so I find it necessary to help the class grasp the idea of folklore by anchoring it to items and to group these items. Consequently I write on the board, and have done so (with variations) since 1963, the following "categories" of folklore:

1) Transcribable (usually verbal) material
2) Belief and value systems
3) Actions, behavior systems, and customs
4) Technology and its products (material culture)

This gives the class some sense of the "what" of folklore. I point out that these are not mutually exclusive categories. In fact, I like to take an item at the end of this lesson—such as the mountain dulcimer, and show its interrelationships amongst the categories. The dulcimer is "clearly" from category 4 since it is a traditionally made item (often), but it has a folk aesthetic about its looks and how it is played, and there are beliefs about whether or not it is "sinful" to use it for dances or singing (category 2). There are given places and times when it is played (gatherings and festivals) and the manner of playing it is traditional (category 3). The playing is judged good or bad by a knowledgeable audience (category 2 again), and often there are words used to explain how to build it (perhaps mnemonic devices to know what woods to use in making it), as well as sayings involving a dulcimer, terms for its various parts, or words to songs sung with a dulcimer (category 1).

The dulcimer example has only limited utility, for it reenforces the stereotype of folk group as "them" (point downward). The next step is to ask the class what groups they belong to—for all groups have folklore. (If this is too threatening, I ask what groups their friends belong to.) Various categories are at once recognized by: ethnic, linguistic, regional, age, sex, and others are the most obvious. It is always fun to ask the class in what group they would place students. They are clearly not an ethnic group, and they are not a geographical group on a commuter campus, but are they a "work," "leisure time," or "life style" group? The fact that each student has difficulty with this very immediate question shows the inherent complexity of deciding what a "group" is. Yet each class member knows that in the eyes of others she or he is daily classified as a "student." This is a pointed lesson about the intriguing "grey" areas of folklore. I go through the four categories (above) with the class, listing the folklore with which they are familiar from the many groups to which they belong. It often comes as a surprise to some students to see how long the list can be, without even approaching an ending.

There are several assignments I feel are helpful to a beginning folklore class, at least one of which I give before the first exam. I often assign a similar project as part of the final. One of these assignments is to take a given edition of a local paper and find in it examples of items which use folklore. Before the first assignment I have the entire class bring in another edition of a specific paper and we go through the paper examining how folklore is used. There are three steps: identify the folklore, determine if it has been altered or not, and conclude why it appears where it does and how it is used. All sections of the paper are grist for this assignment, and the students' own cultural experience can serve as confirmation of the "changes" made in the material. (There have been documented cases of students actually driven to use the library for this assignment in order to discover more about the newspaper's use of folklore.) I never have failed to find this an exciting and engaging assignment. From the layout of the paper, through "newspaper folklore," through advertisements, want ads, obits, personals, syndicated (and not syndicated) columnists, to the most challenging—the "hard news" stories—the students eventually are able to find folklore everywhere. Once they ask and begin to understand why it is used, they are well on their way to critical thinking.

I also assign the class at least one literary work, one which is generally acclaimed by the current folklore of literary academe to be "good" literature. I ask them to locate and verify the folklore, and then to discuss the reasons the author might have chosen to use folklore or even folk-like material to achieve his or her aesthetic goals. In James's *Turn of the Screw*, for example, it soon becomes apparent that the work would have no effect upon people who did not believe in (or "know about") British and American ghosts, and how they traditionally manifest themselves. The very form of the story, the incomplete frame, adds to the air of mystery since there is no neat "summing up." In this respect, James violates the ghost tale's performed oral folk tradition, thus making his work more dramatic in written form, for we are left with no "present" to which we can return. It becomes clear to students that not only is the very structure of Twain's "The Celebrated Jumping Frog of Calaveras County a folklore form (a hoax—or an acted-out practical joke), but the characters are folk stereotypes used to develop the themes of east versus west and education versus common sense. Twain skillfully uses folk speech as well as various traditional verbal genres and items (such as the joke of the poor loaded frog, or the Munchausen-like tale of the sawed-in-half dog) to achieve his aesthetic goal.

So the newspaper assignment and the "literary" assignment have much the same end. They teach the student to ask important questions: not just where, what, and how, but also "why—given the writer's goals?"

Sometimes I assign each student a summary-critique of one scholarly article published in one of the major folklore journals within the last ten or fifteen years. I ask students to find and read an article which interests them, summarize it and the author's intent, and then discuss whether or not the author was successful. If the student does not understand the article, I ask that the student discuss why this happened. After all, a major part of one's education is to learn what questions to ask. This assignment often forces the student to become familiar with journals other than those consulted during research for the paper, and it also gives me access to differing perspectives on a wide range of articles.

The Necessity of Teaching the History of the Field

I find it necessary in almost every introductory folklore class to give a history of the discipline. Since I feel it is of central concern to teaching folklore, I will explore it at greater length than I do any other section of my course. An historical perspective not only reenforces other material in the course, it also helps to correct misconceptions of the current field. After all, folklorists have no claim to the only interesting and varied history of an academic discipline. The students can see how intellectual vogues have influenced not only folklore but much else, and this naturally leads them to wonder what is influencing their (and others') thinking today. When, for example, students learn that during the National/Romantic period of folklore scholarship in the early nineteenth century Sweden ruled Finland, it is much less of a mystery to them why a country doctor decided to collect and then patch together a national epic, *The Kalevala*, which served well to give Finns a sense of separate national identity.

I begin by discussing the enormous amount of folklore material in libraries, archives, and elsewhere, that predate the acceptance by academic institutions of folklore as a valid discipline. Students should know something about the numerous ancient collections of Eastern traditional materials gathered from oral tradition (the Jataka tales and the Panchatantra, for example). The Western "ancients" seemed to enjoy describing the folklore of other cultures: Herodotus observed and wrote about the folklore of the "barbarians," and later Sophocles interpreted the folklore that everyone who "counted" in Athens already knew.

I point out that almost all literature was oral before (and for quite a while after) Gutenberg's famous 1456 Bible. I also point out that the majority of what is listed in college catalogues as "Medieval literature" is intimately related to (or is) folk literature. Some professors of Old and Middle English feel a bit uncomfortable when their students mention this, but as we know, that is metafolklore manifesting itself in our own subculture. And of course there were adults who simply enjoyed readings, garlands, miscellanies, Perrault's redactions, Basile, and Boccaccio. So history is full of descriptions of folklore, and of redactions of verbal folk tradition, just as museums are full of mute folk artifacts. But the study of these things is relatively new.

Unlike others, who have been influenced perhaps by the past twenty-five years' emphasis on the study of folk narrative (as opposed to folksong), I do not cite 1812 (and the Grimms) as the symbolic beginning of serious folklore scholarship. I cite instead Bishop Percy's successful publication of his *Reliques* in 1765, complete with headnotes and, in an early edition, an essay on the origins of the form of the ballad. For the sake of discussion I divide the periods of scholarship into:

1) The Romantic/Nationalistic period (roughly 1760-1859)
2) The Unilinear Evolutionary period (1859-1920), which would be much simpler to call "the period of Social Darwinism,"
3) The Panic Period (approximately 1920-1960)
4) The Present.

The "Panic Period" lasted roughly forty years, after Social Darwinism was largely discredited, leaving folklore collectors with massive amounts of data, initially collected to amplify the stages of human development or to feed the fires of Historic-Geographic scholarship. I present a clear explanation of why classification systems were needed by comparative folklore scholars. Stith Thompson's valiant attempt at organizing the totality of human experience has been discredited as much as that of Murdock, but I show how Thompson's *Motif-Index* can be used to advantage even by those of use who prefer a contextual approach to folklore.

I generally cite the end of the Panic Period as about 1960, and then describe the various splits, vogues, borrowings, and other approaches to folklore which have since developed. This must be done with a knowledge of each approach's historical antecedents (i.e Propp in Structuralism or von der Leyen and Phillips Barry in psychology and psychoanalytic interpretation). With each approach discussed, I give the students citations of work done, so the bibliography for the course is presented in context.

One of the greatest values of these lectures is that they present students information with which to evaluate the material they encounter. The lectures leave students with some knowledge of the intellectual climate which helped produce a particular work. Even more important, just as past versions of a ballad may continue to be sung alongside of newer ones, some older intellectual modes still influence present works.

As an example of this ongoing influence, I simplify matters by temporarily leaving the Romantic/Nationalistic period aside (although it still exerts influence), and draw a simple chart on the board to show how the Unilinear Evolutionary school, using Compte's stages of Savage, Barbarous, and Civilized, predisposes us to think that folklore is the province of children and is created by homogeneous groups. One of the most insidious elements of this thinking, still held by many folklorists (and unfortunately found in subtle ways in Toelken) is that the folk create as a group, "unconsciously," while "civilized" people produce "art" which is rational, individual, and creative. This is the chart:

BEHAVIOR AT ASCENDING CULTURAL STAGES

	Savage and Barbarous	*Civilized*
Creativity	group	individual
Psychology	childlike	adult
Creative Process	unconscious	conscious
Literature	folklore	art

Once students understand this mind-set they are able to understand why many people feel that folklore is for children and why folklorists initially combed only the "backward" areas of the world for folklore. Understanding the history of folklore scholarship helps us be aware of our own habits of thought. If nothing else is learned in a folklore course, knowing that we have such habits and that they are vividly seen in our treatment of, and attitudes toward, what we call "folklore" makes the effort for both student and teacher worthwhile.

The Course

The assignments for the course are required readings which must be covered by all students. However, I find it best if the course remain flexible so that strict adherence to the weekly discussion topics can be broken for various reasons, such as matters of current interest which might be better teaching vehicles than the assignments.

I find assigning certain articles at the beginning of the course very helpful. Kay Cothran's articles are especially compelling as thoughtful and sensitive examples of research. I feel it necessary to help the student recognize that a folk item without its context is no more than a Rorschach test without a subject—often embarrassing to the researcher who substitutes his thoughts for those of the "subject." To make this point and others, I include in my course tapes and film first without and then with explanations, many from my own research. I also include in the assignments "listenings" which are tapes of materials from my own work, my colleagues' work, or from other recorded sources. Such assignments reenforce both the need for an item's context and the concept that a major component of folklore is performance.

The reading list is included here. Possibilities for any course are great. I suppose that the most difficult thing in a course such as this is to set limits. The field is exciting, and it is difficult not to overreact to the enthusiasm of new students by asking too much of them. The secret I have discovered is to remember that in their own "context" students do take other courses as well.

Given the above outline of the history of the course, the description of my goals and objectives, and my discussions of some of the course content, the following syllabus should give the reader an idea of the kind of introductory course I teach. The broad outline of the course remains fairly constant, but many of the specifics vary from term to term. The field of folklore is wide and folklorists are constantly adding to and refining the scope of what they do. It may look to some who read only catalogue titles that we teach the same thing over and over, but that is hardly the case.

ENGLISH 5481: INTRODUCTION TO FOLKLORE (Fall 1983)

Texts:
Toelken, Barre. *The Dynamics of Folklore*. Boston: Houghton Mifflin, Co., 1979.
Brunvand, Jan, ed. *Readings in American Folklore*. New York: W.W. Norton, 1979.

Supplementary Texts:
Dundes, Alan. *Interpreting Folklore*. Bloomington, Indiana: Indiana University Press, 1980.
Kaufman, Gloria, and Blakely, Mary Kay. *Pulling Our Own Strings: Feminist Humor & Satire*. Bloomington, Indiana: Indiana University Press, 1980.

Welcome to the first of two courses entitled "Introduction to Folklore." Either this course, or the second introductory course (English 5482 [which will not be offered next quarter since the Instructor will be on leave]) are required to take English 5483 (which will be offered in the Spring of 1984). In English 5483 each student will do a collection in the field. If you are planning to take the Spring collecting course, it is suggested that you choose a research project for this quarter which will help you acquire preliminary background information for a well-defined pilot field study (to be done in ten weeks).

If you have taken this course with no future plans for folklore research, do not be concerned; this course will be of value to you. Understanding folklore will allow you to experience your culture and other cultures more deeply. It will be helpful to keep in mind that throughout this course each of you will feel a degree of uncertainty; you are in a new field of study, one in which much of the material is in constant flux, responding to the changing values of people, society, and the contexts in which it is perpetuated (performed).

This quarter you will become acquainted with some of the verbal genres of folklore as well as types of folklore which reflect belief and value systems: folk traditions which do not necessarily rely upon verbal communication in "fixed forms" (such as folk medicine, foodways, festivals, tabus, folk aesthetics, and so forth). The student will be introduced to her or his "metafolklore," and will learn the history of how folklore has been studied (and how the study has been regarded by others).

Minimal Readings and other Assignments

Week I (September 27 and 29)
TOPIC: Folklore and Metafolklore. The scope and requirements of the course; A

working definition of folklore as a process vis-à-vis "popular culture"; A discussion of current folk uses of the term.

Week II (October 4 and 6)
TOPIC: The categories of Folklore and Folklore's relationship to culture. The subject matter of folklore; use of bibliographical tools in research; folklore as a force in current society.
READINGS: [Readings must be read by the beginning of the week for which they are assigned.] Brunvand—Kay L. Cothran, "Participation in Tradition," pp. 444-448; Richard M. Dorson, "Folklore at a Milwaukee Wedding," pp. 111-123; Toelken— Chapter 1 "The Folklore Process," and Chapter 2 "Dynamics of the Folk Group." [Always look carefully at the bibliography given at the end of each chapter, just as you should be watching all footnotes in articles and books for potential leads for your own work.] [Optional] Dundes—"Who are the Folk?" pp. 1-19.

Week III (October 11 and 13)
TOPIC: The folk group; the history of folklore scholarship; the way folklore works. Introduction to short verbal forms, including folk speech, proverb, riddle (by this point in class can you think of more?).
READINGS: Toelken—"Introduction," pp. 3-21; Chapter 3, "The Folk Performance," pp. 93-121; Brunvand—Sylvia Ann Grider, "*Con Safos*: Mexican-Americans, Names and Graffiti," pp. 138-151; [Optional] Dundes—"Seeing is Believing," pp.86-92.
LISTENINGS: Carl Sandburg reading from "The People, Yes," in The Learning Resources center in Walter Library—call #: English 1006.

Week IV (October 18 and 20)
TOPIC: Some short verbal and non-verbal genres (in context): folk speech, proverbs, riddles, rhymes, and gesture.
READINGS: Toelken—Chapter 4, "Dimensions of the Folk Event," pp. 123-149. Brunvand—Ronald L. Baker "Hogs Playing with Sticks," pp. 199-202; Kay L. Cothran, "Talking Trash in the Okefenokee Swamp Rim, Georgia," pp. 215-235. Dundes—"Thinking Ahead," pp. 69-85.
DUE: Purchase the Minneapolis newspaper (*Star/Trib*) for Friday Oct. 21st. Find two good examples of how folklore is used to make a point, and bring to class to hand in on the 25th. Attach these two examples to sheets on which you will hand them in. Also submit a few paragraphs showing in each piece 1) where the folklore you discuss is located, and 2) why you feel the writer chose this folklore and, 3) how it works in relation to what the writer wishes to convey in the work. Give proper bibliographic headings on the assignment.

Week V (October 25 and 27)
[Note: the Instructor will be in Nashville for the AFS annual meetings on the 27th; this day graduate students give their reports and are responsible for having a tape recording of the class session—see Instructor for details]
TOPIC: Folksong: methods for understanding; genres.
READINGS: Toelken—Chapter 5, "Community Taste," pp. 151-197; "Appendix: A fieldwork transcript," pp. 369-388; Brunvand—Ida M. Cromwell, "Songs I Sang on an Iowa Farm," pp. 31-52; Bess Lomax Hawes, "Folksongs and Functions:

Some Thoughts on the American Lullaby," pp. 203-214; Tristram P. Coffin, "'Mary Hamilton' and the Anglo-American Ballad as an Art Form," pp. 309-318; Dundes—"Projections in Folklore," pp. 33-61.
LISTENINGS: Ballad tapes (English 1004-1005); blues tape (English 1003); Unfortunate Rake tapes (English 1001-1002). Ask for handouts for listenings.
DUE: ON OCTOBER 25TH, NEWSPAPER ASSIGNMENT (described under WEEK IV).

Week VI (November 1 and 3)
TOPIC: Folksong (continued); Halloween—Urban festival and change.
READINGS: Kaufman and Blakely—Malvina Reynolds's song "We Don't Need the Men," p. 131; Toelken—Chapter 6, "Folklore and Connotation," pp. 199-223; Brunvand—John Q. Anderson "'Miller Boy,' One of the First and Last of the Play-Party Games," pp. 319-323; William A. Wilson, "Folklore and History: Fact Amid the Legends," pp. 449-466; Dundes—"Texture, Text, and Context," pp. 20-32.
DUE: November 3, Preliminary statement for term paper with annotated bibliography (accepted only at the beginning of class).

Week VII (November 8 and 10)
TOPIC: Review for midquarter examination on Nov. 10.

Week VIII (November 15 and 17)
TOPIC: Folk narratives, legends, tales, and myths.
READINGS: Toelken—Chapter 7, "Folklore and Cultural Worldview," pp. 225-261; Brunvand—Judy Trejo, "Coyote Tales," pp. 192-198; Ronald B. Dixon, "Some Coyote Stories from the Maidu Indians of California," pp. 16-21; William Hugh Jansen, "The Surpriser Surprised: A Modern Legend," pp. 64-90; Linda Dégh, "Symbiosis of Joke and Legend," pp. 236-259; Dundes—"To Love my Father All," pp. 211-222.
LISTENINGS: Folktale tape (English 1010)

Week IX (November 22 and 25)
[Class meets only on the 22nd; the 25th is Thanksgiving. Consider this week as an extension of WEEK VIII for all assignments—have a good Thanksgiving]

Week X (November 30 and December 1)
TOPIC: Stereotypes, "isms," revolution, and worldview; or, do we all have prejudices (and must we)?
READINGS: Toelken—Chapter 8, "Being a Folklorist," pp. 263-289; Brunvand—Shirley Marchalonis, "Three Medieval Tales and their Modern American Analogues," pp. 267-278; Dundes—"The Crowing Hen and the Easter Bunny: Male Chauvinism in American Folklore," pp. 160-175; "Into the Endzone for a Touchdown: a Psychoanalytic Consideration of American Football," pp. 199-210. [Please, as with all articles, read these "critically" in the best sense.]; Kaufman and Blakely—Read the two "introductions" carefully and compare them. Read in the text at your discretion and bring to class your notes and your text for discussion.

LISTENINGS: To yourself, others, mass media—write examples of folklore in a brief journal with contexts—a few well-collected items with explanations are better than twenty mysteries. THIS WILL BE DUE DECEMBER 6.

DUE: TERM PROJECT ON DECEMBER 1 (at the beginning of class).

Week XI (December 6 and 8)
TOPIC: Folklore and literature; why all authors must use folklore.
READINGS: Mark Twain's "The Celebrated Jumping Frog...."; Dundes— "Metafolklore and Oral Literary Criticism," pp. 404-415.
DUE: December 6, COLLECTED EXAMPLES OF CURRENT "ISM" FOLKLORE (see Week X above).

Final examination will be held on Wednesday, December 14th from 6:00-9:00 p.m. in this room—UNLESS THERE IS A TAKE HOME EXAMINATION, WHICH WILL BE DUE AT THE SAME TIME AS THE BEGINNING OF THE EXAMINATION.

W. F. H. Nicolaisen

State University of New York at Binghamton

Folklore

The course described here was first offered in the spring semester 1970, mainly in response to my own request after I had, in the previous semester, been appointed to a professorship in the Department of English, with special responsibility for the teaching of courses in the English language. It has since been given in almost every semester and in several summer schools and has been taught by Professors Jane Mobley and Elizabeth Tucker. As described here, its particular shape is only that of the version taught by myself, and even then the description provided here does not reflect any actual realization of its scope and aims but rather a kind of norm or general framework which, as in all good folklore, allows for variation and flexibility. It has never been the same in any two semesters although its basic concept and tenets have remained relatively unchanged.

Initially the course was devised with students in mind for whom it would be, in all probability, the only academic contact with the subject matter in their undergraduate careers. For many of these students, such contact would be almost accidental in so far as *Folklore* would be chosen by them from an extensive menu of course offerings available to fulfill distribution requirements in the humanities for students in the School of Arts and Sciences (Harpur College) or English requirements for students in some of the professional schools. Although offered by the Department of English, the course attracted, in these early days, very few English majors; most of the students enrolled were majoring in the sciences, social sciences, nursing or business. This situation changed only very little when the Department of English instituted a "Specialization in English Literature and Folklore" several years ago, for the number of students who avail themselves of that option has always been small. Nevertheless, it has become a second important function of the course to serve the needs of this small group of students as their starting point and most fundamental requirement. Its overriding purpose has, however, remained the introduction to folk-cultural matters of students who would, on the one hand, never take another course in the subject and who would, on the other, often very reluctantly wish to conform with certain curricular expectations. *Folklore* is erroneously regarded by many as a comparatively easy or painless way of fulfilling these expectations. It is therefore mainly with such students in mind that the course has been devised and given, and it has not always been easy to reconcile this double function as topical appetizer and prescribed, and therefore suspect, intellectual fare. The processes of winning students over to a subject (or discipline) and of satisfying their curricular needs are not as closely related as may seem at first glance, and it has been my aim to concentrate on the former without neglecting the latter.

As in many other universities and colleges, folklore courses here are almost exclusively offered by the English Department whose chief strength and direction lie in the teaching of literature. In such a setting, teachers of folklore tend to be regarded as fringe personnel whose subject matter is little understood but who, in some disconcerting way, tend to attract fairly large numbers of students. In order to be a viable and recognizable part of the course offerings of the Department of English, the folklore course at SUNY-Binghamton has therefore, ever since its inception, had a strong emphasis on folk-narrative, a choice which happens to suit my own personal academic interests but which may, if not properly understood, be seen as an imbalance or as a distortion of the much more encompassing range of matters usually categorized under the rubric *Folklore*. This apparent over-emphasis is, in reality, more likely to reflect the deliberate selection of examples to illustrate certain basic principles inherent in both the subject matter and the discipline rather than a one-sided approach to the discipline and its principles themselves. It is certainly appropriate in the particular circumstances in which this course is offered.

These circumstances also include class size. Because of the considerable popularity which this course has had over the years—a popularity which, paradoxically, has sometimes made it suspect in the eyes of those whose courses appear to be less attractive to students—the temptation has been great to admit to it as many students as wished to take it, thus gaining as many FTEs as possible for administrative purposes. On the two occasions on which the ceiling was thus lifted under pressure, the consequences were highly unsatisfactory since one of the most important ingredients of the course was destroyed or at least seriously diminished—the intense personal involvement of every student, for, when all is said and done, this course is not so much about others elsewhere but about those within the classroom, instructor and student alike. For this reason, we have tried to keep the course size to about fifty students, small enough to safeguard that vital personal attention and involvement, large enough to bring together a sufficient variety of background, upbringing and predilections, despite the fact that a high proportion of our students are ethnically and socially remarkably homogeneous.

Limited enrollment has also meant that the basic format of the course has been left intact, that curious but effective mixture of instruction and discussion, of induction and deduction, of lecture and seminar which allows the instructor to instruct while enabling the student to respond immediately through question and comment. In my experience, this course loses much of its effectiveness when conducted purely as a survey of theories, ideas and classifications by which, as has sometimes been wryly but aptly said, the notes of the professor become the notes of the student without passing through the heads of either. Without diminishing the crucial role of instructor as instructor and without turning him or her into a mere catalyst, there has to be structured dialogue which permits both spontaneity and calm reflection, both inquisitiveness and widening of vision. To me, it is essential that students contribute their share, however circumscribed and however anecdotal, to the growth of this course so that the intellectual traffic never travels along a one-way street. And it is just as necessary that the instructor be the controller of that traffic who, drawing on his or her own extensive training and specialized research, directs the various thought processes into profitable channels.

I have avoided the terms "teacher" and "teaching" in this context because I am convinced that, among many other academic subjects, one cannot "teach" folklore;

one can only make students aware of its nature, ramifications, and manifestations in the hope that this awareness will continue beyond the classroom and will open eyes to vital facets and dimensions of human life and culture. Perhaps this experience and this point of view in principle disqualify this report from inclusion in an anthology entitled *Teaching Folklore*, but perhaps *Making Students Aware of Folklore* is an acceptably synonymous phrase which simply makes honest allusion to what most "teachers" of folklore do anyhow. Teaching and being taught are not likely to lead to self-awareness and the genuine integration of self which is its almost inevitable outcome; having one's eyes opened to certain phenomena and values in the world "out there" and to the ways in which we both shape and are shaped by them will much more probably lead to that goal, and as a humanist I cannot employ my presence in the classroom to any better purpose.

In order to achieve that purpose, a major portion of my course is devoted to the confrontation and interrogation of texts, both verbal and non-verbal. The three principles of which I want students to become aware—folklore as a behavioral response in a particular cultural register, the notion of folklore as "variation in repetition," and the role of the individual within folk-culture—are successively demonstrated through, or derived from, the substance of individual texts, beginning with the texts of our own lives. We spend more than one class session, for example, in a close reading of William Thoms's famous letter to *The Athenaeum* which coined the English term *Folklore*, extracting from it as much information as possible about the particular world-view and phase in the history of ideas which produced Thoms's personal perception of what folklore is and what is happening to it. We also spend at least three class sessions listening to and analyzing the various verbal and melodic texts of "The Unfortunate Rake," in order to understand the interplay of type and variant and the multifaceted nature of change. We spend practically the whole course comparing and contrasting one artisan's (storyteller's, singer's, quilter's, etc.) version of a folk-cultural product with other artisans' folk-cultural products and modes of behavior, trying to arrive at a satisfying view of the relationships between those artisans and their cultural context. We measure theories and theoreticians against our texts and evaluate their worth on the basis of the material we confront and not as abstract inventions and foibles. In the long run, it is to me more important that students in this introductory course learn what to make of texts than how others, like Olrik, Lévi-Strauss, Propp, Dundes, or Lüthi, have reacted to those and other texts. Of course, they will hear about Olrik, Lévi-Strauss, Propp, Dundes, and Lüthi, too, but only in order to appreciate the variety of approaches possible, and not in order to absorb dogmas. There can never be a definitive view of a non-definitive text, and the best use of other definitions which we can make is to utilize them in honing our own.

Whenever I offer the course, it is my assumption that the students taking it—even those who are acquainted with certain folksongs or who play a "folk" instrument—do not know what folklore is. I am, however, also assuming that all of them have or practice folklore of one kind or another. It is therefore the purpose of the initial section of the course to make them conscious of that knowledge and of these practices in order to give them an opportunity to make constructive contributions to the course from the very beginning and to demonstrate their own involvement in the very subject matter under discussion. The first of three graded assignments (there are no examinations) parallels the thrust of this initial phase: students are asked to collect from their own families, categorize and present anything that might by some stretch of the imagination be called folklore. As a result, we accumulate a considerable body of material, much of it shared with others, with which to illustrate certain more general and more theoretical points in future discussions, while at the same time each student is placed in the role of participating observer instead of disinterested onlooker. In addition, this particular assignment frequently brings about a re-evaluation of the students' family ties and a new appreciation of the grand-parental generation and its importance as a storehouse of family lore. Not infrequently, students are surprised at their findings and begin for the first time to see themselves and their families as having a past as well as a present identity. I therefore regard this first phase of the course as laying a foundation on which the success of the rest of the course will chiefly depend. Unless their own very personal interest is aroused at this stage, students are apt to treat the course as just another requirement to fulfill and never lose a certain aloofness, skepticism or even snootiness which prevents them from appreciating fully what folklore is and does and how it affects their lives.

It is, of course, also in these early phases that the role of the instructor defines itself. In an age when technological aids, especially in the audio-visual field, offer many tempting alternatives and shortcuts, it is easy to be overwhelmed by them and to expect them to be a viable substitute for one's own efforts and skills. I remember clearly falling to that kind of temptation during the early years of this course, by using a large variety of recordings, films, slides, and such like devices, in the hope that they would not only do the work for me but also prove highly attractive to students. Fortunately, I soon discovered that this large-scale use of audio-visual aids had quite the opposite effect. Students brought up in front of television sets quickly became restive, inattentive or even absent, and the glue of my comments was not strong enough to hold these class sessions together and to give them perceptible structure. I have since used such aids much more sparingly, employing them to augment, support and illustrate points I wish to make, issues I wish to raise or principles I wish to suggest, and I have found that this controlled ploy of the great things technology has to offer the humanist serves as an invaluable enrichment rather than as a doubtful substitute. The fact that so much folklore entertains as well as instructs or informs should not mislead anyone into thinking that it is its entertainment value which makes it so attractive in the classroom—far from it. What matters is the intellectual quality and engagement of the instructor and his or her enthusiasm for the subject matter to be conveyed. If these characteristics are present, then the judicious insertion of sound and vision, including live performances by singers, story-tellers, weavers, spinners, Easter egg colorers, etc., may be exploited to the full and to best advantage. It is the analysis and synthesis offered by a well-trained and sympathetic mind that counts in the end, not the prolific or even indiscriminate use of audio-visual dramatics. I find it a condition sine qua non for the success of my folklore course that these quintessential elements be established from the very beginning and that my own presence and direction be made felt throughout the forty-five (or so) hour-long sessions of the course. Naturally, this means much harder work on my part, especially if it is to be translated into the kind of relaxed classroom atmosphere which is so conducive to effective learning. Once the instructor's role and the students' naive but constructive involvement have been established and the basic principles have been outlined and substantiated through suitable examples, the central portion of the course can be tackled. For some of the reasons mentioned earlier, the heart of my own course is devoted to an extensive display and discussion of folk-narrative texts and categories, both spoken and sung. In the course of this undertaking, we try to stay well clear of genre-mongering and use taxonomic handles only very sparingly. Whatever classification system we adopt we try to read out of the texts rather than approaching them with preconceived notions.

It is at this point that the second assignment is introduced to parallel the course matter. It is designed to help students understand through personal experience the all-important relationship of type and variant as one of the basic concepts of folklore. Students are asked to select from their reading of Stith Thompson's *One Hundred Favorite Folktales* one story which, for some reason or other, they have found particularly enjoyable, and to search for two other variants of the same tale type in other publications, most conveniently in the *Folktales of the World* series; the three variants must be from different countries. With the help of tale-type and motif indexes, students are then required to present the three variants in tabular form, episode by episode, and to comment on their relationship to each other. One of the main purposes of this assignment is to acquaint students in a very practical fashion with some of the chief tools of the folk-narrative scholar's trade, without presenting the historical-geographical method which has fashioned these tools as the only or even the most important approach to the study of folktales. This assignment is therefore deliberately intended to explore and utilize library resources and the impressive corpus of primary and secondary literature which our discipline has produced in the course of its growth. While seemingly insisting on old-fashioned methods, it encourages students to discard some of their own ingrained ideas derived from the study of written art literature, and to take a position of their own in the evaluation of products of folk-cultural processes and performances. Even when helpful librarians are available, this is always the most demanding time for me since many students are poorly skilled in the use of library resources and require much guidance in all steps of this assignment. It is also a time-consuming assignment to read and grade and I have several times been on the brink of dropping it in order to make it easier for myself, but have always refrained from doing so because it continues to be essential to the conception of my course.

While students are researching this assignment, classroom work is designed to equip them with the necessary methodology and to indicate the kind of phenomena worth looking for. Not surprisingly, my own teachers Walter Anderson and Kurt Ranke, as well as the writings of Max Lüthi, have done much to shape my thinking for this portion of the course. The influence of Francis Lee Utley is probably also apparent somewhere. My own awareness of these shaping forces is, however, never allowed to prevent me from making this thoroughly my own course and from introducing emphases and choices, perhaps even biases, which have emerged in my own research over the years. I have always felt strongly that one's own latest insights, findings, hunches and preoccupations are by no means too raw or too specialized to be given a place in an introductory course, and this has probably been the major variation in course content and presentation from semester to semester. Whenever I have been intrigued by aspects of time and space in folktales, a considerable portion of my course has been devoted to them, too; whenever the nature of Jack as a folk hero has been of interest to me, Jack has also been given much attention in my course; whenever scholars' pronouncements on incremental repetition in ballads have puzzled me my students have been subjected to a full dose of my puzzlement; whenever the function of legends as behavioral responses has been of concern to me, I have shared my concern with my students; whenever the regionality and spatial distribution of things folk-cultural has occupied my research time, then regionality and spatial distribution became important items in the classroom, too; and so on. I have never seen any point in divorcing research (and publication!) from teaching, not even at the introductory level; in fact, I have found their symbiosis most beneficial and one of the most attractive features of a scholar's life. It is also quite exciting for students to be told that what they have just heard is a very recent discovery or has not been published yet or has yet to be tested on a larger body of material. If it is good enough for my colleagues it is good enough for my students. Furthermore, the inclusion of the results of one's recent or current research activities keeps a frequently repeated course like this one from becoming stale and distanced. The immediacy of its themes and concerns is bound to communicate itself to students in the form of up-to-date relevancy and freshness and as gratifying recognition of the worth of their own minds.

As so much time is spent on the substance and function of folk-narrative, the remaining portion of the course is turned into a kind of coda making brief reference to non-verbal and partially verbal aspects of folk-culture. This may give the whole course the appearance of lopsidedness or top-heaviness, and in certain respects this is probably true. It is, on the other hand, in these late stages of the course that students are required to attend to their third assignment, the collection and presentation of folklore from live informants who are not members of their own families. Since they have known about this assignment from the very beginning of the semester, much perplexity, thought, consultation and argument have gone into the preparation and execution of this task, aided by a complete reading of Brunvand's *The Study of American Folklore*, in order to ascertain the range of items to be considered for possible collection. The classroom concentration on folk-narrative has therefore been conducted against a background of more encompassing study and troublesome attention to categories of folklore only loosely connected with Märchen or legends. Since much of what is collected is shared at the very end of the course, such central facets of folk-culture as custom and belief prominently come into their own, for the majority of the items collected can be classified under these headings. When seen as a combination of work inside and outside the classroom, the course has indeed at this stage begun to round itself out very satisfactorily and, although much has to be excluded, has already incorporated the several major components which are part of human behavior in the folk-cultural register. Even the remaining gaps are not haphazardly left but carefully selected.

In order to counteract this gappiness as much as possible and to provide a final overview, I usually try to let the course culminate, sometimes with the help of films, in the consideration of a folk festival or some other calendar event the commemoration or celebration of which necessitates the combination of many elements of folklore, from the spoken word to ritual procedures and the design and texture of costumes. It is important to me that students should learn not only that folklore, folklife, folk culture—call it what you will—is a mode of behavior appropriate to certain circumstances but also that the many items and several categories of folklore do not usually exist and function in isolation but interact together, often providing a highly complex cultural text the analysis and interpretation of which is the ultimate task of the folklorist because it links the study of process and product, of performance and response, of individual and group, of individuation and bonding, of creativity and tradition, of type and variation, of repetition and innovation, of activity and passivity, of competence and incompetence, of function and aesthetics, of word and wallpaper, of dance and tune, etc. It is, I think, only by focusing on the integrated, interdependent, interlocking, orchestrated combination of folk-cultural features and factors on particular occasions that we can make our students understand what folklore really is, what it means and what purposes it serves in the lives of human individuals and groups, eminently including our own lives and the groups of which we are part. When all is said and done, that is, I presume, the chief aim of my course, and I would regard it as failure if I were to neglect or ignore this side of it. Being able to handle life better because of what we know about folklore and how we use it is perhaps its most important lesson.

Sample Syllabus: English 1500: Folklore

    Day 1 : Organization and Scope of the course
    Day 2 : What is Folklore? (I)
    Day 3 : What is Folklore? (II)
    Day 4 : Who are the Folk?
    Day 5 : Thoms's Letter to the *Athenaeum*
    Day 6 : Evolutionary and devolutionary views of Folklore
    Day 7 : Family Folklore (preparation for first assignment)
    Day 8 : "The Unfortunate Rake" (English versions)
    Day 9 : "The Unfortunate Rake" (New World versions)
    Day 10 : "The Unfortunate Rake" (parodies)
    Day 11 : Type and Variant in the folktale (AT 922)
    Day 12 : Type and Variant in the folktale (AT 922)
    Day 13 : Type and Variant in the folktale (AT 922)
    Day 14 : Sharing of results of first collecting assignment
    Day 15 : Introduction to the Tale Type Index as a library tool
    Day 16 : Introduction to the Tale Type Index as a scholarly tool
    Day 17 : Variants of AT 510B
    Day 18 : Theories of the folktale (I)
    Day 19 : Theories of the folktale (II)
    Day 20 : Close reading of AT 480 (I)
    Day 21 : Close reading of AT 480 (II)
    Day 22 : The nature of legends
    Day 23 : Olrik's "Laws" of folk-narrative
    Day 24 : The Folk Hero (I)
    Day 25 : The Folk Hero (II)
    Day 26 : The problem of Paul Bunyan
    Day 27 : Jack Tales (I)
    Day 28 : Jack Tales (II)
    Day 29 : The Trickster
    Day 30 : Collecting Folklore (preparation for last assignment)
    Day 31 : Mythological Folktales of Africa
    Day 32 : Mythological Folktales of North America
    Day 33 : Ballad text and tune: Child
    Day 34 : Ballad text and tune: Bronson
    Day 35 : Supernatural Ballads
    Day 36 : Dialogue Ballads
    Day 37 : Lyrical Ballads

Day 38 : Disaster Ballads
Day 39 : Folk song and work song
Day 40 : Material culture in the Binghamton area (slides)
Day 41 : Calendar Festivals (films)
Day 42 : Students report on their fieldwork (I)
Day 43 : Students report on their fieldwork (II)

[Note: The exact number of days varies slightly from semester to semester. This syllabus is based on the whole on the version of the Spring Semester 1979.]

Texts

Brunvand, Jan Harold. 1978. *The Study of American Folklore*. 2nd ed. New York: W. W. Norton.

_____, ed. 1970. *Readings in American Folklore*. W. W. Norton. (optional)

Friedman, A. B., ed. 1956. *The Viking Book of Folk Ballads*. New York: Viking Press.

Thompson, Stith. 1968. *One Hundred Favorite Folktales*. Bloomington: Indiana University Press.

Bruce A. Beatie

Cleveland State University

Simulation Techniques in an Urban Folklore Workshop

Background of the Course

Before I can begin to talk about the particular folklore course I teach with some regularity, I need to state briefly how I, a medievalist/comparatist whose dissertation was on metrical forms in medieval Latin and German lyric poetry, got into the business of teaching folklore at all. My only formal training in the field came from Albert B. Lord, whose course (*Introduction to Folklore*) I took at Harvard, and for whom I later served as reader. When I began my first full-time teaching position at the University of Colorado in 1964, I began teaching my own version (with due acknowledgement) of Lord's course.

Over five years I taught the course twice at Colorado and once at the University of Rochester. When I came to Cleveland State University, I planned to offer it again, and scheduled it for the summer of 1971. Enrollment was fairly good: some 25 students. Following my usual first-day-of-class procedure, I asked them to complete questionnaires outlining their educational backgrounds and discovered that only one of the 25 students had had any substantial background of study in literature.

In that first class session—as I skimmed questionnaires while waiting for the others to be finished—I had the sudden realization that the course which I had followed Lord in calling *Introduction to Folklore*, was in fact nothing of the kind. It was really an *Introduction to Traditional Epic*, and it assumed literature majors as its audience. By the end of that hour I realized that I could in no way teach the course I'd intended to teach. Before the next session I'd thrown out my prepared syllabus and, over the summer, created ad hoc my first "real" folklore course.

Since that summer of 1971 I have taught the course a little more than once every two years, and it has changed as I learned more about the kind of student audience I could expect. Cleveland State University is a downtown urban institution almost all of whose students come from Cleveland's own county. Most of them have Balkan or Afro-American ethnic backgrounds (75 and 15 percent, respectively) and belong to the first generation in their families to attend college. Their main reason for attending college is to obtain a vocational "union card."

The first variation of the "real" folklore course created in that summer of 1971 came when, six months later and at the last minute, I was asked to take over a course called *Myths and Holidays* in our First College (an attempt to create a small-college atmosphere within a large College of Arts and Sciences). The *Myths and Holidays* course, which I had helped a colleague design, was an eight-credit workshop intended to comprise half of a student's regular course load; it was specifically designed to take advantage of the ethnic backgrounds expected in its students. The approach to folklore I had worked out the previous summer fit well into my colleague's intended workshop structure. I added field-collection projects as the main focus of the student's work, and the second time I offered it in First College, I renamed it *Introduction to Folklore*.

In 1979 I was asked to modify its syllabus to fit within the parameters of a proposed external degree program intended for adult audiences, and at that point I renamed the course *Urban Folklore Workshop*. The structure developed by 1979 has proven sufficiently viable that only minor changes have been made since then.

Present Structure of the Course

I have offered this course, in its various permutations, to freshmen, upper-level students, and graduate students; in the last several years, the "typical" student has been an adult in early to mid-thirties with a couple of years of college, not necessarily in the immediate past. Since this represents in almost all cases the first folklore course taken, the different levels of different audiences seem to make little difference: for upper-level and graduate students I increase the work expectations and the grading standards, but otherwise make no changes in the syllabus.

In one sense, this course has no real place in the curriculum, save as a humanities elective; it is not a required part of any major program, and only with special departmental permission does it count as part of a major in Anthropology, English, or Modern Languages. It satisfies the general university and college humanities requirements in spite of the fact that, as I teach it, the course belongs as much in the social sciences as it does in the humanities.

When taught within the context of our Extended Campus College, it fills a more specific niche. The ECC program, modeled on the program of the "To Educate the People Consortium" based at Wayne State University, has an integrated cross-disciplinary lower-level curriculum in which students take a year of Humanities, a year of Social Science, and a year of Science and Technology. Each quarter their course load consists of a television course, a weekend conference course, and a seminar meeting four hours weekly. In this curriculum, my *Urban Folklore Workshop* is part of a curricular package in which the television course is called "Humanities through the Arts," and the weekend conference course focuses on "the Arts in Northeast Ohio communities."

The *Urban Folklore Workshop* is usually scheduled as a weekend course, usually meeting for six hours on Saturdays. The first four Saturday sessions are scheduled at the beginning of the quarter, and represent the "content" and "field methods" segments of the course. There is then a four-week break during which the workshop does not meet, though I am available for consultation with the students; there are required assignments which must be turned in during the break period. During the break period, students are asked to complete their folklore collection projects. In the final two Saturday sessions, students are expected to present a brief oral report to the workshop on the results of their collection projects, with handouts and/or demonstrations as relevant, followed by general discussion of the results.

The overt content of the course is never quite the same from offering to offering, because its point of departure is always the kinds of folklore carried by the different workshop participants. This information is collected by means of exercises, questionnaires, and discussion, and is immediately put into a tentative sort of order on the blackboard.

Using the workshop's collective experience as a reference point, I then turn to a brief overview, both theoretical and descriptive, of the nature of folklore and its relationships to other disciplines. A review of the development of folklore as a research discipline provides a transition to the specific topic of urban folklore in general and its particular manifestations in the greater Cleveland community. A catalog of the "Cleveland Folklore Archive," the student collection projects accumulated in my files since 1972, provides a concrete focus for this discussion.

At this point we turn to the individual collection projects the students in the current workshop are expected to undertake, and the remainder of the formal course content focuses on brief but intensive training in folklore field methods. (Since this will be discussed at some length below, I won't comment on it further here.) The training sessions are broken up, both to provide variety and to give additional "subject-matter" perspectives, by audio-visual presentations that change from term to term.

Over the ten years I have been teaching this course, I have tried almost every available textbook, and found none of them wholly satisfactory. In general, I use three texts: an introduction, a field methods book, and an anthology of examples of folklore. The introductory book I have used most recently is J. Barre Toelken's *The Dynamics of Folklore*. As a brief introduction to field methods I use the Smithsonian Institution's pamphlet, *Family Folklore*, edited by Holly Cutting Baker et al., and *Folklife and Fieldwork*, by Peter Bartis of the American Folklife Center. The only anthology I have used more than once is Willard Burgess Moore's *Molokan Oral Tradition*, because of its focus on an urban ethnic tradition.

Students participating in the *Urban Folklore Workshop* are required to attend and participate actively in all workshop sessions (crucial, since the number of contact hours in the course is low), complete all exercises assigned, pass an examination (middle of the term) on the readings, and complete a folklore collection project. The project itself has several carefully-defined stages, at each of which the student must submit written material for comment from me:

> a. Definition of project
> b. Research plan
> c. Bibliography
> d. Collection diary
> e. Oral presentation of collection results
> f. Written collection-project report, with materials, in archivable
>   form.

Simulation Techniques in Teaching Field Methods

Since my only formal training in folklore had dealt with folk literature, my only knowledge of folklore fieldwork methodologies came from textbooks; and the "simulation techniques" which I began to use that summer of 1971 described earlier initially had nothing to do with field methods. My only concern then was to bring into the present consciousness of students with no prior knowledge of folklore and little of literature a sense of what Toelken was later to call "the dynamics of folklore," a sense of folklore as process—and, in part because of my training with Albert Lord and my familiarity with the "oral theory," the dynamic process I was most concerned about initially was that of transmission.

My first experiment in using simulation to bring alive for my students the concepts of transmission and variation in folklore focused on what I have since called "branching" transmission. At an early class session I asked the workshop students to put away all books and writing materials and simply to listen. I then proceeded to tell them orally, in my best tale-teller's style, a short folk tale that I knew well but that I hoped they would not know. In all cases I began with a published text, and usually retold it from memory, with an inconspicuous tape recorder documenting my telling; a couple of times I read a text aloud.

Only after telling the tale did I inform the class that, at a session about a week later, some of them would have to retell it. At that later session I would divide the workshop into groups of some five to seven people. The groups would each choose tale-tellers by lot, and ask the chosen tale-tellers to retell the tale I'd told, as best they could, from memory. Each group was furnished with a tape recorder, and the several retellings were recorded.

Since my concern was to show how oral transmission of narrative resulted in variations, I asked each group first to transcribe from their tape the first five minutes of "their" text, and then to prepare a detailed summary, motif by motif, of the tale as their group had heard it, using the tape recording as basis. Once this exercise had been done, the resulting texts and summaries were presented to the whole workshop for discussion that focused mainly on the nature and possible reasons for the variations that had occurred.

I have experimentally varied the nature of the tale they hear (familiar vs. unfamiliar, highly structured vs. loosely structured, belonging to mainstream European tradition vs. belonging to a very unusual Amerind tradition, etc.), as well as the conditions of transmission (telling the tale more than once, allowing note-taking, etc.). This exercise produced several sets of variant texts and motif summaries which I have used in discussions of variation patterns when I offered the workshop in later years.

I have also experimented with another type of simulation, one that involves what I call "linear" transmission. I have used it a little less frequently, because of the logistics of carrying it out in the workshop situation, and because it is much more tightly structured than the branching transmission exercise. As a basis for this simulation, I use the old "telephone" game. Having set the group as a whole to work on some exercise that will keep them fruitfully occupied for perhaps two hours, I take one member of the workshop off to a separate room where there is a tape recorder, and to that person tell from memory in as good an anecdotal style as I can manage an elaborate joke. (I usually use the "Saran-Wrap" joke which I'd first heard long before I knew what folklore was, with its whole chain of authority.) I record my telling of the joke.

The student to whom I've told the tale is then reminded of how to operate the recorder, asked to go back to the main room and choose another student. The first student takes the second back to the separate room, and tells him or her the joke from memory, recording the telling. The first student then gives the second student the same directions I had given him or her, the second student goes back to the main room and picks a third student as audience, while the first student writes out, as well as he or she can remember, the joke as he or she had told it.

The process continues until we have either gotten through the workshop participants or (which happens more frequently) we run out of available time. At that point, the student who was the final "audience," the end of the "telephone" chain, is asked to retell the joke to the entire workshop. (On one occasion, "Saran-Wrap" had been changed in the transmission process to "Reynolds Wrap" aluminum foil; when this was retold to the whole class, it broke up completely.)

Using the written-from-memory versions which the joke-tellers have prepared, we then analyze at once the process of transmission and variation, noting what kinds of changes occurred and trying to suggest reasons for the changes. The tape-recording remains as evidence for more sophisticated analysis if time allows or need requires it.

When I began using these simulation approaches in 1971, my only concern was to show how folklore transmission operated as a dynamic and creative process. It quickly became obvious, however, that these experiments provided material for extremely effective "hands-on" training in the fieldwork techniques crucial to folklore collection. As my objectives in the course turned more and more toward student collection projects, I began to make progressively greater use of the materials produced by the simulations in fieldwork training.

The simulations themselves provide some training in the use (and the problems of use) of tape recorders. In setting up the simulation sessions I try to use as many different kinds of recording equipment as possible, so that students may not only have experience with different hardware, but also have the chance to see what effects the use of different sorts of equipment has on the resulting recordings.

The greatest value of the resulting recordings for exercises in transcription, editing, and analysis is that the students are already familiar with their contents, so in their practice time they can concentrate on problems of technique and accuracy. In order to give the students extensive practice in transcription and to get the recorded texts transcribed without doing it myself, I require the students to complete at least four handwritten pages of satisfactory transcription from the recordings the simulations produced. The recordings are placed in the Instructional Media Laboratory with log sheets to assure that each student does a separate section of the tape and that the result is a complete transcription of the whole tape.

These transcriptions are then brought back to the whole workshop and the problems of preparing final "edited" versions are discussed at some length. These workshop sessions usually produce "samples" of edited transcriptions; it is seldom that we have time to edit completely any simulation text.

Conclusions and Prospects

As should be obvious from the description of its scheduling, my *Urban Folklore Workshop* is, as university courses go, relatively low in contact hours. It is also, as its "workshop" name implies, a course that lies in the pedagogical spectrum somewhere between the usual lecture/discussion course and a directed-study or tutorial course.

The results which the workshop produces, in terms of solid and sometimes exciting contributions of collectanea to the Cleveland Folklore Archive, suggest that it achieves its pedagogical goals. But one distressing result of the limited contact time is that there is seldom time to exploit fully the materials resulting from the simulations; the area that suffers most is analysis. There is seldom time, over four Saturdays, to do the simulations, transcribe the results, do some tentative editing, and still manage to do more analysis of the results than can be achieved ad hoc through class discussion.

By way of conclusion, therefore, let me comment briefly on what the course I've described, and the simulations methods I've developed for it, might be in the best of all possible academic worlds—in other words, a wish list.

First, as to the simulations. They have proven in themselves an exciting classroom exercise in which students participate with delight, and which accomplish very effectively my goal of giving students a real sense of the dynamic qualities of transmission and variation in oral folklore. They provide materials which allow for extremely effective intensive training in transcription techniques, and thereby make it possible for me, in a very limited time, to give students with no prior experience enough general practice in folklore field methods so they can accomplish solid collection projects within a single quarter.

The simulations could provide material for a thorough introduction, not simply to field methods, but to the whole science of folklore research; but there is simply not enough time within the context in which I have to teach the course for this to happen. They do provide, and indeed have provided, a substantial body of experimental material on the nature of oral transmission and tradition. This material, I believe, provides the basis for some important theoretical conclusions, but I have not yet had the time even to get all the materials transcribed, much less to subject them to the kind of analysis necessary to arrive at such conclusions.

As far as the course itself is concerned, I wish it were more than a one-shot venture, an isolated elective in a curriculum poor in core requirements. The course works well and has produced valuable results; but it leads nowhere, and I cannot in present circumstances build either on it, or on the students I've trained through it. I've worked toward developing, at the least, a minor rather than a major program in folklore that would go along with majors in Anthropology, English, and Modern Languages, but so far I have not been able to secure the needed approval.

Whatever the course's limitations, however, and whatever lovely things I might like to do with it in the best of all possible worlds, it has served my students and the university well. It brings a humanities/social science discipline "home" to them in a way, I believe, no other course offered on campus can. A freshman student some ten years ago, who had collected Polish-German witching customs from her grandmother, came to me after the course was over and said, "you know, I hadn't really talked to my grandmother for ten years. Now I know she's a real person." More recently, an auto-worker in his late thirties, who had just sat through two sessions of student collection reports, exclaimed to the workshop at large at the end of a report on patterns on graveyard head-stones: "Goddamit, folklore's everywhere!"

For me personally, the course has had a value beyond measure. It is a truism that, when education happens at its best, the instructor learns as much as his students. My *Urban Folklore Workshop* has taken an ordinary medievalist and made him over into at least a halfway respectable folklorist and graffitologist—but that last is another tale.

Note:

The only thing I have seen explicitly paralleling my simulation techniques is:

Moyle, Natalie K. "Casey Stengel and Turkish Epic: An Experiment in Oral Transmission." Unpublished paper delivered at the annual meeting of the American Folklore Society, Detroit, November 1977.

Two publications have so far resulted directly from my Urban Folklore Workshop:

Beatie, Bruce A. "De Profundis: Graffiti as Communication," *The Gamut* 5 (Winter 1982), pp. 59-66. (Based on a collection of restroom graffiti made in connection with the course.)

Liedtke, Harriet. 1974. "Recollections of Witching in Poland," *Journal of the Ohio Folklore Society*, N.S. 3:1, pp. 5-16.

Zora Devrnja Zimmerman

Iowa State University

Teaching Folklore in Iowa

Most years, *Folk Literature and Myth* (English 357) is the only course, the one and only course in folklore offered at Iowa State University. One course, given once a year. Pretending that I can cover everything considered significant in folklore in one term, I balance folk genres and group dynamics, motifs and epics, contemporary legends and ancient myths. It is obviously a monumental juggling act. The rudimentary, classic stuff must remain absolute, I firmly believe, so oral epic, ballads, fairy tale, and myth become the core of the course. Yet I shudder at the thought that concentrating on older forms will confirm the notion that folklore is an historical subject, that it is quaint, and nostalgic and very, very old. Consequently, I examine urban legends, superstitions, holiday traditions and adolescent rituals—the living lore most of the students know. The course as I teach it is a collection of mini-courses on at least a dozen subjects. I have taught it this way a long time, rejecting other formats because the integrated approach seemed the best of the several choices before me. The format reflects not only the history of the course and the nature of this enormous, nurturing institution, also my own beliefs about folklore: forms change according to their context, but functions and purpose remain relatively stable. History and context and belief shaped the course, and it may be worthwhile to examine how.

Once upon a time the course was entitled *Introduction to Folklore* and it was offered by the College of Sciences and Humanities as one of its own. That was back in 1975 when I first proposed the course and maintained that it was cross-disciplinary and should be identified with both the humanities and the social sciences. A truly interdisciplinary course, I thought, ought ideally to be taught by someone conversant with each subject involved or it should be team-taught so it can draw its energy from expert sources in the appropriate fields. I had to remind myself that we don't live in an ideal world. There was no infinite supply of expert sources here. Only two folklorist-types walked this campus: James Dow and I. And we both were concerned principally with literature. So I did the best I could. I invited as guests artists, storytellers, mimes, singers, dancers, and collectors; I examined foodways and legends; I observed festivals and crafts. I felt fine about the broad exposure students were getting, but I began to despair as I cut back more and more the very subject I was most interested in and most qualified to teach: traditional literature. There simply was not enough time in a quarter term to do it all. Moreover, even though I still felt dedicated to the spirit of an interdisciplinary course, I did not like teaching material I knew someone else could teach better. I was saved by budget cuts and the university's switch to a semester calendar. The folklore course was transferred to the Department of English in 1978 and within a year I had a chance to redefine the course both in terms of its new home and a new calendar.

Again, several options to choose from, considerable obstacles to overcome. When I think back on the factors that determined the present course, I am amazed to say that those factors still exist. We still do not have a folklore program. We have no advanced undergraduate courses in folklore, not even a regular graduate offering. Every few years or so I may teach a senior seminar in fairy-tale and myth, but it is not a regular course. I taught a one-time only folklore seminar on the graduate level and an honors seminar in the fairy tale but that sort of thing doesn't happen often enough to enable students to plan a sequence. James Dow has also slipped German folklore into a German literature in translation course offered by the Department of Foreign Languages and Literatures. Yet, once again, such an offering is practically hidden and certainly not part of the regular course load he carries. Without additional, more specialized courses in folklore, it seems presumptuous to encourage an Iowa State student to concentrate on the subject. The best I can hope for in my students is a whetted appetite and a new perspective.

When *Folk Literature and Myth* came into being, it solved several of the problems noted above: it provided a broad overview of the discipline, yet concentrated on traditional literature, which I was most qualified to teach and which I loved to teach; the course could be grafted onto existing programs in anthropology, sociology, English, elementary education, journalism, philosophy, psychology, history, and art. For many majors in these subjects the folklore course became the great synthesizer, the course that made sense out of the chaos.

Two other options existed. The first was recommended by several folklorists teaching elsewhere: harness the energies of these students and send them out in droves to collect regional lore. After all, here I was in the heartland, the breadbasket of America, an area rich in traditions that have been virtually ignored. These students could be in the field, learning to recognize and analyze folklore firsthand. But then I would remember the dozens of carefully preserved student papers I had pored over in the Indiana University Folklore Archives: error after error, misunderstandings, ruinous mishandlings of informants, gross lapses in memory, wild generalizations. Were I dealing with more advanced students, students who had learned the rudimentary principles, I certainly would assign fieldwork. As it was, I only felt justified in offering a broad, truly introductory course in the subject. I compromised: students would be free to choose a field project if they wished. (Such freedom means partial slavery for instructors, however, since tutorial guidance is necessary for each student involved in fieldwork.)

The second option was simpler. Why not focus the course on a single genre— on the traditional ballad, for instance, or on oral epic or the folktale? The change to concentrate on a manageable topic, to achieve some depth, to experience for at least a few minutes the illusion of control—all seemed wonderful. But, since I had only one course to give, I would give it to the discipline. Better that I draw into the course the many students who were curious about folklore but intimidated by a possibly elitist, literary English course. In the end I was able to do both: I regularly teach the broader course to a general audience and occasionally offer more specialized seminars for advanced students.

So that's how the present course evolved. By the third time the course was offered, demand was greater than supply. Every year students were closed out. At first the course was labeled experimental, that is to say, a course not yet accepted into the official university catalog. The title appeared in that sacred volume in 1980 and students were able to apply the credit toward the humanities requirement in their degree programs. (Before catalog inclusion the course could count only as an elective.) In 1984 two sections were offered for the first time; both filled. The audience was and is quite varied: about twenty percent are English majors (fewer than I would like), thirty percent from humanities departments, a disappointing seven percent from the social sciences, fifteen percent from math and the natural sciences, and the remaining twenty-eight percent from computer science, engineering, business, art and design, and education. This wide range in student interests contributes significantly to my conviction that the course should remain integrated and broad in its approach.

To provide a foundation and to unify the course, I use Brunvand's *The Study of American Folklore*. Over the years it has proven itself to be the best text for my purposes. Once I substituted Toelken's *The Dynamics of Folklore* and it seemed as though the level of the class's understanding of both process and context in tradition rose remarkably but, simultaneously, I noted a drop in the ability to recognize and identify various genres and types. An atmosphere of confusion about basic definitions and classifications persisted throughout the term. I toyed with the possibility of requiring both texts but decided the cost was prohibitive and the time too limited. When teaching the advanced seminars, however, I insist on Toelken.

In 1983 I added Brunvand's *The Vanishing Hitchhiker* to the reading list and included it this year as well. Descriptions and discussions of urban legends trigger strong reactions in my students; many suddenly recall different versions of a legend and are pleased to know finally how to explain them. All seem to understand better the anatomy of a legend and its origins. As a result of using *Vanishing Hitchhiker*, students seem to obtain a more thorough comprehension of the function and development of versions, the mechanics of transmission, and the role of belief. Students also seem to be more willing to acknowledge the existence of folklore in contemporary society. I try to channel this new excitement into discussions about superstitions, local character legends, memorates, and children's lore. I bring in excerpts from essays and sample texts from various collections. Mullen's comparisons of superstitions among deep-sea and off-shore fishermen, as well as his sketches of local eccentrics in *I Heard the Old Fishermen Say* are quite effective. The Knapps' *One Potato, Two Potato* has also provided me with excellent material. After spending about four weeks on the contemporary lore just described, I focus on riddles and proverbs for a week and then concentrate on traditional narrative and myth for the next six weeks. Earlier discussions on legend and memorates can now be connected to readings in the folktale, oral epic, and fairy tale. The bulk of the narrative material is comprised of selections from Dorson's *Buying the Wind, Folktales Told Around the World*, and *American Negro Folktales*; several sketches from Randolph's *Pissing in the Snow*; a dozen or so Märchen from the Grimm collection; and Fitzgerald's translation of *The Odyssey*. (I taught *Gilgamesh* one year but had to spend an exorbitant amount of time on the background and culture so I, sadly, dropped it.)

Oral composition and the art of the traditional narrative are two of my principal concerns in the course. Lord's *The Singer of Tales* is regularly recommended, but only the rare student ever reads it. I summarize. I also provide eyewitness accounts of epic chanting and I use my personal collection of Serbian epics to help illustrate the composing process. In the last two years I have assigned Hansen's essay on Homeric epic and oral poetry with fine results. A poetic translation of *The Odyssey* is crucial. (I demand the Fitzgerald.) Unfortunately, at least one student per class complains about reading the poetry. Usually the student has never read any serious poetry and can fathom neither the word order nor the vocabulary. I usually tell such students to read a prose summary of the epic first and to read difficult parts of the poem aloud. It seems to help. The vast majority of the students is visibly impressed by Homer and comes away from the epic with considerable respect for oral tradition.

After *The Odyssey*, I tackle myth, and I know that no matter how much time I allot to this genre, I will always only skim the surface. In the last few years, I have concentrated on creation myths, bringing in copies from various collections, comparing and analyzing levels of meaning. One year I assigned Griaule's *Conversations with Ogotemmêli*, using it as a representative text of sacred oral traditions. It is a rich, serious work and I would include it more often had I more time. Always I search for an anthology that will offer a collection of creation myths from several cultures, an anthology that is both generously annotated and oriented toward the folklore student. The ones I find all lack something: folklore notes, or general cultural and historical background, or several versions of a single text, or thematic groupings. So far, the best one for me is Sproul's *Primal Myths*. I bring in xeroxed samples and distribute essays from Sebeok's *Myth: A Symposium*. Somehow it all works, but I know it could be better.

I concentrate on the fairy tale for the next two weeks. This genre, as represented by the Grimm Märchen, proves to be the most stimulating to teach. I approach the tales from various angles, using Lüthi's essays in *Once Upon a Time: Upon the Nature of the Fairytale* as the guiding light, and Bettleheim's musings on the subject in *The Uses of Enchantment* for deliberations on function. (Bettleheim's orthodox Freudian interpretations of individual tales in the second half of the book receive little sympathy from the students.) Comparing versions of a single motif or collection of motifs becomes the mainstay of many student projects and a significant teaching tool. Not only do the comparisons illustrate the importance of versions but the comparing process itself accents the differences between decorative and core motifs, oral and visual verbalizations, and traditional and personalized poetic techniques.

Comparing versions of motifs and oral formulas continues as we move into traditional British ballads. Friedman's *Folk Ballads* still gives the best introduction, in my mind, on ballad styles and subjects. Moreover, his careful presentations of ballad versions and his excellent annotations keep the volume on my reading list year after year. I complement the text with recordings of some of the more popular ballads.

The last two weeks of the term are devoted to student projects. Some are field projects, others are based on questionnaires or library research. I schedule a workshop for the project in the middle of the term and then work with students on an individual basis to help develop appropriate questionnaires, provide guidelines for fieldwork and interviews, or give general advice. In addition to the project, I either require another paper for the course or I substitute two essay exams. I also regularly give a mid-term exam which covers the basic principles and definitions of folklore—the textbook material. But the project is central. For most students—I remember only a few exceptions—developing the project is a memorable and valuable experience. In their course evaluations, many students cite a sense of achievement and the feeling of becoming an expert on a particular subject.

The majority of the papers deal with typical topics: superstitions, tombstone epitaphs, graffiti, quilting patterns, fairytale motifs, oral histories, children's games and stories, folk instruments, crafts, local character anecdotes. The range of topics is considerable. In the last seven years many students have focused on regional traditions, especially Iowa lore. Recent papers have dealt with family legends of a Jesse James kidnapping, stories about a local Bonnie and Clyde shootout, stories of bootlegging whiskey in Templeton during Prohibition, memorates on coal-mining in Madrid, interviews with hoboes in Britt on Hobo Day, foodways among the Norwegians in Story City, the Swedes in Elkhorn and the Danes in Exira, descriptions of old-time threshers in Spencer, and versions of Boone's Kate Shelley legend.

I evaluate and return the reports before the end of the term. Each student gives a brief oral summary of the work to the class, emphasizing methods and results. Since these topics vary enormously, those last sessions are always informative and thought-provoking—a great way to end the semester. Giving an oral description of the project allows each student to apply some hindsight on the experience and to pose some knowledgeable questions to other students.

I still think that at a university like Iowa State, where no folklore program exists and where there is only one regular offering in folklore, a broad, integrated introductory course is best, but it should be one that reflects the special interests of the instructor. If it does not, the course will eventually acquire the aura of a mail-order catalog. To borrow an earlier metaphor: there is a limit to how many objects a juggler can handle. And in the end it's really the rhythm and timing that count.

Larry Danielson

University of Illinois at Urbana-Champaign

A Folk Narrative Course for Non-Specialists

In 1973 I joined the English Department at the University of Illinois, Urbana-Champaign, and inherited a folklore course that had been offered for several years, English 367, *International Folktale*. The university catalog described it as "Origin, nature, and distribution of the folktale." I have taught the course eight times over the past decade, more often than my other folklore courses— *Ballad and Folksong in the U.S., Topics in Folklore*, and various undergraduate and graduate seminars related to folklore studies. Although the assignments and emphases in *International Folktale* have changed, its basic organization, purpose, and types of enrollees have remained much the same.

The course is cross-listed in the Comparative Literature Department and is directed toward juniors, seniors, and graduate students. It can satisfy the "theme, mode, genre, and interdisciplinary approaches" requirement for English majors and serve as humanities credit for non-English majors. For many students, however, it functions as an unusual elective that allows them a change of pace which may or may not be pertinent to their academic concentrations. The classroom usually consists of twenty to thirty students: a few sophomores, many juniors and seniors, and several graduate students. Their majors may be elementary education, art, and history as often as English and comparative literature. Their expectations are diverse and their academic abilities disparate. Very few of them have studied folklore in other courses and most of them upon enrollment believe that folk narratives are quaint stories, children's fiction, or tales that concern "superstition" and "myth," two terms which invariably need to be re-defined and clarified at some point in the semester. The nuts and bolts of folk narrative research, the challenge of clearly defined concepts and theoretical approaches to folktale study, and the rigors of careful textual and contextual analysis surprise many students. By the end of the semester, however, most of them are still interested in the topic and leave the classroom with an understanding of folk narrative genres and the different approaches that can be used in folktale studies. I hope, too, that they are able to apply the ideas and methods discussed in the course to such subjects as belletristic fiction, children's literature, and history. Even more significant for me as a teacher, is that they have become conscious of the importance of traditional narratives in human expressive behavior and the complex functions these narratives serve in their own daily lives.

The course is still titled *International Folktale*, but I teach it as an exploration of traditional oral narrative and include in its organization a variety of genres that range well beyond the boundaries of the internationally distributed tale type. The most recent syllabus for the course explains its goals and content in much the same manner as earlier syllabi:

This course will explore types of traditional oral narrative, including the magic tale, myth, legend, and joke. We will discuss several questions raised by traditional tales, for example, origins, distribution, variation, structure, style, and function. The uses of the folktale in literature, popular print, and film will also be examined. Texts that provide the basis for class discussion will be drawn from Black-American, European, Japanese, Israeli, and contemporary American oral tradition.

I emphasize throughout the course that folk narratives are diverse in form and content; that different scholarly approaches are appropriate to their study; and that they serve multiple functions in our lives. The assignments used to reach these goals vary from semester to semester, but they always involve reading and discussing many kinds of folk narratives from different cultural contexts and several analytic pieces that are good examples of folktale scholarship. In addition to the mid-term and final examinations, class members must complete a research paper, some fifteen to twenty pages in length, and three short writing assignments which make use of a specific research technique.

Graduate students, because they must do additional work when enrolled in an undergraduate course according to university policy, present an oral report to the class, often based on research undertaken for the final project. I think that it is refreshing for the class to see a change of face from time to time and that it is good experience for graduate students to teach, however briefly, in an area outside of rhetoric and introductory literature courses. If there are students enrolled who have special interests and abilities, I encourage them to incorporate their expertise into their presentations. Graduate students in oral interpretation, for example, once performed selections from Anne Sexton's *Transformations*, poems based on the Grimm tales, and a children's literature specialist prepared an elaborate slide presentation of Cinderella illustrations from the latter nineteenth century to the present.

My selection of required texts has become less confined by conventional criteria emphasized in my graduate studies as I have become more sensible about what I want students to learn about traditional narrative. Most of them, after all, are not going to become academic folklorists. I have usually assigned a half-dozen books for the semester in order to represent several folk narrative genres and cultures. The primary criterion for book selection is a practical one: if students can get a good idea of the genre or approach represented by the work in question through a judiciously selected chapter or series of excerpts on library reserve or through a class handout, I have not required the book. For example, Dundes's *The Study of Folklore*, Botkin's *Lay My Burden Down*, and Seitel's *See So that We May See: Performances and Interpretations of Traditional Tales from Tanzania* contain excellent materials relevant to the course. I usually assign readings from them, but I do not use them as required textbooks. If students will use most of the work in class preparation and discussion and if it is available in a paperback edition, I will assign it as required reading.

The last time I taught *International Folktale*, the spring semester of 1983, the required readings included *Once upon a Time: On the Nature of Fairy Tales*, by Max Lüthi; *The Grimms' German Folktales*, translated by Francis P. Magoun, Jr., and Alexander H. Krappe; *Folktales of Japan*, edited by Keigo Seki; *Mules and Men*, by Zora Neale Hurston; *Israeli Humor: The Content and Structure of the Chizbat of the Palmah*, by Elliott Oring; and Anne Sexton's adaptations of selected Grimm tales, *Transformations*. I assigned students texts from Hurston, Grimm, and Seki throughout the semester.

Lüthi's *Once upon a Time*, an impressionistic, literary discussion of the magic tale directed at a non-professional audience, is a non-threatening introduction to the basic differences between Märchen and legend. I use it cautiously, however, because some chapters, e.g., chapter 7, "Animal Stories: A Glimpse of the Tales of Primitive Peoples," deal with folk narrative materials foreign to Lüthi's expertise. Also, a vague Jungian premise informs much of Lüthi's discussion, a matter that deserves comment and evaluation in class discussion.

I do not assign every tale in the Grimm collection. I use it as a required text because I think that the *Kinder-und Hausmarchen* is an important work in western literature and should be included in every home library. The Magoun-Krappe translation is good and includes all the texts from the 1857 edition.

Folktales of Japan offers excellent annotations and straightforward translations by a former graduate school colleague whose abilities I trust. It provides versions of European folktales in forms that students find exotic and indigenous texts that can be correlated with Japanese sociocultural studies.

A less conventional collection is *Mules and Men* by Zora Neale Hurston. I first used it in class with trepidation, but I have continued to assign it for several reasons. It is lively reading and reconstructs tale-telling contexts vividly, even though the folklorist may question the means by which these narrative performances were re-created by Hurston. The collection contains several Black-American folk narrative genres and provokes questions about field research that intrigue the new folklore student. Inevitably questions about personal belief and scholarship and about ethics in fieldwork surface in class discussion of the work, especially its description of Hurston's investigation of voodoo rituals and personal experience stories associated with them. I provide relevant background information about Hurston's writing career, her interests in Black-American folklore, and her goals as a Black-American writer (Hemenway 1978 is a detailed account of Hurston's personal life and professional career) and suggest the value of such works for the non-professional audience. Ten years ago I was too insecure as a folklorist in academe to have devoted so much attention to the book in a public forum.

Oring's *Israeli Humor* serves multiple purposes: it discusses humorous narrative genres, explores cultural definitions of humor, and illustrates how structural analysis can be used to understand relationships between traditional narrative and its cultural context. I once assigned the texts, printed in a lengthy appendix, to be read before the author's discussion of cultural background and analysis of the jokes, thinking that this method would stress the importance of context data in humor analysis. My plan backfired. Most class members ended up resenting the book because they were initially frustrated by reading supposedly humorous narratives that were instead enigmatic. Teachers learn as much in the classroom as students.

I have assigned Sexton's *Transformations* in *International Folktale* for several years. This series of poems based on sixteen Grimm tales excites many students and relates to feminist questions of import in this decade. In these radical treatments of familiar magic tales Sexton at times forcefully explicates folktale themes and symbols that have interested many psychoanalytic critics. In other cases she suggests idiosyncratic interpretations of the Märchen that pertain directly to her personal life.

Writing assignments in the 1983 version of *International Folktale* comprised two in-class examinations, two short essays, a schematic presentation of tale-type variants which relied on the Äarne-Thompson *Types of the Folktale*, the Thompson *Motif-Index of Folk-Literature*, and related works, and a research paper which was based solely on library sources or on field materials supplemented by printed collections and studies. The graduate students enrolled in the course presented oral reports from time to time and I followed my accustomed lecture-discussion format. Once again, I packed too many topics and too much reading into the 45 fifty-minute sessions. The following outline represents the topics and themes developed in the class, pertinent assignments, and explanations or reservations about each unit.

(I)   Some Introductory Questions about Traditional Oral Narrative

The first two class meetings described the course requirements, suggested the relation of folk narrative to the more general concept of folklore, and explored the protean boundaries between folk, popular, and belletristic literature. But most important in this introduction to the course was class discussion of the concept of narrative and its uses in human experience. I sometimes incorporate too many anecdotes and personal experience stories in my teaching, but in class discussion concerning the centrality of narrative in our lives, anecdotes are valuable as illustrations. At this point in the semester they also serve to humanize a potentially intimidating syllabus.

(II) Folk Narrative Genres

In 1983 I spent five sessions introducing different folk narrative genres: the Märchen, religious tale, romantic tale or novella, animal tale, joke, anecdote, formula tale, legend, and myth. Linda Dégh's essay, "Folk Literature," provided helpful information for my lectures in this unit. Reading assignments included selected chapters from Lüthi's *Once upon a Time* and texts from the Grimm collection, *Ghosts along the Cumberland* by William Lynwood Montell, *The Vanishing Hitchhiker* by Jan Harold Brunvand, and *Lay My Burden Down: A Folk History of Slavery*, edited by B.A. Botkin. The final session emphasized the problems of genre classification by asking the class to categorize field texts according to the models described in the preceding lectures. The issue of deductive and inductive classification systems in folk narrative study elicited questions that we returned to later in the semester.

(III) Folk Narrative Sources: Print and Oral Texts

The next four sessions concerned the collection of folk narrative from oral sources, fieldwork methods, and the use of popular print sources in folktale studies, e.g., community histories, local newspapers, and special interest publications like *Fate Magazine*, an occult periodical. Readings that served as the basis for discussions included selections from Hurston's *Mules and Men* and class handouts. A graduate student's description of his development of an Illinois equivalent to the *Foxfire* project supplemented the discussion effectively because his newspaper work entailed interviewing, narrative collection, and editing texts for a non-specialist audience. I assigned two short essays based on the collection of one field text and the location of one traditional narrative in a printed source to conclude the unit.

(IV)   *Folk Narrative Transmission and Distribution*

These four sessions touched on selected origin theories, suggested the difficulty of locating the origins of a particular folk narrative configuration, examined the nature of oral transmission, and focused on comparative research methods in the study of tale type variants. Although the emphasis on comparativist methodology may seem old-fashioned to some folklorists, I think that mastery of research tools like the Äarne-Thompson tale type index, the Thompson *Motif-Index*, and related indices, is important (Baughman 1966 is valuable in this assignment because of its restriction to English language texts). Locating and examining versions of a traditional plot illustrates dramatically the dual characteristics of folk narrative: continuity and change. In addition, comparative research methods are useful in other studies, for example literary criticism and the analysis of traditional elements in historical sources. They constitute a set of research techniques seldom encountered in the literature or history classroom. Although students sometimes complain about difficulties in using the standard indices and locating cited sources, most of them find the work interesting and rewarding. The unit culminated in a written assignment that analyzed in a schematic fashion the differences and similarities between tale-type variants and evaluated the reliability of the text collections used for these versions. (Clarkson's and Cross's *World Folktales: A Scribner Resource Collection* includes information about research tools, representative folktale texts, annotations, and lists of parallel narratives. I was familiar with the work when I assigned the search for versions in 1983. However, because I did not explicitly warn the class against using it as a substitution for their own sleuthing efforts, it provided easy answers to a few students' research frustrations.)

(V)   *Folk Narrative as Literature*

The following four sessions introduced concepts of narrative style and narrative structure, using selections from *Folktales of Japan* and the Grimm collection. I discussed Axel Olrik's epic laws (Olrik 1965) and introduced the concept of syntagmatic structure through lectures on Propp's *Morphology of the Folktale* and Alan Dundes's motifemic sequence model (Dundes 1965). I also worked to explain the concept of paradigmatic structure through an application of Lévi-Strauss' theory of polar opposition mediation to a Japanese folktale (Lévi-Strauss 1971). This exercise argued the value of such an approach in discovering the relationships shared by narrative structure and social structure. The unit is a demanding one and its intensity is modified from year to year by the interest or disinterest of the class members in the mysteries of structure.

(VI) Folk Narrative as Oral Performance

The next three sessions attempted to counter the emphasis on conventional text in the preceding weeks. Examinations of oral performance style incorporated students' attention to one another's story-telling performances. (By this time in the semester, most of us had shared a good many personal experience narratives with one another.) I also discussed Dell Hymes's distinction between reportive and authoritative performance and the number and complexity of variables present in a single narrative performance (Hymes 1975). In this unit I have sometimes used videotapes of students sharing anecdotes about a common topic. The in-class analysis of performance features was valuable in clarifying the concept of performance style. My 1983 schedule, however, did not accommodate the extra time and planning required by such a project.

(VII) Psychologizing about the Folktale

Three sessions did not provide enough time to deal with important psychological approaches to folk narrative. Using selections from Lüthi and Alan Dundes's psychoanalytic analyses of folk narrative (Dundes 1980), I attempted to acquaint the class with the primary concepts used in Jungian and Freudian interpretations of certain folktales. Graduate students were valuable resources in these considerations. For example, one report described and evaluated Bruno Bettleheim's *The Uses of Enchantment*. It also referred to student essays on favorite fairy tales which the graduate student suggested as a writing topic in the rhetoric class she was concurrently teaching. Her innovative presentation enriched students' understanding of psychological responses to the folktale.

(VIII) Folk Narrative and Culture

These seven sessions were anthropological in orientation and attempted to illustrate the complex relationships between folk narrative and its socio-cultural contexts. Oring's *Israeli Humor* is a persuasive study of the joke and anecdote in a specific context, that of the Palmah, an underground militia active in Palestine in the 1940s. The unit also included a graduate student's study of the connections between comic anecdotes about Black-American preachers and Black-American attitudes toward religious institutions and their leaders. Another student discussed the curandera (folk healer) and the bruja (witch) in southwestern Hispanic-American folk belief and legend. Because of the student reports I eliminated speculations about the functions of the urban legend in American society originally planned as part of this unit and always a popular topic in the classroom.

(IX) Folk Narrative and the Visual Arts

Because I teach film as well as folklore courses and the English Department has a well equipped media center, I have always included in the course several sessions on folk narrative in film. They provide a respite from classroom preparation for students at work on their research papers at this point in the semester. Although the materials do not represent "oral traditional narrative" in the strict sense of the term, they do illustrate the continued life of the folktale in the film medium. They also initiate interesting questions about the ways in which different media, e.g., oral performance and film, affect content and audience response to narrative. Once again, a special presentation enlivened the unit, this time by a colleague's wife who showed the class a movie her family had made during summer vacation, a film treatment of a Russian folktale about Baba Yaga, a cannibalistic ogress. Her comments about problems in making the movie and the revision of the story in order to facilitate the filming of live action were especially valuable. (The chicken that refused to walk while its upper body was encased in a cardboard-box "house"—an imaginative effort to recreate Baba Yaga's house, which rests on fowl legs—was the entertaining case in point.) Two films in the unit, *The Fisherman and His Wife* (animated) and *Hansel and Gretel: An Appalachian Version* (live action) were visualizations of popular Grimm tales. Three other films concerned other kinds of folk narrative: *Foster's Release*, a realistic dramatization of the urban legend about the baby-sitter and the hidden assailant; *The Birth of Aphrodite*, an avant-garde interpretation of the myth of Aphrodite; and *Venus and the Cat*, an artistic and adult animation of the Aesop fable of the same name. The unit concluded with a slide presentation of *Playboy* magazine cartoons which alluded to folk narrative motifs. For this session I was indebted to a former student who had researched the topic carefully and enthusiastically.

(X) Folk Narrative and Literature

I had planned to discuss the trickster archetype in literature at this point in the course, using *The Trickster* by Paul Radin and the novel *One Flew over the Cuckoo's Nest*, by Ken Kesey. The interpretation of the novel's protagonist as a trickster figure interests me, but the compacted class schedule did not allow the topic. Instead we concentrated on Anne Sexton's transformations of sixteen Grimm tales. To elucidate the differences between western folk literature and twentieth-century belletristic literature we compared and contrasted Sexton's intense, confessional versions of the stories with the Grimm texts. I supplemented discussion of the poems with biographical information concerning Sexton's troubled life and suggested correlations between the poet's experiences and her interpretations of the Grimm Märchen. (McClatchy 1978 and Sexton and Ames 1977 are important sources in this discussion).

(XI) Conclusions and Questions

The course concluded with several student reports based on their research projects. I chose those that were of special interest to the class and appropriate for oral presentation: a report on local supernatural legends; visual interpretations of Äarne-Thompson 310, "The Maiden in the Tower" (Rapunzel), and 709, "Snow-White," in children's literature; and a family history based largely on oral sources which documented a Jewish family's escape from Luxembourg to Santo Domingo in the early 1940s. This last student project was the capstone of the course for me. It not only illustrated the uses of oral tradition in the reconstruction of the past, but it also provided the student with a positive sense of family heritage and the reestablishment of kinship ties that had become separated in the past generation. Although this unit was to have allowed time for concluding generalizations, it did not. I have yet to avoid scheduling too many topics and too many assignments when I organize a course syllabus.

In retrospect, the 1983 version of *International Folktale* satisfied me as a teacher. The excellent students who worked so hard in preparing class presentations and contributing to class discussions were essential to its success. Conferences about student presentations and bibliographic suggestions related to their topics are important. But it is just as important to exploit, if you will, student curiosities and to encourage their interests in aspects of oral traditional narrative that may or may not fit neatly into the syllabus constructed for the course.

In certain semesters *International Folktale* was not as successful as in 1983. I tend to overemphasize folk narrative genres that interest me, especially the legend, at the expense of other genres, usually the joke and myth. Students and teachers do not always share the same interests. Some classes have found the unit on structural analysis frustrating and irrelevant, a response that probably reflects my own discomfort with a rigorous structural approach to folk literature. Ten years ago I was convinced that the course should survey the history of folktale scholarship, perhaps a good idea if most of the students plan to enter graduate folklore programs. I eventually realized that there were more important matters to teach in *International Folktale* than Theodor Benfey's Indianist theory and Hans Naumann's interpretation of the obstacle flight motif. Significant issues in the history of folktale studies, for example the historic-geographic approach and the psychoanalytic analysis of texts, can be selectively admitted into lectures and discussions without surveying the history of the field. One semester I required as the final research project a collection and analysis of urban legends, which the class apparently enjoyed. The course evaluations, though, revealed some discontent about the lack of alternatives in fulfilling one of the major assignments of the semester. In one case, a student resented that I had forced the class to consider such "disgusting" narratives when folk literature really concerned the "beautiful and uplifting." I had clearly failed to communicate to this student my position that folk narrative takes many forms, both appealing and appalling, and that it serves many functions, both positive and negative.

The next time I teach *International Folktale* the course will change in some respects, depending on the students enrolled in it, my research and reading interests, and the ideas articulated in folklore journals and conference papers at the time. My goals in teaching the course, however, will probably be about the same: to explore the diversity of folk narrative and its multiple functions in the human experience; to relate the subject in some way to other disciplines; and to encourage students to consider the important uses of folk narrative in their own lives.

Robert A. Georges

University of California at Los Angeles

A Required Introductory Graduate Course for Folklore Majors

Most individuals grumble through their required introductory graduate class. While the titles of such courses vary among departments and programs, they tend to be strikingly similar in their aims and structures. They are also (unfortunately) seldom stimulating or satisfying. Most have as their sole objective acquainting students with research resources and techniques employed by professionals in the field. Class participants are usually required to examine assigned reference works, to compile bibliographies, and to prepare and deliver oral reports on books and essays which describe or exemplify selected approaches to the phenomena which serve as data for the discipline. Classroom sessions and course assignments are more often activity- than idea-oriented; and those who can demonstrate familiarity with source materials and an ability to present, document, annotate, synthesize, and evaluate information are usually judged to have done well in the class and to have acquired the necessary background and skills to become serious and successful scholars.

Having suffered through two such classes in my graduate student days (one in English at the University of Pennsylvania and the other in folklore at Indiana University), I was determined to spare students a similar fate if and when I ever offered a comparable course. The opportunity came sooner than I had expected. In 1968, after just two years on the UCLA faculty, I was assigned to teach Folklore 200, "Folklore Bibliography, Theory, and Research Methods." The first graduate-level class for students pursuing the Master of Arts Degree (the only graduate degree offered at the time in folklore and mythology at UCLA), Folklore 200 was not only required, but completing it was also a prerequisite for enrolling in other graduate folklore and mythology courses, whether required or elective. These facts complicated my task as a prospective Folklore 200 instructor, for my responsibility, I realized, was not just to offer a graduate course, but to teach what I judged to be the keystone course in the interdisciplinary UCLA Folklore and Mythology Program curriculum and in the students' and my own field of specialization.

As I pondered the matter, I realized that one of the things which had disturbed me about the comparable courses I had taken was their lack of any organizing principle. In Richard M. Dorson's *Folklore Theory* and *Techniques* courses at Indiana University, for instance, I had read works and heard reports describing the research of a multitude of (mostly contemporary American) folklorists; and I had become familiar with basic reference works, such as the type and motif indices, and had learned how to use them, principally to annotate data. But apart from being told who was, and who was not, a good and respectable folklorist, and what reference works and bibliographies one should, and one should not, consult and cite, I was uncertain about where or how either the individuals or books we discussed fit into a larger scheme of things. Simply put, I had no sense of how folklore studies had evolved over time. I decided, therefore, that the Folklore 200 course I had been assigned to teach would focus upon what my own required introductory graduate folklore course had ignored: the historical and ideological development of folkloristics as a field of inquiry.

Designing the kind of course I envisioned was much more difficult than I anticipated. While my own graduate training had made me aware of the evolution of the historic-geographic method (an awareness I acquired by reading Stith Thompson's writings and by participating in Warren Roberts' two-semester folktale class rather than through instruction I received in my *Folklore Theory and Techniques* courses), I had little knowledge of what had preceded or followed it. Besides my own ignorance, I was hampered by the dearth of books and essays on the subject. The few available publications were descriptive and biographical, characterizing the backgrounds, research, and publications of pioneering and influential investigators, but providing little information about the contributions of individual scholars to the development of the discipline or about the similarities and differences in their conceptions. While I perused works of many investigators whose names I had heard but whose views I had not previously known, I had no clearer conception of the evolution of folkloristics after my wide-ranging reading than I had as a graduate student.

As my mood changed from frustration to despair, Richard M. Dorson's book-length works on the history of folklore studies in the British Isles appeared in print. Although *The British Folklorists: A History* and *Peasant Customs and Savage Myths: Selections from the British Folklorists* (both published in 1968) were more descriptive and biographical than ideological in their orientations, Dorson had discovered that certain individuals could be grouped and discussed together because they seemed to share assumptions, hypotheses, and concepts, even though they often focused upon different kinds of data or upon data from different eras or locales. In addition, Dorson's comparisons and contrasts in *The British Folklorists* of the preoccupations and views of the sizeable number of pioneering folklore researchers, together with the excerpts from their works which he reprinted in *Peasants Customs and Savage Myths*, hinted at something which I had intuited: (1) that despite their varied backgrounds and differing professional fields, multiple individuals often conceptualize folklore in similar ways; (2) that when multiple individuals conceptualize folklore in strikingly similar ways, a model of inquiry can be said to evolve; and (3) that the presuppositions, assumptions, and hypotheses which multiple individuals seem to share lead them to pose similar kinds of research questions, to regard similar kinds of phenomena as data, to utilize similar research techniques, and to propose similar answers to the questions they formulate. Furthermore, once they evolve, models rooted in similar conceptions of folklore are perpetuated through unconscious imitation and formal training; and new models which are generated do not supplant existing ones, but instead are utilized simultaneously by different individuals, with both similar and different kinds of inquiries being pursued at any given time by those with an interest in a seemingly common body of phenomena or set of questions. On the basis of this realization, I decided to make models of inquiry in folkloristics and the concept of folklore underlying them the bases for organizing the Folklore 200 class I was evolving.

Two of Dorson's categorical designations—"The Antiquary-Folklorists" and "The Savage Folklorists"—suggested the first two models which had evolved historically: those rooted in (1) the concept of folklore as survivals from the historical past and (2) the concept of folklore as survivals of prelogical thinking and primitive stages of cultural evolution. A third model was inherent in the work of the articulators and practitioners of the historic-geographic method; its intellectual foundation was the concept of folklore as diffusible entities.

The graduate folklore courses I had taken had all been presented in terms of one or some combination of these models, and most works published by folklorists during the first five or six decades of the current century could also be described and analyzed in terms of one or more of the three. But it was obvious that there were additional models which needed to be considered if the Folklore 200 course I was evolving were to be comprehensive and up-to-date.

From the late nineteenth century on, a growing number of investigators (most of them anthropologists) had conceptualized phenomena identifiable as folklore as aspects of culture, on the one hand, and as correlates of other cultural phenomena, on the other. They tended to take the former for granted, for since human beings create folklore and teach it to, or learn it from, each other, its cultural nature seemed to be an established and indisputable fact. But researchers' discerning and hypothesizing interrelationships between folklore and other cultural phenomena suggested that folklore could be conceptualized as a reflector and refractor of other aspects of the culture of which it was a part. A fourth model, I realized, had evolved among those who espouse such a view—one that has as its foundation the concept of folklore as expressive manifestations of cultures.

Merely tangential to folkloristics, I had been taught and initially thought, was a host of other studies which could not be reconciled with the four models I had already discerned. These included structural, psychological, psychoanalytical, and the then (in 1968) small number of event- or performance-oriented analyses. Pondering the matter, I realized that such works could not be excluded from consideration in an introductory graduate folklore course simply because most folklorists slighted or ignored them or because they did not seem to be rooted in any of the popular or prevalent models that guide other inquiries. Structural studies, I eventually concluded, are distinct, having as their intellectual foundation a concept of folklore as analyzable structures and structured forms. Furthermore, despite their apparent differences, psychological, psychoanalytical, and some of the event- or performance-oriented studies (specifically, those not rooted in a concept of folklore as expressive manifestations of cultures) can be regarded as having a common conceptual base, for all are rooted in the notion that phenomena identifiable as folklore are expressive manifestations of the nature and behavior of Homo sapiens. While Freud and Jung and their followers view folklore as outputs of unconscious psychic states and processes, and some event- and performance-oriented researchers regard folklore as products of pan-human sociobiological processes, their inquiries have a common intellectual foundation because they conceive of human beings collectively as a single species whose individual members have a common nature and exhibit common behaviors, of which examples of folklore are expressive manifestations.

Having uncovered an organizing principle (models of inquiry in folkloristics rooted in different conceptions of what folklore is) that was meaningful (to me), and having isolated what seemed (to me) to be the six models which have guided inquiry in folkloristics (sometimes singly, but most of the time simultaneously, since individuals who are contemporaries may follow different, as well as the same, models, and since the same individual may employ different models at different times), I had conceptualized a way to structure Folklore 200. To introduce students to such a structure, I felt, I had to begin the course by making them aware that bibliography and research techniques cannot be studied or understood independently of what is loosely termed "theory." The model that a researcher employs is not only rooted in what he or she presupposes, assumes, and hypothesizes, but it also determines the nature of the studies in which he or she engages, the research techniques he or she employs, and the published work he or she generates. To make these points in a manner that would place them in a broad and general intellectual context, I concluded, we should begin Folklore 200 with a discussion that was grounded in a philosophically-oriented work which characterizes inquiry in a systematic and comprehensible way. Because of its behavioral, as well as its philosophical, orientation, I selected Abraham Kaplan, *The Conduct of Inquiry: Methodology for Behavioral Science* (1964). The first fifteen chapters (170 pages), I felt, would provide a general, yet comprehensive, introduction to inquiry that could then serve as a point of departure for the kind of historical and ideological development of folkloristics upon which we would focus during the remainder of the quarter.

Once I had settled on Kaplan's book as a way to introduce the structure of Folklore 200, I had no difficulty selecting other course readings. Convinced that graduate students should read primary, instead of secondary, sources whenever possible, I assigned selections reprinted in Dorson's *Peasant Customs and Savage Myths* and in Alan Dundes's *The Study of Folklore* (1965) to exemplify research conducted in terms of models which have as their intellectual foundations the concept of folklore as survivals from the historical past and the concept of folklore as survivals of prelogical thinking and primitive stages of cultural evolution. These included excerpts from the writings of such individuals as Sir Walter Scott, William John Thoms, Thomas Keightley, Max Müller, Andrew Lang, Edwin Sidney Hartland, and George Laurence Gomme. Readings illustrating models of inquiry rooted in the concepts of folklore as diffusible entities and as expressive manifestations of cultures came largely from the *Study of Folklore* and from *Studies of Mythology* (ed. Robert A. Georges, 1968). Among them were works by Stith Thompson, Paul G. Brewster, Franz Boas, W. H. R. Rivers, A. R. Radcliffe-Brown, Bronislaw Malinowski, Ruth Benedict, and Roger D. Abrahams. Periodical essays, either in their original form or as reprinted in the Dundes reader, constituted the sets of readings for discussions of models which have as their bases concepts of folklore as analyzable structures and structured forms and as expressive manifestations of the nature and behavior of Homo sapiens (e.g., essays by Alan Dundes, Claude Lévi-Strauss, Ernest Jones, C. G. Jung, and Clyde Kluckhohn).

From the time of its inception, Folklore 200 was designed to end with a section titled "Retrospect and Prospect in Folkloristics." Readings assigned for this concluding course segment focus upon such fundamental issues as the problem of defining folklore and upon long-established or evolving controversies in folkloristics, such as that which has erupted recently about whether one should study folklore as text or in context. A full listing of readings required for Folklore 200 the last time I taught it (winter quarter, 1982) is included in the copy of the course syllabus appended to this essay.

Just as I believed that folklore bibliography and research methods (techniques) should be examined as manifestations of the models in terms of which folkloristics can be conceived to have evolved historically and ideologically, so did I feel that course writing assignments should be an integral part of the study of those models. The assignments have varied somewhat over the years, but the requirement of two short analytical papers (five to ten double-spaced typewritten pages each) and one exercise has remained constant.

The first analytical paper assignment correlates with readings and class discussions about how early researchers identified phenomena as folklore and configured examples of folklore into sets. I give students two or three folktale or ballad texts which are similar in many respects and different in others. Their task is to read and study the texts, to compare and contrast them, and to advance and defend (with textual evidence) a hypothesis about the probable relatedness or nonrelatedness of the tales or songs of which the texts are records. The objectives of the assignment are (1) to make students aware of the criteria that human beings (including folklore scholars) employ to group (type) and to differentiate "folklore items" on the basis of textual records alone, and (2) to demonstrate to them the problems that can arise when one is forced to defend the judgment one has made about whether examples of folklore which exhibit both discernible similarities and differences are of the same or different types. All class participants are given the same set of texts, and they are encouraged to discuss the data and the problem posed by the assignment with each other as frequently as they wish. Students present the results of their analyses, including the evidence they adduce to support the hypothesis they advance, in essay form.

The second assignment is a written exercise, distributed while the class is discussing the concept of folklore and mythology as diffusible entities. To complete the exercise, the students must familiarize themselves with, and make use of, reference works such as the type and motif indices; Francis James Child, *English and Scottish Popular Ballads*; Archer Taylor, *English Riddles from Oral Tradition*; Bertrand H. Bronson, *Traditional Tunes of the Child Ballads*; Paul G. Brewster, *American Nonsinging Games*; and Wayland D. Hand, *Popular Beliefs and Superstitions from North Carolina*. All these works have as their purposes (1) to facilitate typing, (2) to provide textual data for comparative studies, and/or (3) to facilitate the authentication and annotation of data. While the exercise sheets distributed to all students have the same number of sections and questions within each section, no two are identical, although some of the questions in each exercise are obviously the same. The aim of this assignment is to acquaint students with the objectives, data kind and coverage, organizational scheme, usefulness, and limitations of books which exemplify a commitment to the concept of folklore as diffusible entities and which many consider to be the basic reference works in folkloristics.

The third written (and second analytical paper) assignment is due during the ninth week of the ten-week quarter. The students are given copies of a published essay in which various approaches to, or preoccupations in, folklore studies are characterized and discussed in terms of an organizing principle or organizational scheme which differs from that employed in Folklore 200. (Two essays I have used frequently and alternately are Richard M. Dorson's "Current Folklore Theories" (1963) and "Introduction: Concepts of Folklore and Folklife Studies" (in his *Folklore and Folklife: An Introduction*, 1972:7-47.) Students are asked to read the assigned essay and to analyze it in terms of a set of posed questions. (For Dorson's "Current Folklore Theories" essay, for instance, questions which I have posed from time to time include the following: "What does Dorson mean by 'theory?'" "Are the 'theories' which Dorson describes and discusses properly identified as 'theories,' or is/are some other designation/s more appropriate, and why?" "In what ways and to what extent can Dorson's 'theories' be said to be mutually exclusive, on the one hand, and overlapping or redundant, on the other?") Students present the results of their analyses in essay form.

Folklore 200 concludes with a three-hour written final examination. The exam is designed to enable course participants to utilize the information and to apply the analytical skills acquired in the course of the quarter. One question always requires students to define terms which folklorists frequently use in their writings (e.g., tale-type, motif, oicotypification, diachronic/synchronic studies, syntagmatic/ paradigmatic structural analysis). The other four or five questions require essays as answers. These sometimes ask the respondents to infer and characterize the underlying assumptions or hypotheses about the nature of folklore inherent in quotations excerpted from works other than those assigned for the course; to explicate certain passages in quotations taken from course readings; to compare and contrast multiple researchers' assertions or views about such things as what folklore is or how it originates, is disseminated, or changes; and to generate a "scenario" in response to a hypothetical question. (One such hypothetical question posed in an exam several years ago read as follows: "Assume that Max Müller, Bronislaw Malinowski, C. G. Jung, and Ruth Benedict could be brought together to serve as participants in a panel discussion, chaired by Claude Lévi-Strauss, on the nature and significance of myth. How would each be likely to present his or her views; who would agree and disagree with whom, and how; and how would Lévi-Strauss mediate oppositions and bring the discussion to a meaningful and harmonious conclusion? Write the scenario, being boldly imaginative, yet precise in your answer.")

Folklore 200 is a full and demanding course, particularly since it is taught during a single ten-week quarter (two two-hour class meetings per week). Yet while students often complain about the heavy workload, they give the class high marks in their quarter-end evaluations. From the readings, lectures, class discussions, paper writing, and final examination, students state, they gain a meaningful overview of folkloristics. Since we explore not only the nature of each of the six models, but also the ways in which, and reasons why, each evolved and has been modified or transformed, students usually develop an appreciation for the fact that inquiry in folkloristics (as in other fields) is ongoing and ever-evolving, with new generations of scholars following in the footsteps of their predecessors and puzzling over age-old questions, on the one hand, and building upon the work of their forerunners, posing new questions, and proposing alternative solutions to fundamental problems, on the other.

With a few exceptions, I have taught *Folklore Bibliography, Theory, and Research Methods* during every other academic year since 1968. The colleague and I who currently alternate the teaching of the class organize the course differently, and each of us has his own priorities, emphases, reading and writing requirements, and expectations. But we are agreed that the principal purpose of Folklore 200 should be to help students develop a meaningful conceptual foundation for subsequent graduate folklore courses and for their own inquiries by helping them to understand how folkloristics has evolved ideologically and chronologically and why this has occurred.

In describing the background and evolution of an introductory graduate course for folklore majors which I designed and have taught regularly for the past fifteen years, I have presented what can also be characterized as a description of the generation of what has become, in retrospect, an Urform or archetype. I have not altered the overall structure of Folklore 200 appreciably since I first taught it in 1968, for student feedback and my own self-assessment provide ample evidence to suggest that using models of inquiry in folkloristics as the course organizing principle is effective, defensible, and enlightening. Because I believe that graduate students majoring in folklore should read primary source materials and that they should be familiar with the writings and views of such key scholars as Müller, Lang, Thompson, Boas, Malinowski, Benedict, Lévi-Strauss, Jung, and Freud, I have made few changes in course reading assignments over the years. Because I am convinced that most beginning folklore graduate students do not have the necessary familiarity with basic concepts, preoccupations, and issues in folkloristics to conduct meaningful research in their first graduate-level class (and particularly in a course which is scheduled for only one ten-week quarter), I continue to assign two short analytical papers and an exercise rather than a single, lengthy term paper or field report. Finally, because I believe that examinations are effective instruments through which instructors can test students' understanding of basic concepts, determine their mastery of analytical skills, and prepare them for comprehensive examinations, I continue to make passing performance on a written final examination a heavily-weighted requirement in Folklore 200. Hence, like the phenomena which are its subject, the required introductory graduate folklore course I have here described has remained stable enough over time so that the original is both recognizable in, and reconstructible from, its multiple derivatives.

COURSE SYLLABUS

Folklore 200, *Folklore Bibliography, Theory, and Research Methods*
Winter Quarter, 1982   **Professor Georges**

Required Textbooks:

Dundes, Alan, ed. *The Study of Folklore.* Englewood Cliffs, N.J.:Prentice-Hall, Inc.,
    1965.
Georges, Robert A., ed. *Studies in Mythology.* Homewood, Ill.: The Dorsey Press,
    1968.
Kaplan, Abraham. *The Conduct of Inquiry: Methodology for Behavioral Science.* San
    Francisco: Chandler Publishing Co., 1968.

Optional Textbook:

Dorson, Richard M., ed. *Peasant Customs and Savage Myths: Selections from the
    British Folklorists.* 2 volumes. Chicago: University of Chicago Press, 1968.

Course Description and Assignments

Folklore 200 is a graduate survey course which has as its objectives to increase class participants' awareness, knowledge, and comprehension of the nature and purposes of scholarly inquiry and of the kinds of research questions, techniques, and frameworks folklorists have generated and employ. The course evolves within an historical perspective, with emphasis on the ideological development of folkloristics from its beginnings to the present.

Reading assignments are listed beside the dates on which they are scheduled for class lectures and discussions. Items listed as Text Readings can be found in one of the textbooks required or recommended for the course; those listed as Other Readings are available in the Graduate Reserve Section of the University Research Library (URL) or in the books and periodicals in which they originally appeared. When possible, items should be read in the order in which they are listed on the syllabus.

In addition to the readings, the following are also required of all course participants: (1) two analytical papers, (2) one written exercise requiring the use of reference works on folklore and mythology, and (3) a final course examination (written). Dates on which the papers, exercise, and exam are due or scheduled are indicated below. For purposes of determining final course grades, assignments are weighted as follows: analytical papers, 25% each; exercise, 15%; final examination, 35%.

Tues., Jan. 12 An Introduction to Folkloristics, 1.

Thurs., Jan. 14 An Introduction to Folkloristics, 2: The Nature and Conduct of Inquiry.
Text Reading: Kaplan, chapters 1-14 (pp. 3-125).

Tues., Jan. 19 An Introduction to Folkloristics, 3: Data, Data Gathering, and Data Bases.
Text Reading: Kaplan, chapters 15-19 (pp. 126-170).
Other Reading: Richard M. Dorson, "Introduction: Collecting Oral Folklore in the United States," in *Buying the Wind: Regional Folklore in the United States*, ed. Richard M. Dorson (Chicago, 1964), pp. 1-20.

Thurs., Jan. 21 The Concept of Folklore as Survivals from the Historical Past, 1.
Text Readings: William Thoms, "Folklore," in Dundes, pp. 4-6. Excerpts from writings of Francis Grose, John Brand, Walter Scott, Hugh Miller, Thomas Wright, and Thomas Keightley, in Dorson, vol. 1, 1-51.

Tues., Jan. 26 The Concept of Folklore as Survivals from the Historical Past, 2.
Text Readings: Excerpts from writings of Max Müller and George W. Cox, in Dorson, vol. 1, 67-119, 136-158. Richard M. Dorson, "The Eclipse of Solar Mythology," in Dundes, pp. 57-83.

Thurs., Jan 28 The Concept of Folklore as Survivals of Prelogical Thinking and Primitive Stages of Cultural Evolution, 1.

Text Readings: Excerpts from writings of Andrew Lang and Edwin Sidney
Hartland, in Dorson, vol. 1, 192-207, 230-251, 273-317.

Tues., Feb. 2 The Concept of Folklore as Survivals of Prelogical Thinking and
Primitive Stages of Cultural Evolution, 2.
Text Readings: Excerpts from writings of Alfred Nutt, G. Laurence Gomme,
William Alexander Clouston, in Dorson, vol. 2, 403-436, 470-476.
Other Assignment: ANALYTICAL PAPER #1 DUE.

Thurs., Feb. 4 The Concept of Folklore as Diffusible Entities, 1.
Text Readings: Excerpts from writings of Moses Gaster and Joseph Jacobs, in
Dorson, vol. 2, 488-514. C. W. von Sydow, "Folktale Studies and Philology:
Some Points of View," in Dundes, pp. 219-242. Paul G. Brewster, "Some
Notes on the Guessing Game, How Many Horns Has the Buck?" in Dundes,
pp. 338-368 (skim). Stith Thompson, "The Star Husband Tale," in Dundes,
pp. 414-474 (skim).

Tues., Feb. 9 The Concept of Folklore as Diffusible Entities, 2.
Text Readings: Franz Boas, "The Growth of Indian Mythologies," in Georges,
pp. 15-26. W. H. R. Rivers, "The Sociological Significance of Myth," in
Georges, pp. 27-45.

Thurs., Feb. 11 The Concept of Folklore as Expressive Manifestations of Cultures,
1.
Text Reading: A. R. Radcliffe-Brown, "The Interpretation of Andamanese
Customs and Beliefs: Myths and Legends," in Georges, pp. 46-71.
Other Reading: Bronislaw Malinowski, "Myth in Primitive Psychology," in
Magic, Science and Religion and Other Essays, ed. Robert Redfield (Garden
City, N.Y., 1954), pp. 93-148.

Tues., Feb. 16 The Concept of Folklore as Expressive Manifestations of Cultures,
2.
Text Readings: Ruth Benedict, "Introduction to Zuni Mythology," in Georges,
pp. 102-136. Clyde Kluckhohn, "Myths and Rituals: A General Theory," in
Georges, pp. 137-167. William R. Bascom, "Four Functions of Folklore," in
Dundes, pp. 279-298.

Thurs., Feb. 18 The Concept of Folklore as Expressive Manifestations of Cultures
3
Text Readings: John C. Messenger, "The Role of Proverbs in a Nigerian Judicial
System," in Dundes, pp. 299-307. Betty Wang, "Folksongs as Regulators of
Politics," in Dundes, pp. 308-313.
Other Readings: Roger D. Abrahams, "Playing the Dozens," *Journal of American
Folklore*, 75 (1962), 209-220. William A. Wilson, "The Paradox of Mormon
Folklore," in *Essays on the American West*, ed. Thomas G. Alexander, Charles
Redd Monographs in Western History, No. 6 (Provo, Utah, 1976), pp.
127-147.

Tues., Feb. 23 The Concept of Folklore as Expressive Manifestations of Cultures,
4.

Text readings: Raymond Firth, "Oral Tradition in Relation to Social Status," in Georges, pp. 168-183. Edmund Leach, "Myth as a Justification for Faction and Social Change," in Georges, pp. 184-198.
Other Assignment: WRITTEN EXERCISE DUE

Thurs., Feb. 25 The Concept of Folklore as Analyzable Structures and Structured Forms, 1.
Text Reading: Alan Dundes, "Structural Typology of North American Indian Folktales," in Dundes, pp. 206-215.
Other Readings: Robert A. Georges, "Structure in Folktales: A Generative-Transformational Approach," *The Conch*, 2 (1970), 4-17. Robert A. Georges and Alan Dundes, "Toward a Structural Definition of the Riddle," *Journal of American Folklore*, 76 (1963), 111-118.

Tues., Mar. 2 The Concept of Folklore as Analyzable Structures and Structured Forms, 2.
Other Readings: Claude Lévi-Strauss, "The Structural Study of Myth," in *Myth: A Symposium*, ed. Thomas A. Sebeok (Bloomington, Ind., 1958), pp. 50-66. Claude Lévi-Strauss, "The Story of Asdiwal," translated into English and reprinted in *The Structural Study of Myth and Totemism*, ed. Edmund Leach (London, 1967), pp. 1-47.

Thurs. Mar. 4 The Concept of Folklore as Expressive Manifestations of the Nature and Behavior of Homo sapiens, 1.
Text Reading: Ernest Jones, "Psychoanalysis and Folklore," in Dundes, pp. 88-102.
Other Reading: Alan Dundes, "Earth-Diver: Creation of the Mythopoeic Male," *American Anthropologist*, 64 (1962), 1032-1051.

Tues., Mar. 9 The Concept of Folklore as Expressive Manifestations of the Nature and Behavior of Homo sapiens, 2.
Text Reading: Clyde Kluckhohn, "Recurrent Themes in Myths and Mythmaking," in Dundes, pp. 158-168.
Other Readings: C. G. Jung, "On the Psychology of the Trickster Figure," in Paul Radin, *The Trickster* (New York, 1966), pp. 195-211. Carlos Drake, "Jungian Psychology and Its Uses in Folklore," *Journal of American Folklore*, 82 (1969), 122-133.

Thurs., Mar., 11 The Concept of Folklore as Expressive Manifestations of the Nature and Behavior of Homo sapiens, 3.
Other Reading: Robert A. Georges, "Toward an Understanding of Storytelling Events," *Journal of American Folklore* 82 (1969), 313-328.
Other Assignment: ANALYTICAL PAPER #2 DUE

Tues., Mar. 16 Retrospect and Prospect in Folkloristics.
Text Reading: Alan Dundes, "What Is Folklore?" in Dundes, pp. 1-3.
Other Readings: Dan Ben-Amos, "Toward a Definition of Folklore in Context," *Journal of American Folklore*, 84 (1971), 3-15. D.K. Wilgus, "'The Text Is the Thing,'" *Journal of American Folklore*, 86 (1973), 241-252. Steven Jones, "Slouching Towards Ethnography: The Text/Context Controversy

Reconsidered," *Western Folklore*, 38 (1979), 42-47. Dan Ben-Amos, "The Ceremony of Innocence," *Western Folklore*, 38 (1979), 47-52. Steven Jones, "Dogmatism in the Contextual Revolution," *Western Folklore*, 38 (1979), 52-55. Robert A. Georges, "Toward a Resolution of the Text/Context Controversy," *Western Folklore*, 39 (1980), 34-40.

Thurs., Mar. 18 Course Conclusion and Examination Review

Tues., Mar. 24 Final Course Examination, 8:00-11:00 a.m.

W. Edson Richmond

Indiana University

The English and Scottish Popular Ballads and their Continental Counterparts: English L715/Folklore F715, 1947-1983

Plus ça change, plus c'est le même chose

This title is particularly appropriate for an essay descriptive of a ballad course, and especially for this ballad course, for the very essence of balladry is its continual change, and yet the change results in more of the same thing. Moreover, what is true of ballads themselves is also true of the course which, although it has changed considerably during the past three decades, "c'est la même chose." Approaches to folklore may shift from year to year and decade to decade, but it is important to remember that if one is concerned with texts and genres, one must first understand what they are before he or she decides upon an approach for studying them. What follows is the history of a seminar in ballads, a seminar which focuses upon texts and the definition of genre; it is also an explication of the manner in which the course evolved with relation to a changing student body.

The English and Scottish Popular Ballads and Their Continental Counterparts (English L715/F715) at Indiana University replaced a course taught by Stith Thompson in the 1930s and the early 1940s. I never saw a syllabus for Stith's course, and I have a sneaking suspicion that there never was a syllabus. I do know, however, that Stith was a firm disciple of George Lyman Kittredge in two areas, those of the Medieval Romance and of the ballads, that his interest in the former was temperate and in the latter minimal (viz., his few references to ballads in the *Motif-Index of Folk-Literature*, and that he always looked upon ballads as a form of oral literature). He happily accepted L. C. Wimberly's title *Folklore in the English and Scottish Popular Ballads* as appropriate. Folklore appeared in ballads, but ballads were not folklore per se. In short, Stith taught the ballad, as he first taught the folktale, as a curious literary phenomenon subject to the same approach and the same sort of analysis as a medieval manuscript.

Shortly after I joined the faculty of Indiana University in the summer of 1945, Stith, learning that I had written a dissertation centered on ballads, asked me to develop both an introductory undergraduate course in ballads and folksongs and a graduate seminar in ballads. As a member of the faculty of the Department of English—the Folklore Program, staffed primarily by faculty from English, Modern Languages, and Classics, had been instituted only three years earlier and was still largely a paper program with a minuscule summer budget—I developed courses pointed toward literary studies. The students for these courses were drawn primarily from English with an occasional stray from German and the Classics and, even less commonly, an errant French or Spanish major (Comparative Literature, though already fertilized, was still in the womb).

Since that time, of course, the situation at Indiana University has changed tremendously. Summer Folklore Institutes grew into a Folklore Program in which it was possible to get a graduate degree, the Folklore Program grew into a Folklore Department with its own faculty, a department which could confer undergraduate as well as graduate degrees, and finally, the Folklore Institute was created as a research arm of the department, though at times it seemed as though the department were the cart instead of the horse. Moreover, the man responsible for the direction taken by the department of Folklore at Indiana University, Richard M. Dorson, successor to Stith Thompson, had even less interest in the ballad than did Stith and at one time he said to me that his favorite song was "Those Wedding Bells are Breaking Up That Old Gang of Mine." Disc jockeys might call this a ballad. I would not, nor incidentally, would Dick have, but the remark reflected an attitude which conditioned the evolution of the ballad course and its relationship to the liberal arts curricula at Indiana University.

Despite Stith's muted interest in ballads (incidentally, he played a fine rendition of the traditional tune of "Mary Hamilton" on the guitar and an even more impressive one on the cello) and Dick Dorson's frank antipathy toward the genre, during the first decade and one-half of its existence, *The English and Scottish Popular Ballads and Their Continental Counterparts* was, along with a course in "The Folktales," required for every Ph.D. candidate in Folklore. As a consequence, during its first fifteen years the course was given at least once each academic year. It should be noted, however, that during these years the number of students who were candidates for the folklore doctorate were far fewer in number than was later to obtain. Ph.D. candidates in Folklore had to take the course, but they were, even then, always outnumbered by students from the various literary disciplines. During the next five years, after an abortive attempt (not mine) to move the course from the Department of English to Folklore, the course was given but twice, that is, once every two years. Subsequently, the course returned to its original schedule of being given once each academic year, though at times this meant that it was given during summer sessions which often enrolled students from the Education School. Throughout its history, however, the ballad seminar has averaged an enrollment of from eight to ten students per class, with the minimal enrollment being four students, the maximum an inconceivable (and horrific) twenty-three! Today, however, the course regularly enrolls from eight to eleven students (the latter being the maximum allowed by Indiana University in a graduate seminar).

The attempt to move *The English and Scottish Popular Ballads and Their Continental Counterparts* out of the Department of English and into the Department of Folklore was the result of deep philosophical differences between the director and me. The discipline of folklore was beginning to emphasize the nominal adjective "folk" in "folklore" and to see the noun "lore" in the compound as fundamentally subordinate, as a means of identifying and interpreting "folk." In essence, however, and in spite of the reformation, protestantism and evangelism of folklore, I remained an orthodox Catholic. I approached the ballad in 1947 and I approach it now as a devotee of literature and the Historic-Geographic, Finnish method. My seminar (I no longer teach the undergraduate course, leaving it to those who prize people more than texts) is devoted to the analysis of textual relationships and the history of ballad scholarship. As a consequence, the bulk of the students who take the course come from the departments of English, Modern Languages, and Comparative Literature. Only the occasional folklore student finds what I do of interest. I suspect, however, that for this very reason, since few universities have departments of folklore, what I have to say may be of some value. Ballads, willy-nilly, are a part of the English and Western European poetic anthology, a unique form of English and European literature and as worthy of study as the poetry of Chaucer and Milton, Herder and Rilke, or Eliot and Pound.

The basic text for the course has always been F. J. Child's *The English and Scottish Popular Ballads*. Even in the early years when these volumes were beyond the financial reach of the ordinary student (before Dover reissued them in a relatively inexpensive paperback form) and when the student was required to purchase Helen Child Sargent's and George Lyman Kittredge's abridged Students' Cambridge edition of Child or later MacEdward Leach's *The Ballad Book*, every student was asked to become thoroughly familiar with the Child volumes—texts, notes, appendices, and all. In addition, from the earliest times to the present, all students have been required to read Gordon H. Gerould's *The Ballad of Tradition*. Other texts have been employed from time to time in ways which will be later discussed, but *The English and Scottish Popular Ballads* and *The Ballad of Tradition* were originally and remain today central to the course. From them hang all the law and the prophets.

Despite the retention of these basic texts, the course has not remained static. It has changed in direct relationship to the students' familiarity with the genre. When I first taught the course, before what Albert Friedman calls "the ballad renaissance," I found it necessary to employ what in those days was called a Victrola or a phonograph and to play innumerable records, usually of an entirely commercial nature, for these were what were available, often to the amusement of upper-middle-class students—the usual student of those days—who found Richard Dyer-Bennet delightful, Burl Ives quaint, and my few "race records" hilarious. Then, during the 1950s a new breed of students appeared, nurtured in coffee houses and familiar with what passed for truly traditional material, scornful of Dyer-Bennet, condescending to Burl Ives, and enamored of Leadbelly, Joan Baez and Woody Guthrie. Today, however, the students are more sophisticated than those of the 1940s and less critical than those of the 1960s. They still don't know much about ballads, but they are willing to consider them as a part of our literary heritage, which, of course, ballads are.

Not only are ballads a part of our fundamental literary heritage, they are a unique part. Generally, the students who take *The English and Scottish Popular Ballads and their Continental Counterparts* today and who know anything at all about the genre have made their acquaintance through reading a baker's dozen of texts in a survey literature course, usually appended, wrongly, to the medieval portion of the anthology which they read. Most students find these "poems" exciting. In addition, a rare number of students—and they are strangely few in number—become familiar with ballads through recordings, radio, and concerts. But none of these students seems aware of the fact that ballad texts as we know them have been created in a manner entirely different from that of the poetry of Wordsworth, Goethe, and Auden, nor do they care. They are, in fact, completely unaware of the processes of oral transmission, the phenomenon which distinguishes traditional poetry from art poetry, the process which makes ballads unique as a genre. That a ballad is a product of people, not of a person, is a matter of no concern to them, a fact which makes the students closely akin to ballad transmitters who seldom if ever give the matter a thought.

Indeed, that a ballad is the product of people, not an individual, is central to the course, but it is also true that *The English and Scottish Popular Ballads and Their Continental Counterparts* takes as its point of departure for the genre the concept that an original text for each ballad type was composed by an individual. The texts which we now know through the publications of F. J. Child, Svend Grundtvig, and subsequent collector-editors achieved their form by means of oral transmission or by means of typographical transmitters themselves thoroughly immersed in the processes of oral transmission. The term "ballad" thus does not refer to a poetic text in the same way that we refer to a particular poem by Coleridge or Blake, but to a conglomerate of poems, song-poems if you will, all deriving from a single original which may well be lost and which probably can never be reconstituted because the transmitters had to rely upon their own imperfect memory of something which they had heard.

All of this sounds as if I were tracing the footsteps of George Lyman Kittredge, who in turn was treading on the heels of F. B. Gummere, his one-time student but leader in ballad theory. But the course is not now, nor was it ever, a course in "the beginnings of poetry." It is now, and it always has been, a course in the evolution of a poetic genre. At first it centered on what has come to be known as "the Child ballads," but as I became more aware of the essence of the genre I came to realize that the English-Language representatives were so closely allied to Scandinavian materials that the Danish, Faroese, Norwegian, Swedish and Swedo-Finnish exempla had to be studied along with the English-language materials. At the same time I became convinced that though narrative folksongs of a very similar sort abounded in Western Europe, they differed in significant ways from the genre perpetuated in the Western- and North-Germanic languages. As a consequence, students in the course now do not only have to become familiar with F. J. Child's *The English and Scottish Popular Ballads*, but also with basic Scandinavian, and to a lesser degree, German, materials. Pragmatism requires that this familiarity be acquired in translation in spite of the fact that, in general, I am unhappy with many of the translations which often reflect preconceptions of the translators rather than the texts themselves.

One final note before I move to a description of each of the three basic patterns which I have developed for the course. Years ago, when George Lyman Kittredge wrote the introduction to the Student's Cambridge Edition, entitled *English and Scottish Popular Ballads*, an abridged edition of Child's *The English and Scottish Popular Ballads*, produced in collaboration with Helen Child Sargent, F. J. Child's daughter, he wrote that ballads were immeasurably ancient and that the age of ballad creation was long past. With the first statement I am in violent disagreement, but with the second I agree entirely. The popular ballad of tradition is a product at the earliest of the very late middle ages, and texts of the sort produced during the sixteenth, seventeenth, eighteenth, and early nineteenth centuries ceased to be created by the middle of the nineteenth century, which, coincidentally, was the great age of collecting. Thus my concern in the ballad seminar has always been with a body of material which is fundamentally static, a corpus which is expanding only in that additional texts of the already know "types" are often discovered. In brief, song-poems like "Jesse James," "Springfield Mountain," and "John Henry," for example, are not grist for my mill. They are not truly traditional ballads but what the Scandinavians call efterklang, "echoes," almost, but not quite, the same thing. Essentially, I deal with a closed corpus.

Throughout the nearly four decades that I have taught this course, I have thought of my students as potential professional scholars. This means that I expect students to be thoroughly familiar with libraries, with books, with the techniques of research on the one hand and documentation on the other, and with the history and evolution of their discipline. I have no patience with their reinventing the wheel. I insist that they familiarize themselves with various theories of ballad origins; I insist that they know about the editorial practices of such dissimilar editor/collectors as Thomas Percy, Sir Walter Scott, William Motherwell, and John and Alan Lomax; and I insist that they know how the editorial and critical theories of Pastor M. B. Landstad, Svend Grundtvig, F. J. Child, F. B. Gummere, Gordon H. Gerould, and later Bertrand Bronson, David Fowler, and David Buchan fit into the cultural milieux which produce them. I have, in other words, always emphasized library work over field work. Indeed, though when I taught the undergraduate course, field work was often required, the graduate seminar included it only once, a dismal failure which resulted in much sound and fury signifying nothing.

With the exception of the first two or three years during which it was given, the course nearly always has required two pieces of investigation: the first a semi-formal oral report centered on ballad texts or on a particular book of criticism, the second a formal paper presented orally to the class and, in a revised, written form, to the instructor at the end of the semester. The purpose of the former is to force students to a close reading of the bulk of the English-language ballad corpus, though sometimes this purpose is accomplished by a close, analytical and critical reading of a particular scholarly investigation of the genre. The purpose of the second investigation is to train the students in the techniques of scholarship and to teach them not only about ballads but also how to write the kind of paper suitable for publication in the usual scholarly journal and for oral presentation at meetings of professional associations. Thus, for this latter paper, the students have to become aware of (1) a rigorous, twenty-minute limit for its oral presentation, (2) the fact that they will have to defend their theories and hypotheses against sometimes aggressive opposition, and, in addition, (3) that the written form of their paper must conform to the stylistic requirements of the journal to which they wish to submit it. One hopes as well that in the process of developing this project they will come to realize that oral and written reports are two different genres, something of which few established scholars seem aware.

There is one additional constant. Though *The English and Scottish Popular Ballads and Their Continental Counterparts* has been assigned a mystical 700 number, which at Indiana University is akin to 007, thus presumably a license to kill, and which identifies the course as an advanced seminar presumably directed to highly informed students, I have always found it necessary to begin the course with a series of lectures defining and limiting the subject. In these lectures, during which students are invited to ask questions, I first define the word "ballad" as it is employed in the course and describe the fundamental characteristics of the genre;

I then sketch the history of ballad scholarship from the late fifteenth century in Scandinavia through the great age of collecting in the nineteenth century to the present day; and, finally, I compare with specific exempla English-language ballads with the genre as it is found in Western Europe and especially in Scandinavia. Such lectures are absolutely necessary to give cohesion to the course. Normally, a 700 course at Indiana University, a seminar say in "The Minor Poems of Geoffrey Chaucer," "Transformational Phonology," or "The Lesser Poets of the Post-Neo-Augustan Age," enrolls a cohesive body of students, all thoroughly familiar with the material to be studied. As has been noted earlier, the students in the ballad seminar are not only not well-informed about the genre but they also come from very different disciplines; thus my introductory lectures must be the equivalent of an undergraduate survey course and must establish a common foundation on which to build.

In 1947 when the ballad seminar was first given, what I have briefly described as the introductory lectures were really the core of the course, and they extended far beyond the three or four meetings I now allot to them. During the time given over to lectures, the students were required to read Gerould's *The Ballad of Tradition* and extensively in Child's *The English and Scottish Popular Ballads* and, while doing so, to consider carefully a research project to be presented as a term paper toward the end of the semester. The next two or three class meetings were devoted to individual consultations about the subject for the proposed research paper, and the final meetings consisted of oral progress reports which also served as the bases for class discussion and allowed each student to take advantage of the comments of his peers and the instructor before writing his final report. When the course was structured in this manner, most students compiled editions of particular ballad types, developed brief historic-geographic studies of particular ballad types, or wrote papers with such titles as "Ballads and Medieval Romances," "The Nature of Ballad Heroes," "The Language of the Border Ballads," "The Editorial Practices of Thomas Percy," and the like. When so structured, the course ended with a final examination based primarily upon required readings and class lectures. This proved to be, as most final examinations are, pedagogically worthless, and it was soon dropped.

At the time when the course followed this pattern, it worked reasonably well. It was a course given in the Department of English and the pattern was familiar to the students. The work required of the participants was essentially the same as that required in a seminar in *Beowulf* or *Victorian Literature*, and the students, coming as they did, from departments of modern languages and literatures, were comfortable with it. It had the fault, however, of fitting the conventional pattern of a seminar in literature so well that it unfairly emphasized the similarities between ballads and art poetry and neglected the unique aspects of the genre. In spite of reading or hearing about F. B. Gummere's *The Beginnings of Poetry, Old English Ballads*, and *The Popular Ballad*, and becoming thoroughly acquainted with Gerould's *The Ballad of Tradition*, the students failed to grasp the significance of oral transmission in the creative process, not because it wasn't a constant topic of discussion but because the course itself was completely conventional, no different, really from a seminar in the works of Wordsworth and Coleridge.

Moreover, insidiously, the student body was changing. Even though officially enrolled in departments of English, Classics, French, German, Spanish, History and their ilk—and they could do no other since neither Folklore nor Comparative Literature had degree programs as yet—graduate students were invading the hinterlands of Indiana from the coffee houses in the environs of Harvard, Columbia, and Berkeley. In addition, an occasional anthropology major condescended to investigate the course. For such students the old pattern was no longer suitable. A compromise had to be made.

It was made, and it was truly a compromise: the fundamentals of the course did not change, but the approach did. *The English and Scottish Popular Ballads and Their Continental Counterparts* did not loosen its affiliations to literature, but it shifted its emphasis to analyses of scholarly investigations of ballads. The introductory lectures remained about the same, as did the requirements for a final research paper, but during the middle portion of the course, attention was turned to the work of other scholars. Each time the course was given, a particular volume of ballad criticism or history of ballad scholarship was chosen for microscopic dissection. After being exposed to my introductory lectures and to some reading of Child, each student was assigned a number of pages (usually a chapter) from the book selected for the semester and asked to examine these pages in minute detail. They were first asked to summarize the content. They were required to check the documentation with care, and when doing this, they were also required to check not only the accuracy of the quotations but also the accuracy of indirect quotations, paraphrases, and summaries, to ask themselves whether what they were checking was faithful to its sources. Finally, the students were asked to give their own opinions about the material which they had read.

The books used for this exercise have varied over the years; they include G. H. Gerould's *The Ballad of Tradition*, M. J. C. Hodgart's *The Ballads*, D. K. Wilgus's *Anglo-American Folksong Scholarship since 1898*, Wells's The Ballad Tree, Fowler's *A Literary History of the Popular Ballad*, and David Buchan's *The Ballad and the Folk*. The choice was often limited by availability. F. B. Gummere's *The Popular Ballad* and W. M. Hart's *Ballad and Epic* would have been ideal for such analyses, but they were both out-of-print and out-of-stock long before the course came into being. Moreover, an exercise such as this does not lend itself to the use of one or two copies of a text on the reserve shelves of a library, for the texts being analyzed must be consulted constantly, scribbled in occasionally, and carried from library card file to library shelf and back again and again.

The exercise culminated in both an oral presentations of the students' findings and informal written papers outlining the results. Usually, three oral reports were given each seminar meeting and the students not actually involved in the presentation were expected to have read the material covered by the various oral presentations. This often resulted in lively discussions about interpretations (both of the source and the student's analysis) and was probably the most effective device I yet have found for instigating class participation. Moreover, it had the value of making the students not only read a basic book but also of making them think about it and how it evolved and was related to its predecessors.

Nor was this the only advantage to the exercise. I found that in addition, students truly became more involved. They realized, as they never had before, that professorial omnipotence does not necessarily imply omniscience, and that a great deal of nonsense had been written about ballads. As a consequence, they turned to their own research papers with enthusiasm, and these papers came to be more than simply seminar exercises. The oral "progress reports" were enlivened, for both the presenters and the other members of the class realized that they had something to contribute. At this time I became aware that it was unwise to schedule evening classes. Daytime classes have a *terminus ad quem*; evening classes do not, and if evening seminars never lasted into the wee small hours, they often extended because of the vitality of discussion into the larger two-digit hours. Moreover, during the time that the course employed this format, it was unusual if at least one student did not in time see his or her research paper published in one of the major folklore or literary journals.

In spite of the success of this format, about six years ago I decided that changes were needed. I had just completed work on *The Types of the Scandinavian Medieval Ballad* and my interests had shifted to matters of age and definition. To the class I posed the question "What, really, is a traditional ballad?" Though I did not eliminate the lecture portion of the course, I shifted it to the middle and modified the lectures to merge with assignments made initially. Fundamentally, these assignments were for each student to read a number of texts in Child's *The English and Scottish Popular Ballads*, usually the texts of from ten to twenty different types along with all headnotes, footnotes, and appendices. The ballad types assigned to each student were carefully chosen to represent the entire spectrum of materials published by Child. Each student was then asked to construct a definition of the genre based upon his or her readings of the texts assigned and to present this definition, supported by specific references to particular ballad types, to the class as a whole and at the same time to present me with an informal, written summary of his or her conclusions. Normally, three "definitions" were delivered each class meeting, and this allowed approximately equal time for class discussion. It should also be noted that all of the students in the class were expected to be familiar with the texts that formed the basis for each report at the time it was delivered. Thus, in theory at least, by the time these reports were completed, all students had read the bulk of the materials in the Child collection, and each had scrutinized from ten to twenty types closely. The effect was to shift the emphasis in the course from a study of ballad scholarship to a study of ballads themselves.

In this, as in all formats, of course, the seminar culminated with a research paper (I require "term papers" in all of my classes, not only those in literature and folklore, but also in language and grammar classes). As in the earlier patterns for the course, students first presented oral progress reports, and then, after presumably profiting from the seminar discussions revolving around the oral reports, gave me on the last day of class a manuscript of the sort which could be sent to a learned journal. The emphasis upon ballad texts led, of course, to a different sort of final paper, a fact that was also conditioned in part because my lectures began to emphasize David Buchan's *The Ballad and the Folk* and David Fowler's *A Literary History of the Popular Ballad* more than Gordon H. Gerould's *The Ballad of Tradition* even though every student in the seminar was required to read the last. Though a few students chose to compile editions or historic-geographic studies of particular ballad types for their papers, most turned to analyses of ballad language, ballad structure, and, *mirabile dictu*, the repertoires of particular ballad transmitters. These papers were more sophisticated than those produced in the initial course, but somehow less interesting than those written during the immediately preceding pattern; yet they did center their attention upon ballad texts and a number appeared in print, a consummation devoutly to be desired.

In reading what I have written to date, I see that I have neglected to mention that as early as 1950 I supplied each student with a reading list consisting originally of 100 titles and later expanded to 150 items. This annotated book list is divided into a number of categories—General Studies, Bibliographies, The History of Scholarship, Criticism, Collections, and the like—and cross-referenced. It has, moreover, been revised, revised, and revised. The latest updating took place in 1981. It was my feeling originally, and it is still my feeling, that the ballad bibliography is so vast, students need a basic, limited guide to available materials. In addition, also around 1950, I made available to the students in the seminar a seven- or eight-page mimeographed pamphlet entitled "Characteristics of the Popular Ballad of Tradition." In one sense, these handouts are the core of the lecture portion of the seminar and allow students to apply what I have been saying to their own research. In another, they also serve to emphasize the fact that the seminar is concerned primarily with stanzaic, narrative, folk poetry which is dramatic in its structure, concentrated in a single episode, impersonal in its approach to this episode and its characters, and transmitted orally in such a way that change is inevitable.

I note, too, that though I have frequently quoted the title of the course—*The English and Scottish Popular Ballads and Their Continental Counterparts*—I have said very little about the "Continental Counterparts." I do, however, devote at least one hour's lecture to these materials and require the students to read Chapters VI and VII ("The Scandinavians and Their Kin" and "Svend Grundtvig and the Modern School in Denmark") in S. B. Hustvedt's *Ballad Books and Ballad Men*, Knut Liestøl's "Scottish and Norwegian Ballads," and my own "'Den utrue egtemann': A Norwegian Ballad and Formulaic Composition," as well as translations of some of the Scandinavian analogues of English and Scottish ballads from Eric Dal's *Danish Ballads and Folksongs* and Axel Olrik's *A Book of Danish Ballads*. The emphasis upon Scandinavia not only reflects my own competence and interest, but it also reflects my firm conviction that the narrative folksongs of English-language areas and Scandinavia are of the same specie and need to be studied conjointly.

I am limited, too, by the need for translation. Very few of the students who enroll in the seminar are at home in any language except English. Of those who are, even fewer are capable of reading dialect material, that is, the non-received-standard dialects of a given language. Most ballads appear in such dialects. As a consequence, I must turn to those linguistic areas whence come reasonable translations. To overcome this problem, I strongly recommend that each student read Entwistle's *European Balladry*, even though much of what Professor Entwistle discusses is only remotely related to the genre. On the other hand, I also strongly encourage the occasional student who has sufficient linguistic competence to center his or her attention upon a comparative study when writing a research paper.

Finally, I am fully aware that ballad tunes and ballad music in general are virtually ignored in this course. The reasons for this are manifold. First of all, I am not competent to handle music. More importantly, however, it is my opinion that it is not necessary to study ballad tunes and ballad texts conjointly in order to understand the genre. A tremendous portion of English renaissance lyric poetry was composed for a musical setting; yet few students of these materials concern themselves with the tunes and none considers them essential for a critical interpretation. Moreover, ballads have been transmitted by recitation as well as by singing for centuries. We all know that Bell Robertson, one of Scotland's most prolific contributors to our knowledge of balladry, recited her ballads, and I can add to this the fact that Hæge Bjonnemyr whose contributions to the Norwegian ballad corpus were exceeded only by that of her mother, Jorun, always recited ballads. Thus, I disagree with Bertrand Bronson's dictum that a ballad is not a ballad unless it is accompanied by music; on the other hand, were I competent to do so, I certainly would include musical analyses in the course.

In many ways, the ballad seminar at Indiana University has, like its subject matter, been the product of communal re-creation. It has never lost its identity. It has always centered its principal attention upon ballad texts of the sort that appear in the editions of Child and Grundtvig. At the same time, it has occasionally shifted its approach, not in relation to the fads of a particular time but in relation to the capabilities, backgrounds, and knowledge of the participants. However, as I said of the course at the beginning of this essay, *"plus ça change, plus c'est la même chose."*

Linda Dégh

Indiana University

The Legend

Background

Since 1965, F455: *The Legend* has been a core course in the graduate curriculum of the Folklore Institute at Indiana University. Every other year I teach this course during the first semester in sequence with F786: *Folktales and Allied Forms* during the second. The two courses combined constitute the subject of the Folk Narrative doctoral qualifying examination.

Folktales and Allied Forms played a prominent role in the history of folklore studies at Indiana University, and more generally in the education of folklorists in the United States. Stith Thompson, the founder of the program, introduced folklore theory and methods along the lines of his own research interests in the historic-geographic approach to the folktale. Thompson began teaching the folktale on the graduate level in 1922, and began specifically training professional folklorists in oral narrative in 1937. Exporting European narrativistics to America, he attracted students from home and abroad. Thompson became the first professor of English and Folklore in the United States and also managed to establish a folklore library and a publication series. In 1947 the training program began to award Ph.D. degrees in folklore. Following Stith Thompson's retirement, Warren Roberts, who had earned the first American Ph.D. degree in Folklore, taught *Folktales and Allied Forms* until I joined the Folklore faculty in 1965.

Several reasons prompted me to change and expand *Folktales and Allied Forms* in order to accommodate all prose narrative genres from the simplest "true" or "everyday story" to the Märchen. Educated in the European tradition, I was primarily an ethnographer who collected folk narratives and looked at social functions and meanings and interrelations of the different genres discernible from the interaction of tellers and listeners. My field experience among peasants and peasant migrants to the cities in a period of rapid technological change taught me that nothing is sterile and stable, and the traditional genres sensitively react to social change by assuming new roles and expressing new meanings. My first-hand observations made it impossible for me to view texts extricated from reality. Methodologically and theoretically, functionalists and sociologists in related fields impressed me most; phenomenologists from Jolles to Lüthi, dealing with narrative genres, taught me to identify shift of world-view and goal as causes for generic transformation. I succeeded in setting up two courses, dividing narrative according to the two basic contrastive categories—the fictional tale and the truth-claiming legend ("Grundformen," Lüthi, 1961) of oral narration.

Before I began teaching the legend in 1965, I had participated in the work of the Legend Commission of the International Society of Folk Narrative Research (Dégh, 1963, 1965). My experience was limited to the European peasant tradition; thus, my first course at Indiana University represented this stage in my learning. Students in the 1965 class were asked to identify and scrutinize national legend bodies, compile bibliographies and attempt classification using the provisory international categories agreed upon by a board of scholars at the Budapest meeting of the Legend Commission (*Tagung der Sagen Kommission*, 1964). At that time I did not know more of the American legend than what Wayland Hand stated in his two international meetings reports (Hand, 1961, 1963).

Development of a New Course

In a way, I became a part of a laboratory in which folkloric information was exchanged. My students and I learned new forms of folklore and new interpretations, and constructed new hypotheses built on them. (The way F455 is directed resembles methods of Greverus [1980] and Kottak [1982]). My classes not only introduced me to the inexhaustible sources of American folk legendry, but also helped me gain new insights and try new methods and theories. My works from then on were tested in the classroom context. This provided me with the assurance that my assumptions are based on relevant sociocultural conditions. As in spontaneous legend-telling sessions among folk-groups, the legend class participants precipitated controversies, generated new legends, and developed interpretations according to their different degrees of involvement and creativity.

Where did it all begin? I taught F101 *Introduction to Folklore* to college students who were not desperately interested in folklore scholarship. They hoped that I would play the guitar and sing, tell them how to get rid of the poltergeist in the dormitory, and they would earn an easy A grade. In those years, enrollment did not exceed 80 to 100 and I had only one assistant to help grade bluebooks. To spice my lecture on scholarly classification systems, I told stories from my old recordings about shepherds who claimed to have seen ghosts. One of the students interrupted my story: "Why shepherds in old Europe? This same thing happened to me and it is true." This statement turned the class into a legend-telling community. Class participants took turns filling me in on the most popular legends of Indiana. We passed the hour, no one heard the bell ring, stories kept coming. This was the moment when I realized that the legend is much more than just an extraordinary story, limited to archaic peasant conditions: any social class, permanent or occasional group in the industrial world can be its bearer. I realized also that legends are indexes of current social concerns, and complexities increase their usefulness to express these concerns.

Rightly or wrongly, I decided to give up my original plan to introduce F101 students to folklore theory. Instead, I taught them how to identify and collect folklore, particularly legends, most prevalent in Hoosier (or better: Midwestern) tradition. F101 students learned the skill of collecting, thus contributing to the enrichment of the Folklore Archives with what we did not have: dependable material.

While reading collections turned in by F101 students, the problem of archival storage, preservation, classification, and scholarly utilization was raised. With the aid of the folklore archivist (a graduate student in my legend class), as a part of the legend class assignments, we rearranged legend items according to the new international system of classification. Placing materials collected by F101 students into the proper categories became a routine legend class assignment. In 1969 I gave up teaching *Introduction to Folklore*, which now enrolls 350-400 students per semester and employs several assistant instructors. By continuing to assign legend collection to their students, assistant instructors in F101 help increase our archives.

Over time, subsequent F101 classes were able to amass thousands of texts with necessary information concerning tellers, situation of telling and interpretation of meaning by the tellers and their support groups. Scrutiny of new materials became central to the legend class, which in 1967 began to function as a workshop, exchanging field experiences, identifying and analyzing types and the extent of their variability and avenues of dissemination.

In 1968 I founded the journal *Indiana Folklore* to serve as a forum for the publication of authentic legend materials fit for scholarly use. The first issue was the first published product of the joint effort of the legend class. Its purpose was to set a standard format for collecting, describing, comparing and analyzing legends and local legend repertoires and commentaries by the tellers concerning sociocultural background and meaning. As collecting and analyzing methods were refined, the format was greatly improved. At the time the legend class was engaged in this work, folklorists knew little about legend because no adequately recorded materials existed. Most of the legends were buried between miscellaneous collections in archives labeled as "myths," "traditions," or "superstitions," or worse: they filled story books labeled for lay audiences according to the editorial principles of the Grimm brothers. Professional folklorists knew of local spooks that haunted cemeteries; they also knew of the most widespread current scare legends such as "The Hook," "The Boyfriend's Death," "The Stolen Grandmother," "The Hatchet Man," yet no properly recorded versions could be found in academic holdings.

The Course

Following accumulation of substantial field materials, evaluations, and experiments within the framework of F455, I introduced in 1971 the current format of the course. The course design is flexible enough to allow slight modifications in order to accommodate fresh materials and keep abreast with the latest developments in legend scholarship. The outline also permits me to pick a particularly timely focus around which research papers are coordinated each time the course is offered.

F455 Course Outline

I: Introduction: Some guidelines to legend study. Preliminary operational definition.

II: A brief survey of legend scholarship
1. Sources: archive materials and printed collections
2. Collecting legends: the fieldworker's responsibilities; what to collect and how?
3. The problems of classification—the elusive text and its context
4. Past and still lingering theories.

III: The legend as a story and its interrelations with and differentiability from
         other genres
         1. The "true" or experience story
         2. The joke and the anecdote, the humorous, the weird and the
         grotesque.
         3. The Märchen-magic and the legend
         4. Custom, ritual and drama
         5. Verse Poetry
         6. The historical, etiological, magical, and religious aspects of the legend
IV: Processes of legend formation: techniques and channels communication
         1. Formal elements, structure and style
         2. The question of aesthetic qualities
         3. Form and content, transmission and composition procedures
V: The "legend climate": worldview, folk religion, sociology and psychology of
         the legend
         1. Content ingredients, potential and manifest legend cores derived
            from objective and subjective facts
         2. Individual and collective experience. The parapsychological point of
            view
         3. The dialectic nature of the legend
VI: The legend in everyday life of today. The current phenomenon of "legend
         explosion" and its indicators. Tradition and mass media.
         1. The sociocultural background
         2. Active and passive bearers
         3. Legend-telling groups and their audiences
         4. Media legend channels
VII: Conclusions

My purpose in teaching this intensive course is to introduce and illustrate a
complex folkloristic method of approach, one also applicable to the study of any
other folklore genres. I use the legend and not another genre for exemplification
because the legend is one of the earliest recognized forms of folklore and has been
studied since the time of the Grimm brothers. The large international body of
collections from traditional and modern societies is easily accessible and reveals the
historic development of folklore research methods up to our times. Most
importantly, the legend is more flexible and viable than most of the classic genres
created by and attached to specific preliterate or pre-industrial population groups
and socioeconomic conditions. In studying the legend we also address questions
concerning the existence and role of folklore in mass society. Orienting ourselves
to the present, equipped with the knowledge of the past, we attempt to understand
the fantastic proliferation of the legend and its vigorous resistance to changing
times, and its role in the formulation of human thoughts, acts and mass
movements.

Simply stated, the course follows a thread in quest of an adequate definition
for the legend. In the introduction I expose the problem created by the failure of
generations of folklorists to find an acceptable definition and delimitation of the
legend and the reasons for trying afresh in light of changing human conditions
(Dégh, 1978). Following an operational definition, I continue with all I think needs
to be known about past scholarship to prepare the class for a first identification of

legends by contrasting them with similar or identical stories belonging to other genres. After considering generic relationships and the criteria that make a legend a legend, we explore the genre as (1) texts in terms of form (style and structure), content (narrative motifs and episodes) and the creative compositional processes; (2) product of sociocultural and ideological milieu; and (3) as function (performance resulting from interaction of tellers and listeners in transmitting and manipulating materials). In the final week of class meetings we return to the original goal and reconsider the elements of definitions in the light of the learning experience over the semester. For two hours everyone is welcome to participate in the discussion with questions, criticism, new ideas and interpretations. I insist that any idea or theory must be supported by properly documented hard data, not just stated as a belief or feeling.

It may seem narrow to build a course around definition, but I have found that the constant search for stable and variable features opens broad vistas for surveying data critically and flexibly in view of the genre as a process, particularly if it concerns the study of living legends. My own interest in the legend called for liberation from the bonds of traditional, often ambiguous definitions which stubbornly persist in academic tradition despite contrary findings. Thus it often comes as a surprise to students that legends may not always be orally told stories and that there are many other channels to consider than immediate face-to- face communication, and that the existing categories are increasingly failing to fit the diffuse body of legendry in constant flux under modern mass media stimulation. (The attempt by modern folklorists to change—by using terms like "urban legend," "modern legend," and "urban belief"—the common opinion that legends are situated in the rustic and old fashioned countryside, has not, in my opinion, been useful. These terms are meaningless because they pertain to legends known before urbanization. What kind of scholarly purpose calls for categorizing stories on the basis of locus? Does it make any difference if the ghost in the scary story appears to a housewife in the department store's parking garage or to a peasant woman in the barn? Or if the horse-drawn buggy or a motor car was stolen with grandma's corpse in the trunk?)

To find new formulations and to encourage critical thinking and interpretation of materials during the learning process, first-hand familiarity with current legendry is a *sine qua non*. I wanted to shape a course based on the living legend as it exists in society. Class members are expected to look at the sociocultural, psychosocial and situational contexts while considering traditional convention, individual and group contribution.

F455 is a lecture course with periods set aside for discussions. Classes meet twice a week for an hour and a half with a ten-minute break in the middle. I tried to make it a once-a-week course to accommodate more discussion but this way we accomplished less because intensive attention required by the theory-oriented themes cannot be sustained for three hours.

Each time we begin with twenty minutes recapturing and discussing the materials from the previous class meeting, and at the end I allow fifteen minutes for questions and comments. It is quite usual that more interesting themes result in more discussions and there are times when we cannot finish by the end of the hour and continue at my office or in the library cafeteria. It is not unusual for students in the class to call me at home if an idea occurs to them or from a fieldwork site if they need guidance.

F455 is a rather demanding class, so I never minded if students dropped out because they were not ready to do the work. The relatively low course number allows undergraduates to attend, but they are given a lighter load based on individual consultation. Those who accept the challenge usually do well. The majority who enroll are graduate folklore students but in years past there always were students from other disciplines, mostly from anthropology, sociology, comparative literature, English, history, education, psychology and library science. I discuss readings separately with each member of the class and advise them on choosing a term paper theme and I check occasionally on their progress.

The Reading List

The structured bibliography is extensive and informative, including most of the useful writings on the legend with emphasis on the latest theoretical essays. The bibliography contains required and recommended readings, grouped together thematically. There are reference and encyclopedic works, textbooks and indexes, book-length monographs, and theoretical essays. All these are to be consulted as needed for the preparation of term papers and take-home exercises. The rest of the readings are articles or marked-out book passages and are required reading. The close reading of legend texts is absolutely required because they are the source materials basic for the course. I have chosen a representative sample of texts to show different techniques of recording, transcribing, publishing, annotating and interpreting by collectors. The bibliography is too lengthy to reprint here, but the following list includes most of the primary readings:

Baker, Ronald L. *Hoosier Folk Legends*. Bloomington: Indiana University Press. 1982.

Brunvand, Jan H. *The Vanishing Hitchhiker: American Urban Legends and Their Meaning*. New York: W. W. Norton. 1981.

Buchan, David. "The Modern Legend." In *Language, Culture, and Tradition*, ed. A. E. Green and J. D. A. Widdowson, pp. 1-15. 1981.

Dégh, Linda. *Indiana Folklore: A Reader*. Bloomington: Indiana University Press. 1980.

_____. "Processes of Legend Formation." *Laographia* 22 (1965):77-87.

_____. "UFO's and How Folklorists Should Look at Them." *Fabula* 18 (1977): 242-248.

Dégh, Linda and Andrew Vazsonyi. "Legend and Belief." In *Folklore Genres*, ed. Dan Ben-Amos, pp. 93-124. Austin: University of Texas Press. 1976.

_____. "The Memorate and the Proto-Memorate." *Journal of American Folklore* 87 (1974):225-39.

_____. "The Crack on the Red Goblet or Truth and the Modern Legend." In *Folklore in the Modern World*, ed. R. M. Dorson, pp. 253-272. The Hague: Mouton. 1978.

_____. "Magic for Sale: Märchen and Legend in TV Advertising." *Fabula* 20 (1979): 47-68.

Dorson, R. M. "Defining the American Folk Legend." In R. M. Dorson, *American Folklore and the Historian*, 157-72. Cambridge: Harvard University Press. 1971.

Fine, Gary Alan. "Cokelore and Coke Law: Urban Belief Tales and the Problem of Multiple Origins." *Journal of American Folklore* 92 (1979): 15-40.

Gilbert, Helen. "The Crack in the Abbey Floor: A Laboratory Analysis of a Legend." *Indiana Folklore* 8 (1975): 15-40.

The German Legends of the Brothers Grimm. Ed. and trans. Donald Ward. 2 vol. Philadelphia: ISHI. 1981.

Hand, Wayland D. "Status of European and American Legend Study." *Current Anthropology* 6 (1965):436-46.

_____. *American Folk Legends: A Symposium*. Berkeley and Los Angeles: University of California Press. 1971.

Honko, Lauri. "Memorates and the Study of Folk Belief." *Journal of the Folklore Institute* 1 (1965):5-19.

Jason, Hedda. "Concerning the 'Hysterical' and 'Local' Legends and Their Relatives." *Journal of American Folklore* 84 (1971):134-45.

Klein, Barbro. "The Testimony of the Button." *Journal of the Folklore Institute* 8 (1971):127-46.

Kosko, Maria, *Le fils assassiné (At 939A): Étude d'un theme legendaire.* Helsinki 1966.

Lindow, John. "Rites of Passage in Scandinavian Legends." *Fabula* 19 (1978):40-61.

Luomala, Katherine. "Disintegration and Regeneration. The Hawaiian Phantom Hitchhiker Legend." *Fabula* 13 (1972). 20-59.

Lüthi, Max. "Aspects of the Märchen and the Legend." In *Folklore Genres*, ed. Dan Ben-Amos, pp. 17-34. Austin: University of Texas Press. 1976.

Mitchell, Roger E. "The Press, Rumor, and Legend Formation." *Midwestern Journal of Language and Folklore* 5 (1979):477-82.

Mullen, Patrick B. "Modern Legend and Rumor Theory." *Journal of the Folklore Institute* 9 (1972): 95-109.

Requirements

The course requirements are manifold and varied in nature. My aim here is to teach many skills and techniques to the students and challenge them to try their hand in interpretation and theorizing. To secure gradual acquisition of knowledge, assignments are carefully planned and timed in coordination with the succession of themes in the course outline. By completing the assignments in the legend class, students acquire a number of abilities: taking notes; compiling bibliographies;

recording and transcribing field, archive, and library data; doing comparative text analysis, editing and writing articles.

Everyone is expected to take notes and keep a log of the readings on 3x5 cards. From time to time I check class notes and expect them to be turned in with the log for evaluation at the time of the final class meeting. Occasionally the class helps clear the backlog of the F101 collections in the Folklore Archives by identifying and abstracting legends for the card catalog; although useful in acquainting students with the legend holdings, this activity did not work out as a regular assignment.

Four take-home exercises are given at three to four week intervals. The first, given before the students become exposed to (and confused by) theories, proved to be extremely successful. Its purpose is to utilize personal encounter with the legend and turn it into ethnographic data for scholarly discernment, thus converting laymen into researchers. In this "self-survey" (guided by a set of questions I prepared, see Appendix I) students act as informants by recalling legends, or what they thought were legends, from their earliest memories (in the home environment, in school, etc.) to the present. After the completion of the self-survey, the material must be subjected to folkloric analysis, providing commentaries, type and motif number as routinely done in the collections used as models. It is interesting to note that the self-survey works as some kind of spontaneous psychological experiment which leads many students to analytic recollections and reveals sensitive—almost numinous—moments (fears, daydreams, nightmares, second sights, suppressed beliefs). In addition, this repertoire also tells much about the students' regional, ethnic, and religious cultural heritage and affiliations. I have found that the legend reveals the diversities of Americans who were exposed to the same educational system. Folklore students doing this exercise discover themselves as carriers of a specific cultural tradition.

The second assignment is rather simple: a critical survey of past scholarship based on the readings of Wayland Hand's 1965 assessment, and the American Folk Legend Symposium which was held in Los Angeles in 1969. The only difficulty here is to teach students how to be creatively critical, how to form an opinion without using current slogans to debunk earlier trends. I want them to evaluate those earlier trends fairly by the standards of their time.

The third assignment concerns analytical assessment of the legend: form, content, meaning. Taking departure from the class discussion of genre relationship, the question to be raised is: what turns an identical story into a true story, a drama, a joke, a Märchen, or a legend? I usually choose cross-generic plots for this exercise. For example, AT 939A, "Killing the Returned Soldier" (Kosko, 1966) is an excellent case because the same plot coexists in epic, ballad and legend forms and displays diverse tendencies in various cultural areas. Some students draw spectacular charts to show affinities, others do statistical listings of identical and culture-specific elements. What I expect is not the dissecting of a coherent story into minimal narrative units but rather the more difficult task of providing an interpretive description of formative processes.

The fourth exercise is the monographic study of a chosen legend on the basis of its variants. Any set of interrelated variants can be used: those coming from one area, one country or from two diverse countries. The purpose is to discover the substantially stable and variable elements of the core story and their relationship to social and cultural factors. In one instance, American and German devil legends were compared, tracing the significant differences between the image of the devil in both countries. In another, the regional subtype of a road ghost legend was established as related to a violent crime and a curiously shaped marker where the crime occurred.

During the third week of classes, after the completion of the two-phase self-survey, the students must begin to plan their term papers. Ideally, I expect that the self-survey gives them a sense of what the legend is all about and how to look at it from the inside-out and the outside-in. Ideas of a paper might also occur by the careful examination of the reading list. The paper may be based on individual collection in the field or on materials found in the archives or library. When considering a theme for the paper, the student has to make sure that there is plenty of material to work with, that the material is easily accessible and completion is feasible within the given time. To ensure success, I expect a two-page outline of the project, with a preliminary bibliography. After I have read the proposals, accepted them with or without revision, research can begin. The paper has no required number of pages; it must be finished two weeks before the period of final examinations, so that I can read and evaluate them before the class meets for the final discussion.

The legend class does not conclude with an oral or written class demonstration. By this time I have a pretty good idea of the quality of everyone's work. The last meeting consists of a communal assessment of what we did and what we did not accomplish, what theories and methods were found useful, and what ingredients of definition need further improvement. Since class members work pretty closely with each other and the exchange of ideas is always a part of the meetings, I usually ask everyone to present a short summary which is then followed with general comments. My observations conclude the sessions.

My ideas and methods for the seminar keep changing as the world that produces legends is changing. I still feel challenged to experiment, particularly if the students are ready to participate. One year the whole class assisted in the investigation of the occult phenomenon and its legend connections. I established contact with the Indianapolis headquarters of a group which held annual psychic fairs attended by local groups from the Midwest. We attended the year's psychic fair and developed individual projects working with diverse occult groups. Another year an exorcist renowned for her power to expel spirits from haunted houses moved to Central Indiana. We examined her activities and interviewed her clients and supporters in Bloomington, Martinsville, Gosport, and Camp Chesterfield (the oldest spiritualist camp in the United States). In 1982 the central research theme of the class was the legend at Halloween. Several term papers and articles in *Indiana Folklore* originated in similar class projects.

Over the years *Indiana Folklore* became the outlet for the best term papers of the legend class. Collecting, analyzing, and presenting are the three steps professional folklorists take in their creative work. I designed the legend course to teach students how to make these three steps. They are given a free hand to deal with their own collection as it best fits their personality and the nature of the data they find. My role is to help interested students to turn their term papers into publishable manuscripts. During the semester they learn editorial skills and techniques necessary for the preparation of articles. Associate instructors for the F101 course (who often are also members of the legend class) call my attention to valuable collections. In many cases I contact the collector and encourage him to do further work under the guidance of a volunteering legend class student. With the addition of comparative notes and commentaries excellent coauthored articles have appeared; in other cases the undergraduate's authorship was fully recognized with an editorial note identifying editorial contributors. Sometimes we had to engage in a long search for a potential author who graduated and left Indiana University. Once a partner in a law firm in Chicago expressed surprise and delight that we wanted to ask his permission to publish the term paper of his junior year.

F455 is a course which prepares folklorists for independent research. I feel this is what graduate education in folklore should provide in general. It seems to me that the ubiquitous legend, with its persistence and strong ties to everyday existence of modern humankind, including ourselves, is more appropriate for this kind of education than a number of other folklore forms. I always opposed educators who routinely published their student's class contributions with no recognition for the fieldworkers other than a simple listing of their names. I not only avoid this kind of exploitation but urge class members to publish their own worthy materials.

Some F455 students were successful in choosing term paper topics for which the raw data was easily accessible for them. Deanna Sliney, for example, recorded legend-telling of Indiana Bell telephone operators with whom she worked part-time (Sliney, 1974); Sylvia Grider, as dormitory counselor, observed the development, blossoming and decline of a scare legend among freshmen (Grider, 1973); Margie Cohee was a grade school teacher in a rural school when she made her pupils describe and draw pictures of ghost legend events; Kenneth Thigpen explored the repertoire of students in the high school class of his wife in a small town (Thigpen, 1971).

Newspaper reports sometimes led us to bona fide legends and legend-cycles on noble robbers, underground railroads, haunts, lunatics, crazy killers, witches and UFOs. A 1966 report on cemetery vandalism and cruelty toward animals led to a rich find of legendry about a Black Lady ghost or witch watching over her baby's grave in Stepp cemetery (Clements and Lightfoot, 1972). The newspaper account of chain links growing every full moon on a tombstone to reveal the death by strangulation of an innocent wife pointed to a local legend complex (Clements, 1970). F101 students helped their associate instructor describe a case of legend-performance by driving with him to the legend site, while reciting pertinent stories in turn (Hall, 1973). The psychic fair led Janet Langlois to an unusual dramatized form of the Vanishing Hitchhiker legend in a Catholic School in Indianapolis (Langlois, 1978).

Every time I teach F455 I feel the urge to improve the class project, to add something new, to change the emphasis and reach out for a new key to the riddle of my own interest: the meaning of the legend. Some of my students were attracted to this genre and did fine doctoral dissertations illuminating some of the important aspects. Sylvia Grider wrote about sixth graders' supernatural narratives (1976); Elizabeth Tucker described girl scout stories in two different social groups (1977); Louise Russell analyzed Mexican-American children's legend repertoire persisting in an Anglo community (1978); T. Bullard pursued the UFO legendry through the ages (1982); Janet Langlois wrote on the local spread of stories about Belle Gunness, the Lady Bluebeard (1977). I am always hopeful for new devotees.

Appendix

Guidelines for legend self-survey.

1. Your name, place of birth, age, ethnic and sociocultural background and the places of your school education.
2. What legends do you know? Describe all stories (about witchcraft, ghosts, miracles, dream messages, strange encounters, precognitive experiences, telepathy, U.F.O. sightings, E.S.P., horrible stories about monsters, killers, lunatics, etc.). Indicate which of the stories impressed you most. Answer all following questions as they pertain to each single legend you know.
3. Which are the sources of your information? PArents, friends, classmates, newspaper, radio, TV, or other?
4. When did you hear the legend? At an early age, before you were six, grade school, or later?
5. At what occasion (slumber party, scout camp, dormitory, bull session, visit to a "spooky" place, or at a specific event, like Halloween)?
6. How many people were present?
7. What kind of people were there (male, female, old, young, of what occupation)?
8. What effect had the story on you and the others in your company (did it stimulate fear, depression, humor, confusion, indifference, negative feeling)?
9. Did your informant believe the account?
10. Did you believe the story was true?
11. How about others?
12. Indicate if you ever repeated the legend heard from others or if there are some that you like to tell.
13. Did you ever visit scenes of legend events (haunted house, cemetery or other)? Did you go along or in a group? How many people of the same and opposite sex?
14. If you went with others, how many were you? Did you walk or drive? Describe preliminary preparations for the trip, the scene and group reaction.
15. What was expected to happen at the time of the visit?
16. Did you, or somebody else you know, experience the expected event (appearance of a spook, strange noises, lights, etc.)? Give details of the experience.
17. Apart from all this, did you ever have a supernatural or strange experience that you could not explain?
18. If so, try to describe it and explain it. Do you or did you ever talk about it with others? Do you generally like or dislike to remember it and discuss it?

Neil Rosenberg

Memorial University of Newfoundland

Introduction to Folksong

I have been teaching the *Introduction to Folksong* course on the graduate level for most of the fifteen years that I have been at Memorial University. The form of the course has varied considerably during that period. At one point it was a class which mixed graduate and undergraduate students; it has sometimes been a reading course; and it often combines students with varied backgrounds. The course presently meets three times a week over a thirteen-week semester; this seems like not enough time to cover the ground I think ought to be covered. Some of my colleagues teach their graduate seminars in thirteen three-hour blocks; I prefer the larger number of one-hour segments, though this too has its drawbacks—a good discussion may be cut off by the end of the class. On the other hand having thirty-nine separate blocks of time gives one the opportunity to make changes, additions and deletions. In the following pages I sketch my outline and explain what I try to do. But first a few special problems.

Music

Until quite recently Memorial had no school of music, and there are still no music appreciation courses for those who are not full-time music students. Consequently, one problem which I constantly face is lack of knowledge about music. This problem is compounded when (as happens every few years) I have in the class a student with extensive training in music. The only practical solution is to devote a week's worth of lecture, reading and discussion to the principles of music, including Charles Seeger's points about the problems of using a prescriptive system for descriptive purposes, and various schemes of tune classification and analysis. I drag a toy electric organ into the classroom and use it when discussing intervals, scales, modes and the like—a trick I learned from George List at Indiana University.

Examples

Another problem is providing examples for students. In an introductory folklore course one can easily trot out proverbs, riddles, legends and other forms—you can tell them yourself and assign readings. But because most students are not musically literate it is not easy for them to get the full impact of printed examples, and I don't really enjoy singing in class. The alternative is to play records, but I have found that very time-consuming. Moreover, because of the textural multiplicity of folksong performance one is never sure, without much time-consuming explanation, that the students are hearing what you want them to hear when you play an example. So, while I occasionally play examples, I have for some years used a device known as "The Annotation Project" to get students to listen to and read folksong texts. For this project, each student is given a tape containing ten songs—field recordings from the Memorial University of Newfoundland Folklore and Language Archive. The student must: (1) transcribe the text of each song; (2) prepare a précis describing the plot or contents of the song in the manner of those in G. Malcolm Laws's two books; and (3) prepare an annotative statement, discussing how their text compares with other versions of the song as they are able to document it through research in published and archival collections or, if they find no other versions, discussing the form and contents of the song in terms of similar songs they have noted in their research.

The project has a number of benefits. Most importantly, it forces students to listen closely to folksongs. Because of the transcription process they become familiar with style in a way that they would not otherwise. In addition they must then search through a large number of collections looking for the songs they are trying to annotate. I try to make the project as realistic as possible by encouraging them to consult with other students and faculty members, to think about phonograph recordings (most of the ten-song anthologies they are given include everything from Child ballads to Hank Williams songs, not to mention local compositions), and to try whatever angle they wish in their research. The result is that they poke around the corpus of collected folksong in a way that they would not bother to do if they were merely told to familiarize themselves with it.

I devised this project knowing from my own experience in annotating joke and song collections that one learns more about collections when one is looking for something than when one is given them as an assignment to plow through for a course. In addition to this project students are required to do a term paper of some kind and are given a final exam.

Focus

Because the course is offered as part of a folklore graduate program my major focus is on folksong as a type of folklore and folklife. While folksong study, particularly the study of the ballad, was a central part of our discipline in its early history, recent trends have seen it move from the center. Furthermore, as our discipline has become more professionalized, it has also become more specialized. Hence my aim is to indicate to our students, many of whom intend to specialize in fields other than folksong, the ways in which theoretical and procedural concerns in their specialty are manifest in folksong studies.

Like most folklorists of my generation, I found the ethnography of speaking approach to folklore studies exciting and liberating. It has certainly made teaching the various genres of folklore to introductory classes much easier. But folksong remains a difficult nut to crack using that approach. This is, I think, because while one can see how narratives are really an aspect of conversational contexts—storytelling events, if you will, which grow out of conversation and can be seen in terms of rhetoric and the like—the folksong remains a bounded form, clearly delineated, if not by yodels and the sound of instruments, then by music and poetics. Hence, I believe, the tendency toward an interest in folksong (since it is so easily separated from context) on the one hand and folksinging traditions on the other. The course begins with folksong and moves toward folksinging, that is, the customary or folklife settings for music.

At the outset I raise a number of special problems. For example, how is one to interpret music? While we all can agree that song texts have meaning (although we may disagree about aspects of that meaning) there is in my opinion no conclusive proof that musical units can be seen as semantic units. Another way of saying this is that folk music and folksong constitute an aspect of folklore in which affect is particularly difficult to discuss.

Another problem I like to raise here is that in comparison with many other genres, folksong is particularly specialized; there is a relatively smaller number of active singers or musicians in a community than of proverb tellers, game players, or personal experience narrators.

And we must deal with a related problem: because folksong is so often a form of entertainment it is relatively easy for it to become popular song and its specialists professionals. Closely related to this is the way in which folksong frequently is chosen as the type of folklore to be utilized in a symbolic way by those interested in reviving or revitalizing traditional national, regional or ethnic culture.

Texts

I have found no single textbook which suits my purposes for this course. Presently I use a combination of texts. These reflect several of my concerns. First, because Newfoundland lies so strongly in the orbit of the British Isles (not just historically but also in terms of the cultural influences which shape its folksong traditions), I have wanted to maintain some emphasis upon British folksong. Second, because this is the only English language folklore program in Canada, I felt it necessary to make this course a sort of introduction to Canadian folksong, particularly the English-language traditions of Eastern Canada. Since most of the students will either do research in the region or are from the region, it makes sense to use examples which are relatively familiar to them. Occasionally I include readings and lectures on Afro-American music, since there are so many interesting parallels to be drawn and contrasts to be made between Afro- and Anglo-American musics.

The three texts I use are Maud Karpeles, *An Introduction to English Folksong*; Edith Fowke, *Penguin Book of Canadian Folksongs*; and Glassie, Szwed and Ives, *Folk Songs and Their Makers*. Karpeles may seem an odd choice, but I find it most useful in the opening weeks of the course since it lays all the platitudes right out in front, so that they can be discussed, elaborated, and in some cases argued. Ms. Karpeles, charming lady that she was, is delightfully wrong-headed about many things; in using this book I follow Francis Bacon's dictum that "Truth emerges more readily from error than from confusion" (Kuhn, 1970: 18). And it includes a brief useful survey of the earlier British folksong collections. The Fowke volume, a collection of tunes and texts, is used at various points in the course to demonstrate music, text, and local traditions. It is also useful to students in the annotation project. Both Fowke and Karpeles are relatively inexpensive. The Glassie, Szwed and Ives volume is used later in the course because it contains a considerable amount of information about folksong performance contexts and repertoire logic, as well as about song-making. The disagreements between the three authors about the role of the songmaker and its pathological implications in cultural terms make this book, like Karpeles, a useful tool for sparking debate in class.

An Outline

In the following pages I sketch the outline of the course as I am teaching it this time (fall semester, 1983). I begin with a survey of the history of the collection and study of English-language folk music, starting first with definitions (such as the IFMC definition given in Karpeles and discussed also by A. L. Lloyd).

1. **Definitions**
   Karpeles, vii-11; Abrahams and Foss, 4-11; Herzog; Lloyd, 11-90.

Following this is a consideration of the history of scholarship and the various assumptions about the nature of folksong which this history reveals. This entails a forced march through the last two chapters of Wilgus, as well as consideration of chapters seven through eleven in Karpeles. At the end of this section, which usually takes about two weeks, I turn to the annotation project. In following the annotation project, students read at least some of the published collections discussed by Wilgus and Karpeles, becoming familiar with that literature in a close way, as I discussed earlier.

2. **Collections, Scholarship and the Annotation Project**
   Karpeles, 68-104; Wilgus *Anglo-American*, 123-343; Lovelace; Beck.

Two weeks are devoted to the examination of what I call typology. I also consider the history of scholarship but focus on a particular aspect of it, namely the way in which students of the genre categorize and organize texts and tunes for analysis. It is in this section that we look at how Child selected his 305 ballads, and the construction of the syllabi of G. Malcolm Laws. We also discuss the problems connected with modal analysis of folk tunes and other aspects of the way in which music description is plagued by the use of a prescriptive system.

During this section of the course the discussion tends toward a description of the ways in which classificatory systems and other typologies reflect the specialized interests and assumptions of the researchers who construct and use them. I suppose that I bring to this particular section of the course an archivist's point of view, having long since abandoned attempts at using finely tuned subject and type indexes as finding devices. I believe that it is important to inculcate in the students at this point a healthy skepticism about the universality of tune and text analysis systems, by pointing out the extent to which they reflect theories about historical origins, limited conceptions of ethnographic reality, and other assumptions of researchers. Of course all systems, be they old-fashioned typologies or new-fangled process models, must be seen as tools which may or may not fit the job at hand.

3. **Typology: Text**
   Dundes; Wilgus, "A Type Index"; Karpeles, 39-67; Toelken; James; Ellis.

4. **Typology: Tune**
   Karpeles, 19-38; Anne and Norm Cohen, "Tune Evolution"; Lomax, "Folk
   Song Style"; Köngäs-Maranda.

In the fifth section, the class turns to studies by Burns, Coffin, Renwick, Long
and others to discuss the way in which folksong scholars have attempted to come
to terms with processes of variation. Variation in itself has been a primary concern
of ballad scholars and other students of folksong for some time, but remained
something of a mystery until beginnings were made at looking at the human factors
lying behind it. The study of variation is a perfect bridge for the movement in the
focus of the course from the song to the singer and singing traditions. Articles like
Long's point to the advisability of understanding processes of performance and
other aspects of the singing tradition in order to understand the way in which texts
are varied or change through time.

5. **Variation**
   Wilgus, "The Text is the Thing"; Burns; Coffin, pp. 1-19; Renwick in
   Coffin, pp. 189-205; Long; Buchan, pp. 51-61.

The next section of the course deals with the singer in terms of roles and
attitudes. Here I begin with a group of early articles by Herbert Halpert, ground-
breaking works which present the words of the singer, describing his ideas about
and experience with singing. It is in this section that we begin to look at such
things as the personality of the singer and its effect upon the tradition (as in
Abrahams' article comparing two female singers); the interesting dichotomy
between private or domestic and public or assembly singing traditions suggested
by the work of Edward D. Ives and the Cohens; and differences in gender roles
which those two scholars and Pocius suggest.

6. **The Singer: Roles and Attitudes**
   Halpert, "Singer Speaks"; Halpert, "Truth"; Halpert, "Michigan Lumberjack";
   Abrahams; Ives, "Lumbercamp Singing"; Anne and Norm Cohen, "Folk and
   Hillbilly"; Pocius.

Discussion in section seven entails a closer look at the way in which individual
singers utilize repertoire. Here we discuss Goldstein's active and inactive article, the
work by Casey, myself and Wareham on repertoire categorization, my own study
of a ballad songbook collector, and Cohen's work on Tin Pan Alley songs. In
considering repertoire we also move into the question of how new songs are
introduced into oral tradition, hence the inclusion of Cohen's article.

7. **The Repertoire: Learning, Transmission, Use.**
   Goldstein; Casey, Rosenberg and Wareham; Rosenberg, "Hobby"; Cohen,
   "Tin Pan Alley."

A logical next step is to look at one particular aspect of repertoire acquisition;
namely, songmaking. Here we examine the interesting and somewhat conflicting
points of view in *Folksongs and Their Makers*. In a sense this section is a review,
from a different perspective, of material covered in the section on variation, since
it deals with the role of personality in the creation and transmission of folksong.

In addition to the three articles in the textbook, I also use an article by Narvaez on parody and one by Wilgus on the professional songmaker, Andrew Jenkins.

8. The Repertoire: Songmaking
Glassie, Szwed and Ives; Narvaez "Folk Parodist"; Wilgus, "Andrew Jenkins."

The material in section eight, especially that of Glassie and Ives, leads into section nine on performance contexts. Here we examine in more detail the ways in which specific situations for the singing of folksong reflect a mediation between tastes and interests of the performer and the social milieu in which the performance is placed. I use Doucette's survey of the Gatineau Valley, and Koning's very interesting article on the fieldworker as performer, which indicates the way in which such individuals become part of the performance situation. Kodish's recent study demonstrates the relationship between content, on the one hand, and social and personal concerns on the other, in the repertoire of a woman singer from Newfoundland.

9. Performance Contexts
Doucette; Koning; Kodish.

The following week we turn to professionalization. In introducing this section I utilize a model which I have been teaching for some time and which is currently in press along with a collection of articles on folklore and popular culture to be published by the Popular Culture Press. The burden of my argument is that the process of the movement of folksong and folk singers into popular song and popular singing context is a gradual one, a series of steps or moves. The model spells out the changes in repertoire and style which accompany such moves, and discusses the ways in which singers characteristically balance decisions about professionalism versus amateurism in economic and social terms. Readings in this section vary considerably as I find interesting new material dealing with interrelationships between folk and popular music. In particular I have in the past used material on country and western music and still use such material from Atlantic Canada. I have also recently introduced readings on conjunto music of Texas and on various kinds of ethnic music in the United States.

10. Professionalization
Narvaez, "Country and Western"; Rosenberg, *Country Music*; Peña; Spottswood; Slobin; Keil; Baily.

The final section has to do with the process of revival. Here we turn to a historical consideration of the North American folksong revival, and discuss this and similar movements in terms of several useful models constructed by Anthony F. C. Wallace and Richard Peterson. The phenomenon of folk festivals and folklorists' involvement in it is also considered.

11. Revival
Wallace; Peterson; Reuss; Engle; Camp & Lloyd.

Direction and Content Angst

This is my course outline as I am teaching it this semester. The reality of the classroom situation is such that I very often find myself engaged in digressions which I either find too interesting to halt in spite of their marginal relevance or which deal with topics to be covered much later in the course. When I began teaching, this sort of thing bothered me very much but I now feel it is the sign of a developing consensus in the seminar which is in the end fruitful and necessary for a healthy graduate class.

Even if we hewed closely to these readings and the orientations they imply, I think that it is not difficult to see how one could improve, add to, or alter the course in various ways. Some topics and orientations I think about as ones which really should be covered in more detail than they are—at least in this year's version of the course—include the following:

(1) *Occupational song.* There are good works available on cowboys and their music, on the lumberwoods (I do in fact touch on this through Ives), on sailors and chanties, and on Afro-American work songs. Related to this topic in a number of ways, but also treated as a special category in their own right, are labor and industrial songs.

(2) *Children's song.* An interesting age group, and one in which specialization is not as important as it is in other song categories. Again there is much useful material in print on this topic.

(3) *Religious song.* This is a topic about which much interesting new research is being done, particularly in the southeastern United States. And there is a considerable depth to the literature, particularly in the work of Jackson on white spirituals and shape-note singing, and in the many works on Afro-American spirituals and gospel songs.

(4) *Instrumental music.* A considerable amount of useful literature concerning fiddling has appeared in the past decade. From time to time I have included sections on this topic in my introductory course. Particularly interesting is the growth of fiddling associations and the spread of contest fiddling. The commercial and professional dimensions are also of interest.

Another dimension to the problem of fitting it all in is the time it takes me to digest the new literature in the field. Even as I am teaching this year's seminar I find myself alluding frequently to two relatively new books I've been reading, David Evans's *Big Road Blues* and Roger Renwick's *English Folk Poetry*. Both give useful new perspectives on close textual analysis based on historical and ethnographic research. I think that the next time I teach the course I will probably integrate some of this material into the syllabus—how and where, I'm not quite certain yet. So it goes.

BIBLIOGRAPHY

Abrahams, Roger D. "Creativity, Individuality and the Traditional Singer." *Studies in the Literary Imagination*, 3 (1970), 5-34.

______, and George Foss. *Anglo-American Folksong Style*. Englewood Cliffs, N.J.: Prentice-Hall, 1968.

Baily, John. "Cross-cultural Perspective in Popular Music: The Case of Afghanistan." *Popular Music*, 1 (1981), 105-122.

Beck, Horace. "Folksong Affiliations of Maine." *Midwest Folklore*, 6 (1956), 69-77.

Buchan, David. *The Ballad and the Folk*. London: Routledge, Kegan Paul, 1972.

Burns, Thomas. "A Model for Textual Variation in Folksong." *Folklore Forum*, 3 (1970), 49-56.

Camp, Charles, and Timothy Lloyd. "Six Reasons Not to Produce Folklife Festivals." *Kentucky Folklore Record*, 26 (1980), 67-74.

Casey, George J., and Neil V. Rosenberg and Wilfred W. Wareham. "Repertoire Categorization and Performer-Audience Relationships: Some Newfoundland Folksong Examples." *Ethnomusicology*, 16 (1972), 397-403.

Child, Francis James. *The English and Scottish Popular Ballads*. New York: Houghton, Mifflin and Co., 1882-1898.

Coffin, Tristram P. *The British Traditional Ballad in North America*. Austin: University of Texas Press, 1977. Rev. ed. with "Supplement," pp. 189-297, by Roger deV. Renwick.

Cohen, Anne and Norm. "Folk and Hillbilly Music: Further Thoughts on their Relationship. *JEMF Quarterly*, 13 (1977), 50-57.

______. "Tune Evolution as an Indicator of Traditional Musical Norms." *Journal of American Folklore*, 86 (1973), 37-47.

Cohen, Norm. "Tin Pan Alley's Contribution to Folk Music." *Western Folklore*, 29 (1970), 9-20.

Doucette, Laurel. "Gatineau Valley Singing Tradition: A Contemporary View." *Canadian Folk Music Journal*, 7 (1979), 18-22.

Dundes, Alan. "Texture, Text and Context." *Southern Folklore Quarterly*, 28 (1964), 251-265.

Ellis, Bill. "The Blind Girl and the Rhetoric of Sentimental Heroism." *Journal of American Folklore*, 91 (1978), 657-674.

Engle, David G. "A Sketch of the German Folk Revival Singer, Katzi Ritzel." *Lore and Language*, 3 (1981), 67-79.

Evans, David. *Big Road Blues*. Berkeley: University of California Press, 1982.

Glassie, Henry, and Edward Ives, and John F. Szwed. *Folksongs and Their Makers*. Bowling Green, Ohio: Popular Culture Press, 1970.

Goldstein, Kenneth S. "On the Application of the Concepts of Active and Inactive Traditions to the Study of Repertory." *Journal of American Folklore*, 84 (1971), 62-67.

Halpert, Herbert. "The Folksinger Speaks." *Hoosier Folklore Bulletin*, 3 (1944), 29-35, 48-55.

______. "A Michigan Lumberjack Singer." *Hoosier Folklore Bulletin*, 1 (1942), 81-84.

______. "Truth in Folk-Songs—Some Observations in the Folk-singer's Attitude." In *Traditional Ballads and Folk-Songs Mainly from West Virginia*, ed. George Herzog, Herbert Halpert, and George W. Boswell, pp. xiii-xx. Philadelphia: American Folklore Society, 1964.

Herzog, George. "Song: Folk Song and the Music of Folk Song." In *Standard Dictionary of Folklore, Mythology and Legend*, ed. Maria Leach and Jerome Fried, vol. 2, pp. 1032-1050. New York: Funk and Wagnalls, 1950.

Ives, Edward D. "Lumbercamp Singing and the Two Traditions." *Canadian Folk Music Journal*, 5 (1977), 17-23.

James, Thelma. "The English and Scottish Ballads of Francis J. Child." In *The Critics and the Ballad*, ed. MacEdward Leach and Tristram P. Coffin, pp. 12-19. Carbondale: Southern Illinois University. Press, 1961.

Karpeles, Maud. *An Introduction to English Folk Song*. London: Oxford University Press, 1963.

Keil, Charles. "Slovenian Style in Milwaukee." In *Folk Music and Modern Sound*, ed. William Ferris and Mary L. Hart, pp. 32-59. Jackson: University Press of Mississippi, 1982.

Kodish, Debora. "Fair Young Ladies and Bonny Irish Boys: Pattern in Vernacular Poetics." *Journal of American Folklore*, 96 (1983). 131-150.

Köngäs, Maranda, Elli. "Deep Significance and Surface Significance: Is Cantometrics Possible?" *Semiotica*, 2 (1970), 173-184.

Koning, Jos. "The Fieldworker as Performer: Fieldwork Objectives and Social Roles in County Clare, Ireland." *Ethnomusicology*, 24 (1980), 417-429.

Kuhn, Thomas S. *The Structure of Scientific Revolutions*. Chicago: University of Chicago Press, 1970.

Laws, G. Malcolm, Jr. *American Balladry from British Broadsides*. Philadelphia: The American Folklore Society, 1957.

______. *Native American Balladry*. Philadelphia: American Folklore Society, 1964.

Lloyd, A. L. *Folk Song in England*. London: Lawrence & Wishart, 1967.

Lomax, Alan. "Folk Song Style." *American Anthropologist*, 61 (1959), 927-954.

Long, Eleanor R. "Ballad Singers, Ballad Makers, and Ballad Etiology." *Western Folklore*, 32 (1973), 225-236.

Lovelace, Martin. "W. Roy Mackenzie as a Collector of Folksong." *Canadian Folk Music Journal*, 5 (1977), 5-11.

Narvaez, Peter. "Country and Western in Diffusion: Juxtaposition and Syncretism in the Popular Music of Newfoundland." *Culture and Tradition*, 2 (1977), 91-105.

______. "The Folk Parodist." *Canadian Folk Music Journal*, 5 (1977), 32-37.

Peña, Manuel H. "The Emergence of Conjunto Music, 1935-1955." In *"And Other Neighborly Names": Social Process and Cultural Image in Texas Folklore*, ed. Richard Bauman and Roger D. Abrahams, pp. 280-299. Austin: University of Texas Press, 1981.

Peterson, Richard A. "A Process Model of the Folk, Pop and Fine Art Phases of Jazz." In *American Music: From Storyville to Woodstock*, ed. Charles Nanry, pp. 135-151. New Brunswick, N.J.: Transaction Books, 1972.

Pocius, Gerald L. "'The First Day I Thought of It Since I Got Wed': Role Expectations and Singer Status in a Newfoundland Outport." *Western Folklore*, 35 (1976), 109-122.

Renwick, Roger deV. *English Folk Poetry*. Philadelphia: University of Pennsylvania Press, 1980.

Reuss, Richard A. "American Folksongs and Left-Wing Politics: 1935-36." *Journal of the Folklore Institute*, 12 (1975), 89-111.

Rosenberg, Neil V. *Country Music in the Maritimes: Two Studies*. St. John's: Memorial University of Newfoundland (Department of Folklore Reprint Series, No. 2), 1976.

______. "'It Was a Kind of a Hobby': A Manuscript Song Book and Its Place in Tradition." In *Folklore Studies in Honour of Herbert Halpert*, ed. Kenneth S.

Goldstein and Neil V. Rosenberg, pp. 315-333. St. John's: Memorial University of Newfoundland, 1980.

Seeger, Charles. "Prescriptive and Descriptive Music Writing." *The Music Quarterly*, 44 (1958), 184-195.

Slobin, Mark. "How the Fiddler Got on the Roof." In *Folk Music and Modern Sound*, ed. William Ferris and Mary L. Hart, pp. 21-31. Jackson: University Press of Mississippi, 1982.

Spottswood, Richard. "Ethnic and Popular Style in America." In *Folk Music and Modern Sound*, ed. William Ferris and Mary L. Hart, pp. 60-70.

Toelken, J. Barre. "An Oral Canon for the Child Ballads: Construction and Applications." *Journal of the Folklore Institute*, 4 (1967), 75-101.

Wallace, Anthony F. C. "Revitalization Movements." *American Anthropologist*, 58 (1956), 264-281.

Wilgus, D. K. "Andrew Jenkins, Folk Composer: An Overview." *Lore and Language*, 3 (1981), 109-128.

______. *Anglo-American Folksong Scholarship Since 1898*. New Brunswick, N.J.: Rutgers University Press, 1959.

______. "'The Text is the Thing.'" *Journal of American Folklore*, 86 (1973), 241-252.

______. "A Type-Index of Anglo-American Traditional Narrative Songs." *Journal of the Folklore Institute*, 7 (1970), 161-176.

Bruce Jackson

State University of New York at Buffalo

Epic

Those who run in a race should not be hobbled. Many critics have sought for rules in Homer which are assuredly not there. Since the Iliad and the Odyssey are of entirely different types, the critics have had much difficulty in reconciling Homer with himself. To make the confusion even greater, Virgil used the plan of the Iliad and the Odyssey in composing the Aeneid, forcing the critics to establish still other rules to make Virgil agree with Homer. . . .

It is necessary in all of the arts to guard against fallacious definitions which exclude the unknown for which custom has not yet set a standard. The arts, especially those which depend upon imagination, are not like the material universe. We can define metals, minerals, elements, and animals because their nature is always the same; the works of man change like the imaginations which produce them. . . .

Voltaire "Essay on Epic Poetry," 1733

The Genre in Question

Epic is a master form. Describe a work as "epic" and people know what you mean—sort of. The word *epic* is applied to the earliest surviving narratives (*Gilgamesh, Enuma Elish, Iliad, Exodus*), artful and considered literary examinations of the human condition (*Aeneid, Paradise Lost, Jerusalem, Ulysses*), memorable films (*Hell's Hinges, Stagecoach, Lawrence of Arabia, Once Upon a Time in the West*), and to abominable attempts at verse and execrable squandering of filmstock (any poem by Colley Cibber and any muscle film starring Steve Reeves). Not one of these epic things is quite like any other, and any set of defining terms that covers them all glosses over what really makes them matter.

Epic is, therefore, a spectacularly imprecise term; its meaning is always defined contextually. Like the term *Romanticism*, which most academics in the humanities can more or less define and for which most definitions overlap only partially, only after you tell us which epics you're talking about can we have any idea of what you mean by *epic*.

That imprecision is not without value. The term implies a congeries of specific narratives and narrative modes. It provides a starting point for thinking about stories of an impressive sort, a forum for discussing ideas about artistic creation, memory, structure, order, and the interrelation of major cultural forms across genres and through time.

Descriptive generic examination has a venerable history; it is, after all, the way Aristotle approached tragedy when he set about writing the most perdurable literary essay of all time. Failing to find a prescriptive definition of tragedy that worked, he labored, in the *Poetics*, to find what worked in the best of the plays people had called tragedies.

Benedetto Croce rejected the utility of the concept of genre for literature studies and of late folklorists have questioned its applicability to folklore studies. But I doubt we'll ever be free of the notion of genre, and that's probably a good thing. Artists perform, audiences respond, and critics interpret in terms of notions of genre. Genre is a cultural map. The map is fuzzy, ambiguous, and ever mutable, but those are characteristics of genre, not faults in it. Faulting genre for being unstable in definition or execution is like blaming giants for being big or thunder for being noisy.

Purpose of the Seminar

I want students to get three things out of this seminar: familiarity with the particular artistic and scholarly works we examine during the term; a grounded idea of how objects named as *epics* by their makers or audiences have comprised a tradition that crosses the boundaries of folk, art, and popular culture; and an acute sense of the way genre functions for artists, audiences, and scholars. I also want them to be aware of the privile accorded to print by those literary scholars who claim to be aware and respectful of the legitimacy and different character of oral traditions (e.g., Ong 1982).

We examine a wide range of objects that have been called epics, and we discuss what makes them valuable or important and what relations they have with other things of their kind. We deal with some of the critical issues related to the texts, such as the various arguments around the Parry-Lord theory of oral-formulaic composition, the relation of texts in time, and the relation of texts across genres.

The seminar is about major narrative modalities. It deals with some materials any folklorist would be comfortable with, and it also deals with literary and film material and scholarship. It provides students an opportunity to deal with the vital interrelationship of oral, print, and film narrative. The interrelationship is commonplace in ordinary life outside the classroom, where the boundaries between folk, popular, and high culture turn out to be far less substantial than academic divisions of labor usually suggest.

The Departmental Context

The official name for this university is "State University of New York at Buffalo," but everyone calls it "UB" (for "University of Buffalo") which was what people called it before it joined the state university system nearly 30 years ago.

Memos from SUNY bureaucrats in Albany to faculty members here would have "SUNY/B" or "SUNY/Buffalo" in the address box; letters going back would have "UB" in the return address box. It's like what happened when the UN moved from San Francisco to New York at the end of World War II. The New York City government officially and with great pomp and publicity changed the name of Sixth Avenue to "Avenue of the Americas." All the old street signs from the bottom of Manhattan to Central Park South were torn down and replaced. The changes meant nothing: no New Yorker refers to that street as anything other than Sixth Avenue and everyone knows that anyone who refers to an address on "Avenue of the Americas" is either a visitor or a silly person. Here in Buffalo, the local university administration recently conceded to the power of folk nomenclature: the top line of our campus letterhead now reads "University at Buffalo" so the letterhead is in tune with the spoken word. UB it is.

UB is one of four graduate centers in the SUNY system. Along with the centers at Stony Brook, Albany, and Binghamton we maintain nearly all of SUNY's Ph.D. programs and do most of the funded research. When the system was organized, Stony Brook was to have the concentration in physical sciences and Buffalo the concentration in humanities. The imbalance has been somewhat redressed over the years, but some difference in focus still exists. Buffalo is the largest unit in the SUNY system and it has the largest humanities faculty. The English department at UB comprises 57 full-time faculty and 175 full-time graduate students (105 of them funded). The department has been flexible in faculty assignments and student requirements: in addition to the usual run of English department offerings, we usually offer more folklore seminars than Anthropology, more film seminars than Media Studies, more comparative literature seminars than Comparative Literature, and more drama seminars than Theatre.

This department has never differentiated graduate seminars and graduate classes; they're all called "seminars" and the registration was, until a year ago, limited only by the room size. A seminar by Leslie Fiedler or Robert Creeley would have 25 and sometimes even more students. For me, a lecture class is one in which nearly all the talking is done by the professor; a seminar is a class in which the responsibility for conversation is at least partially shared. I dislike teaching graduate level lecture classes, whatever euphemism is used for them, so I schedule all my graduate classes for the office of the Center for Studies in American Culture. We've convinced the university computer that the room cannot endure more than 12 students, which, not-coincidentally, is the size I prefer for seminars.

Dennis Tedlock, Diane Christian, and I are the core faculty in the English Department's Ph.D. Program in Folklore, Mythology, and Film Studies. The Program offers methodological guidance for graduate students interested in one or more of three areas of study which relate variously to traditional literature, which deal with the major non-print forms of narrative and mimetic art, and which share historical, anthropological, and sociological concerns. Students in the program may take seminars in several other departments within the university and, under certain circumstances, at other universities. About 25 faculty members at this university and 15 faculty members at other universities are associated with the program. About one third of the students in our seminars are concentrating or doing a minor in FM&FS; the remainder are other graduate students, mostly from English but also from Comparative Literature, American Studies, Communications, and Anthropology.

In addition to *Epic*, my current repertoire of graduate seminars consists of *Traditional Narrative*, *Documentary*, *The Western*, and *Fieldwork*. *The Western* and *Documentary* seminars are primarily about film, but both include materials from other genres as well. In *The Western*, for example, we deal with iconography, myth, text, development, and influence. We discuss paintings by Frederick Remington, Charles Russell, John Bierstadt, and George Catlin; fiction by Owen Wister (*The Virginian*) and Michael Ondaatje (*Collected Works of Billy the Kid*): autobiographies by Charles Siringo (*A Texas Cowboy*) and Andy Adams (*Log of a Cowboy*); travel accounts by Mark Twain (*Roughing It*) and George Catlin (*Letters and Notes on the Manners, Customs, and Conditions of the North American Indians*); and so forth. When possible, Tedlock, Christian and I try to tune our seminars so they create logical sequences or combinations for graduate students especially interested in the FM&FS program (this currently involves Christian's *Mythology*, *Literature and Film*, and *Blake* seminars, and Tedlock's *Mythography*, *Orality and Literacy*, *Translation*, and *Ethnopoetics* seminars.

Seminar Requirements

Students in the *Epic* seminar are required to do two oral class presentations and a term paper. The first oral presentation is a discussion based on one or two critical, historical, or ancillary works; the second is a summary of the term paper. I ask students to hand in two copies of the term papers; one copy is returned to them with my comments, the other is kept on file for a year for any of the other seminar participants who want to read it. A few years ago I started asking students to prepare annotated lists of the interesting/useful works they encountered while working on their term papers, whether or not those works made it to the paper bibliographies. We xerox those lists so everyone, including me, finishes the term with a number of potentially useful references to a wide range of scholarship as well as tips on works we can probably afford to avoid.

The term paper summaries are given at the last two meetings of the seminar. I ask the students to keep the presentations to 15 minutes so we can have 15 minutes for discussion; occasionally we get through a paper in 35-45 minutes, but an hour seems more the norm lately. A good deal of often interesting material is covered in these summaries and discussions, and the students don't seem to mind the extra hours consumed in the process. [1]

The book discussions (a device I adapted from Edson Richmond's ballad and medieval romance seminars) are spread throughout the term and are keyed to assigned texts or discussion topics. In one recent seminar, students reported on Snell's *The Discovery of the Mind* and Dodds's *The Greeks and the Irrational* as part

---

[1]We usually do the first of the two sessions as a regular seminar (our seminars run slightly under three hours), and we have the second session at my house so we can have a lunch or dinner along the way. The last session of my most recent seminar ran from 6:00 p.m. until slightly before midnight; two people had to leave before we were finished; five of the others stayed around talking until about 2:30 a.m. The longest class meeting I remember had a lunch, a dinner, and a late night snack; it occurred at the end of an NEH Summer Seminar for College Teachers in *Traditional Narrative*. I think the discussion part ran some 12 hours and a few of the participants continued the conversation until the birds started making obnoxious pre-dawn noises.

of the discussion of the *Iliad*, and Tigay's *The Evolution of the Gilgamesh Epic* as part of our discussions of *Enuma Elish* and *Gilgamesh*. Later in that term, other members of the seminar discussed *Feud in the Icelandic Saga* (Byock), *The Epic Film: Myth and History* (Elley), *Homer and the Nibelungenlied* (Fenik), *The Babylonian Genesis* (Heidel), *Showdown: Confronting Modern America in the Western Film* (Lenihan), *Blake's Composite Art: A Study of the Illuminated Poetry* (Mitchell), *Nature and Culture in the Iliad* (Redfield), and *The Spoken Word and the Work of Interpretation* (Tedlock).

There are always more books on the suggested list than students in the seminar, and sometimes students will suggest books I hadn't thought of or known about. The books on my list and those I accept as alternates are there because they present critical data or discuss or raise what I think are important methodological questions or hermeneutic positions. The reports usually provide several handles for small lectures by me and for discussions involving members of the seminar. This is perhaps less efficient a technique than straight lecturing, but I think the process involves the students earlier and more critically in the imaginative work of the seminar than would otherwise be possible or likely. It also forces them to engage the argument of a work, something I suspect they rarely do when they're scanning a book as background or for quotations they might work into a term paper.

If they find in a work just what I find in it, I don't say much and we go on to the next discussion. But that rarely happens: sometimes they home in on aspects very different from those I thought critical and sometimes they home in on the same parts I would have selected but they weigh or read them differently. Those discrepant readings often lead to useful discussions. If no one selects a work I think especially important, I'll find a way to work it into our discussions of the primary texts.

Sometimes they'll discuss an epic not on my list of texts for the class. One student a few years ago who was interested in Carolingian narratives did a session on *Chanson de Roland*. Another was writing on Joyce; her hour-long talk on *Ulysses* was so good I went back and read it again for the first time in at least a decade.

The assigned texts, the week-by-week readings, provide us common ground upon which to discuss the relationship between oral narrative and written narrative, between oral narrative and the print or film versions of the same narrative. They let us consider the different capacities of the different media to tell stories. They let us examine questions having to do with structure, influence, style, tradition, form, immediate cultural referents and larger abstract ideas. They let us engage a range of questions dealing with composition, performance, and understanding of simple and composite forms.[2]

Seminar Organization

I've organized this seminar two ways, neither of them really satisfactory: chronologically (beginning with the earliest and ending with the most recent of the

---

[2]Blake's engravings, for example, don't *illustrate* his text; they are coequal with and essential to it. And Sergio Leone doesn't use musical and sound effects tracks to *enhance* the action of his narratives; music and sound effects are part of the action of his narratives. Sometime I'd like to do a seminar on composite forms, with *Turandot, Jerusalem, Once Upon a Time in the West,* and that year's Superbowl as the primary texts.

included epics) and in order of what seems to be increasing generic awareness and reflexivity. The author of the Homeric texts, for example, was in all likelihood aware of a wide range of oral narrative traditions, but Virgil and Dante and the other authors of literary epics were aware not only of oral narrative traditions but also of specific literary documents. Epic was a matter of *choice* for them, one narrative option among many, and they were free to alter the genre to fit their antecedent plans. In *Ulysses* Joyce operated at a further remove, this one ironic, and in *The Bridge*, Hart Crane operated at an aesthetic remove that rendered his major work nearly inaccessible.

I like the notion of primary (folk), secondary (literary), and tertiary (reflexive literary) epic (the primary and secondary epic categories go back at least to Schiller; Fowler added tertiary [Fowler 1982:160-162]), but I am careful to point out to students that the model isn't very precise; it probably works only for people who don't know much about the way oral narrative really works or about the inadequacy of most printed texts of oral performance. Our texts of the *Odyssey* and the *Iliad*, the premier examples of primary epic, are literary redactions of oral epic, and we have no idea how aware the designers and redactors were of the tradition in which they functioned. In creating so sophisticated a narrative in the *Iliad* and so complex a congeries of forms in the *Odyssey*, the Homeric poet(s) may have already been functioning in what Schiller would have called the secondary stage.

Taking the works chronologically is easier—the temporal linearity of it is reassuring to the students and it is simpler mechanically for me, which is nice in a class covering so wide a range of materials—but it's not a meaningful principle of organization. Blake is probably closer in imagination to Leone than to Whitman, Pound, Joyce, or Crane; and *Gilgamesh*, which was assembled from a number of separate stories into a single coherent narrative about 2000 B.C., is closer in composition to *Kalevala* than to the Homeric epics.

Whichever model I adopt for the class, I discuss the other and try to point out the light it sheds and the light it obscures. I remind them that we're not building supersonic aircraft; our models can be imperfect so long as we are aware of their limitations. Students have told me that our discussions about the simultaneous utility and inadequacy of two models have been useful to them in the preparation of their own classes in a variety of subjects.

For one recent version of the seminar, the booklist consisted of *Gilgamesh*, (I use the Sayers translation rather than the raw text in Pritchard), the *Odyssey* (I still like Robert Fitzgerald's translation even though it's more than 20 years old), *The Epic in Africa* (Okpewho), *Exodus*, the *Aeneid*, *Njalsaga*, Dante's *Inferno*, and Hart Crane's *The Bridge*. I also made available to the class xeroxes of *The Mwindo Epic*, Laura Bohannon's "Shakespeare in the Bush," and passages from Joyce's *Ulysses*. I scheduled screenings of *Stagecoach* (John Ford), the 1923 silent and 1956 sound *Ten Commandments* (Cecil B. De Mille), and *Once Upon a Time in the West* (Sergio Leone).

The first meeting is a general introduction to the seminar: the usuals about format of the class and my sourness when someone doesn't show up for a scheduled oral performance or doesn't get the paper in by the end of the term without evidence of something dreadful. I make some general remarks about the use and limitations of genre and genre theory and the limits of what we can legitimately say about texts used in translation. I pass around a xerox of a classical text in several English translations. I note the tendency to map texts from other cultures with our own values and I usually say that such mapping is reasonable enough—not only are we incapable of reading the *Inferno* as it would have been read by a contemporary of Dante, but there's no reason we should read it that way; a goodly portion of what makes any work important is the relevance and resonance it finds in one's own culture. But we're not reading for fun only; we're scholars and we are concerned with knowing something about the original resonance. So, I tell them, we'll sometimes read the texts with a split sensibility, one partly grounded in what we think the historical reality was, and partly grounded in our own world. I give them a xerox of the best thing I've ever seen on the problem of cultural chauvinism and relativism: Laura Bohannon's "Shakespeare in the Bush."

The second week we discuss *Enuma Elish* and *Gilgamesh*. Both poems are interesting in their own right, and our discussions of them foreshadow matters that will come up later in the term: *Enuma Elish*, a written text that had been in its present form for several hundred years by the time the tablets used for our translations had been made, has a great deal of formulaic and thematic repetition. We'll come back to that later in the term when we discuss some of the more extravagant claims made by the Parry-Lord apologists. *Gilgamesh* gives us a chance to begin discussing a variety of narrative themes that will appear in many of the other works, as well as the matter of how we regard an assembled narrative. (At this meeting, students select their discussion books.)

The third week is usually a dinner at my house.[3] We'll most likely discuss the Homeric tradition at this meeting and the meeting that follows it. I used to do *Iliad* one week and the *Odyssey* the next, but over the years I found more and more things I wanted to talk about in both poems. Things were getting quite out of hand, so I decided to have one or two class sessions focusing on one of the Homeric poems and I'd alternate them—one year *Iliad*, the next year *Odyssey*. The two poems have vastly different structures and styles—*Iliad* is linear and *Odyssey* is appositive—but there's quite enough to discuss, such as the Parry-Lord hypothesis and its uses and limitations.

In the fifth week we talk about *Exodus*—the Biblical text and Cecil B. De Mille's two film spectacles entitled *The Ten Commandments*. The 1923 version (a silent) was daring, setting the Mosaic exodus story within a modern morality play about atheism and greed. The 1956 version (starring Charlton Heston) was introduced by a long pious prologue by De Mille. Both film redactions read their own times as well as the Biblical story; both were huge popular successes. (Imagine a Moses iconographical lineup with Americans and Europeans over 40 as the witnesses: how

---

[3]My wife, Diane Christian, and I usually have our seminars over at least once each semester. We used to do it just once at the end of the term, but then we realized that many of the students didn't really engage one another in conversation until that dinner, so we started having a dinner early because it sped up the warming of the class. (When we're both teaching graduate classes we'll have Diane's class one week, mine the next; if we're having the seminars to the house for another dinner at the end of the term we'll do the same thing.) Since we often get students taking seminars with both of us in the same term, and sometimes those students have had other seminars with us previously, one student might have seminar dinners at our house eight times in the course of two or three semesters. We used to try to vary the menus, but big dinners in term time are a lot of work, so we settled on two basic menus, which we alternate. No one has complained about culinary redundancy.

would Michelangelo's Moses fare next to the celluloid Moses De Mille made of Charlton Heston?).

In the next several weeks we talk about the other assigned texts and deal with the reports. I try to introduce theoretical materials in relation to specific works. I bring up Bakhtin's assumption that epic is monologic, for example, in the context of our discussion of African narrative; I talk about Derrida's assumption that epic has unidirectional narrative linearity in our discussion of the *Aeneid* and *Once Upon a Time in the West*.

I save composite epic until late because I like to use it to feed into the discussions of film. We'll read Blake's *Jerusalem* about the twelfth week (Diane Christian takes the class for this session). *Jerusalem* is a nice bridge to modern times because it is a visual and verbal epic which in form anticipates film and in content at once echoes Milton and initiates the modern epic of self-consciousness.

The final regular session of the seminar focuses on iconography, myth, text, development, and influence in film Westerns. Westerns, America's contribution to the epic imagination, are of a piece with important aspects of American painting and imaginative and autobiographical writing of the nineteenth century. After the film industry moved to California, cowhands who had driven cattle herds to California stayed on to work in movies about cowhands, so the representation and the reality often involved the same people. Tom Mix had been a cowpuncher, Texas Ranger, and deputy U.S. marshall before becoming a rodeo performer and then a famous actor. William S. Hart (born in 1880 in Newburgh, NY) worked as a trail-herd cowboy; his close friends included Wyatt Earp, Bat Masterson, Charles Russell and former outlaw Pat O'Malley. John Ford also knew Masterson and Russell; he collected Russell's paintings and used them for film ideas. The Western provides us an opportunity to see the epic in process and in context; its brief history recapitulates the historical range of epics we've considered in the previous eleven weeks.

The final two meetings of the seminar are the paper summaries and discussions.

A term is not long enough to deal adequately with the enormous company of literary and filmic works that have been called epic, or even to deal adequately with the best oral, literary, and film epics. My assumption in any graduate seminar is that in a single semester you can never cover everything that matters, or even everything that's interesting; all you can do is look at some exemplary texts through a variety of critical approaches and consider some of the pending questions.

Sometimes I'll switch off: we'll read the *Iliad* instead of the *Odyssey*; we'll do another saga instead of *Njalsaga* or we'll drop it entirely and read Appolonius's *Argonautica* or Lucan's *Pharsalia* instead. If Diane is teaching *Exodus* and showing the De Mille films in her seminar, my seminar might do *Chanson de Roland* or *Beowulf*. We might do John Ford's Monument Valley films or Francis Coppola's *Godfather* films or Abel Gance's *Napoleon* instead of Leone. That doesn't rid us of the problem of sketchy coverage, but it does keep me from getting stale. I assume I've done a good job if the term papers deal with topics and use approaches and sources that are new to me. The new stuff tells me that the students have become sufficiently interested to go beyond what happened in the classroom and they've learned how to ferret things out on their own.

Bruce Jackson

State University of New York at Buffalo

Fieldwork Seminar

The large part of literary and historical research is predicated on documents already in place: books on a library shelf; manuscripts and letters collected, catalogued, and boxed. But warehoused documents are not the only sources for literary and historical scholars, and they aren't even the primary sources for scholars in folklore, oral history, anthropology, sociology, and recent biography and history. For those scholars, most of the information to be analyzed and interpreted comes from interviews with and observations of living people—from fieldwork.

A graduate seminar in fieldwork theory, methodology, and practice has an obvious place in any folklore Ph.D. program. "The folklore archive," Richard Dorson said in his 1962 *Fieldwork* seminar, "is to the folklorist what the library is to the literary scholar. And the most important contribution to the archive comes from fieldwork." I was new to folklore studies then and I thought Dorson's comment off the mark: what mattered most were the collections people were making, the data that was being gathered; the stuff in archives was primarily there for reference. Later, I came to understand that Dorson's analogy was correct: the archive provides the folklorist materials to understand pattern in time and space; it allows understanding of the careers of items and genres and even contexts. Literary scholars can go get primary data: they can interview writers and their friends, they can buy books in a bookstore, they can visit what may be the real places utilized in the fictional settings. But it is the library that provides access to the books no longer in a bookstore and to the letters of and studies about writers and friends no longer available for interview. Folklorists, Dorson said, had to do fieldwork because it provided the primary information upon which their studies rested. After I had been teaching for a number of years I realized there was another reason for doing fieldwork: only by having had some fieldwork experience can a scholar begin to understand the real character of collections of field data.

A few years ago I decided that a fieldwork seminar had as much place in an ordinary English department as in a folklore program. Study of the fieldwork process involves students in critical examination of the claims to truth underlying many of the historical and analytical studies upon which their own work, whatever area, is and will be based. Doing fieldwork and organizing the results involves them in basic questions of genre, presentation, analysis, editing, representation and reality.

The department in which I teach, as I noted in my discussion of the *Epic* seminar, has an optional Ph.D. program in Folklore, Mythology, and Film Studies. Students in the program make up about half of the registrants in *Fieldwork*

Seminar; the others are English department students doing regular English department concentrations, and they are students from American Studies, History, Media Studies, and other departments. If we had no FM&FS doctoral program, the *Fieldwork* seminar would fill with energetic students anyway. The seminar can easily be tuned to the interests, experience, and needs of the students taking it in any particular term.

The seminar examines how fieldwork is done, the uses to which field-collected data are put, and the ethical considerations engendered by the gathering, editing, and publishing processes. We read several texts about fieldwork and several major documents resulting from fieldwork. It is as much a class in the character of documentary authority, the claim to truth, as it is in practice. Students have two specific assignments: (1) a field project of their own devising, and (2) a discussion in class of a text resulting from fieldwork or the work of a particular fieldworker (recent discussions have focussed on Frederick Wiseman's films, Zora Neale Hurston's *Mules and Men*, George Catlin's *O-kee-pa*, Truman Capote's *In Cold Blood*, John A. Lomax's *Adventures of a Ballad Hunter*, the book and film versions of Norman Mailer's *The Executioner's Song*, Henry Mayhew's *London Labour and the London Poor*, the row that followed publication of Derek Freeman's *Margaret Mead and Samoa*, and the photography of Edward S. Curtis).

The subject matter and media of the projects are entirely open. Since the seminar is made up of students from several fields, our discussions about the selection of projects and initial project design provide occasions for consideration of how researchers in different fields may document and map the same event, and how those researchers may even differentially define what the event is. The seminar is, therefore, enormously useful in providing graduate students a sense of cross-disciplinary understanding that goes far beyond what they get from a sampling of readings in another field. Folklorists can always get a good idea what oral historians do by reading what oral historians write, but I think they get a far more accurate idea by seeing how oral historians delimit what they think matters in a situation and how they select out of the raw data they've collected what they think matters.

Each project has two parts: collection of data, and organizing the data in a form other people can see or read or use. Recent projects have dealt with Grateful Dead parking lot action, suburban Buffalo lawn decoration, Seminole quilting, a campus preacher in Illinois, a folk poet, a Buffalo theater company preparing for a new production, interviews with a writer, etc. We have equipment available for those who want or need it: Sony 8mm video camcorders and VHS decks to edit on, 35mm still cameras, and audio recorders with excellent Sennheiser microphone systems.

I'm not much concerned with the success of the fieldwork project—a failed project that results in real understanding of some aspect of the fieldwork process is more valuable than a successful project that merely ratifies antecedent assumptions. One of the lessons in this seminar is that the reports we get to see based on fieldwork are based on fieldwork successfully done and on subjects that were susceptible to fieldwork methods.

Since this is more than a seminar in simple practice, I solicit help in some of the discussions. Campus colleagues who have done a great deal of fieldwork often visit the seminar and discuss their own work. Diane Christian has described her work on two films and how the fieldwork caused her to revise important initial assumptions. Dennis Tedlock discussed fieldwork in Guatemala and the complex and subtle process of translating the uttered word to the printed line.

The basic practical manual for the class is my own book on the subject, *Fieldwork*. I prefer not to assign my own books in class, but not assigning this one would have been silly. Having them read the book means there is an enormous amount of stuff about the mechanics of fieldwork we don't have to talk about in class at all, and our discussions of purpose and editing and ethics can begin much further along than would otherwise be possible. The other texts I used last time were *The Last Kings of Thule* (Malaurie), *Self, Sex, and Gender in Cross-Cultural Fieldwork* (Whitehead and Conaway, eds.), *Let Us Now Praise Famous Men* (Agee and Evans), *Writing Culture: The Poetics and Politics of Ethnography* (Clifford and Marcus, eds.), *Tell My Horse* (Hurston), and *Black American Street Life* (Rose).

We begin discussing possible projects at the first meeting, but it's not until the fourth meeting that they have to deliver a written project proposal—what they're going to look for or at, how they're going to do it, what they expect to wind up with, why anyone should give a hoot. We'll do this again and again throughout the term: we'll have interim reports, revision reports, and eventually we'll look at or read or hear the results and we'll talk about what happened between initial plan and final product and what was learned about getting what you want and convincing yourself that you wanted what you got.

I had read Dan Rose's *Black American Street Life* only a few weeks before the semester began, but I immediately decided to make it our opening text. Better than any other modern ethnographer, Rose lets us see him in the act of seeing and coming to terms with his material; he reveals his changing self in the field. The extremely well-written narrative begins with a student who is idealistic and naive; it ends with cracked but still-valued ideals and a sad wisdom. Along the way, we see an ethnographer at work and we learn something about how the material encountered in his everyday life in the field is transmuted into the ethnographic text.

The next week we deal with some of the essays in Clifford and Marcus. The subject of the reflexive fieldworker is highly fashionable in folklife and associated studies these days, and this collection of essays articulates the range of concerns better than anything else around. Some of the essays are brilliant; some (e.g. Vincent Crapanzano's "Hermes' Dilemma") are precious and silly. There's enough of a range here for us to touch on what seem to me items of interest and possible risk in the developing student projects.

The essays in the Whitehead and Conaway anthology are particularly good for helping the students become aware of how notions about gender, race, status, and such modulate all human interactions. For obvious reasons, women and minorities tend to be far more aware of this than men, so this session of the seminar often turns into a fairly heated discussion grounded in personal experience. It's a terrific teaching point because at the end of the session I try to get everyone to pull back and think about what this tells us about the operative unarticulated texts modulating the field encounters they've had thus far.

Malaurie's *Last Kings of Thule* and Agee's and Evans's *Let Us Now Praise Famous Men* provide the ground for discussions of narrative voice and the assumed differences between scientific and literary writing. We talk about Apollonian and Dionysian styles in the field and at the typewriter. When we're discussing these books I also have them read my "What People Like Us Are Saying When We Say We're Saying the Truth."

As the term progresses, the students are getting deeper into their projects. They're running up blind alleys, finding that things they thought would be complicated are simple and things they thought simple are impossible. They're learning about the problems of achieving a preconceived idea and about the difficulty of abandoning a preconceived idea in favor of what they're encountering in the world. They're learning about adapting their curiosity to the mechanical limitations of their recording devices. And they're learning a good deal about whatever subject they've chosen for their projects.

For me, the most important product of the seminar is an enhanced sensitivity to aesthetic and truth value of documents claiming their validity from some purported relationship to the world of the real. Even if they never do another bit of fieldwork again, students in this seminar will have an enhanced critical understanding of folklore and oral history, of journalistic accounts of complex events, of television and print documentaries. They will be able to deal in a far more useful way with any piece of work that claims to represent that elusive butterfly called reality.

Works Cited

Äarne, Antti, and Stith Thompson. 1964. *The Types of the Folktale*. Helsinki: Folklore Fellows Communication No. 184.

Abrahams, Roger D. 1977. "Toward an Enactment-Centered Theory of Folklore." In *Frontiers of Folklore*, ed. William R. Bascom, pp. 79-120. Boulder: Westview.

Adams, Andy. 1903. *The Log of a Cowboy*. Boston: Houghton Mifflin.

Agee, James, and Walker Evans. 1980 [1941]. *Let Us Now Praise Famous Men*. Boston: Houghton-Mifflin.

Auslender, Leland. 1971. *The Birth of Aphrodite*. Color, 16mm., 13 min.

Bakhtin, Mikhail. 1981. *The Dialogic Imagination*. Ed. Michael Holquist, trans. Caryl Emerson and Michael Holquist. Austin: University of Texas Press.

Bartis, Peter. 1979. *Folklife and Fieldwork: A Layman's Introduction to Field Techniques*. Washington D.C.: American Folklife Center.

Baughman, Ernest W. 1966. *Type and Motif Index of the Folktales of England and North America*. The Hague: Indiana University Folklore Series No. 20.

Bettelheim, Bruno. 1977. *The Uses of Enchantment: The Meaning and Importance of Fairy Tales*. New York: Alfred A. Knopf.

Biebuyck, D. and K. C. Mateene. 1969. *The Mwindo Epic from the Banyanga*. California.

Bohannan, Laura. 1966. "Shakespeare in the Bush." *Natural History* 75:7, 28-33.

Bosustow, Stephen. 1977. *The Fisherman and His Wife*. Color, 16mm., 10 min.

Botkin, B. A. 1958. *Lay My Burden Down: A Folk History of Slavery*. Chicago: University of Chicago Press.

Bourek, Zlatko. 1971. *Venus and the Cat*. 16mm., 10 min.

Brewster, Paul G. 1953. *American Nonsinging Games*, Norman: University of Oklahoma Press.

Bronson, Bertrand H. 1959-71. *The Traditional Tunes of the Child Ballads with Their Texts*. 4 vol. Princeton: Princeton University Press.

Brunvand, Jan Harold. 1978. *The Study of American Folklore*. 2nd ed. New York: W. W. Norton.

_____. 1979. *Readings in American Folklore*. New York: W. W. Norton.

_____. 1981. *The Vanishing Hitchhiker: American Urban Legends and Their Meanings*. New York: W.W. Norton.

Buchan, David. 1973. *The Ballad and the Folk*. London: Routledge and Kegan Paul.

Bullard, Thomas Eddie. 1982. "Mysteries in the Eye of the Beholder: UFOs and their Correlates as a Folkloric Theme Past and Present." Ph.D. diss. Indiana University, Bloomington.

Byock, Jesse. 1982. *Feud in the Icelandic Saga*. California, 1982.

Capote, Truman. 1965. *In Cold Blood*. New York: Random House.

Catlin, George. 1967. *O-Kee-Pa: A Religious Ceremony and Other Customs of the Mandans*. Ed. John C. Ewers. New Haven: Yale University Press.

_____. 1973 [1844]. *Letters and Notes on the Manners, Customs, and Conditions of the North American Indians*. 2 vol. New York: Dover.

Child, Francis James. 1965 [1882-1898]. *The English and Scottish Popular Ballads*. 5 vol. New York: Dover.

Clarke, Kenneth and Mary Clarke. 1965. *A Folklore Reader*. New York: A.S. Barnes and Co.

Clarkson, Atelia, and Gilbert B. Cross. 1980. *World Folktales: A Scribner Resource Collection*. New York: Charles Scribner's Sons.

Clements, William M. 1969. "The Chain on the Tombstone." *Indiana Folklore* 2:90-96.

_____, and William E. Lightfoot. 1972. "The Legend of Stepp Cemetery." *Indiana Folklore* 5:92-141.

Clifford, James, and George E. Marcus, eds. *Writing Culture: The Poetics and Politics of Ethnography*. Berkeley: University of California Press.

Coffin, Tristram P. 1968. *Our Living Traditions*. New York: Basic Books.

Coffin, Tristram P. 1961. *Indian Tales of North America: An Anthology for the Adult Reader*. Philadelphia: American Folklore Society, Bibliographical and Special Series, Vol. 13.

Cohen, Hennig, ed. 1979. *American Folklore* (Cassette Lecture Series). Deland, Florida: Everett-Edwards, Inc.

Crapanzano, Vincent. 1986. "Hermes' Dilemma: The Masking of Subversion in Ethnographic Description." In Clifford and Marcus, pp. 51-76.

Creighton, Helen, and Edward D. Ives. 1962. "Eight Folktales from Miramichi as Told by Wilmot MacDonald" *Northeast Folklore* 4:51-60.

Cutting Baker, Holly, et al., eds. 1976. *Family Folklore*. Collected by the Folklore Program of the Festival of American Folklife. Washington, D.C.: Smithsonian Institution.

Dal, Erik. 1977. *Danish Ballads and Folksongs*. Trans. Henry Meyer. Copenhagen and New York: Rosenkilde and Bagger for the American-Scandinavian Foundation.

Davenport, Tom. 1975. *Hansel and Gretel: An Appalachian Version*. Color, 16mm., 16 min.

Dégh, Linda. 1963. "A Systematic Ordering of the Hungarian Legends." In *Tagung der "International Society for Folk-Narrative Research" in Antwerp*, pp. 66-74. Antwerpen: Centrum voor Studie en Documentatie.

_____. 1965. "Processes of Legend Formation." *Laographia* 22:77-78. (Proceedings of IV International Congress for Folk-Narrative Research, ed. G. A. Megas.)

_____. 1969. *Folktales and Society: Story-Telling in a Hungarian Peasant Community*. Bloomington: Indiana University Press.

_____. 1972. "Folk Narrative." In *Folklore and Folklife: An Introduction*, ed. Richard M. Dorson, pp. 53-83. Chicago: University of Chicago Press.

_____. 1978. "The Legend and the Sparrow." In *Studies in Turkish Folklore in Honor of Pertez and N. Boratav*, ed. Ilhan Basgöz and Mark Glazer, pp. 77-88. Bloomington: Indiana University Turkish Studies.

Derrida, Jacques. 1976. *Of Grammatology*. Trans. G.C. Spivak. Baltimore: Johns Hopkins.

Dickinson, Emily. 1955. *The Poems of Emily Dickinson*. Thomas H. Johnson, ed. Cambridge: Harvard University Press.

Dodds, E. R. 1951. *The Greeks and the Irrational*. Berkeley: University of California Press.

Dorson, Richard M. 1963. "Current Folklore Theories." *Current Anthropology* 4:93-112.

_____, ed. 1964. *Buying the Wind: Regional Folklore in the United States*. Chicago: University of Chicago Press.

_____. 1967. *American Negro Folktales*. Greenwich, Conn.: Fawcett.

_____. 1968 *The British Folklorists: A History*. Chicago: University of Chicago Press.

_____, ed. 1968. *Peasant Customs and Savage Myths: Selections from the British Folklorists*. 2 vol. Chicago, 1968.

_____, ed. 1972. *Folklore and Folklife: An Introduction*. Chicago: University of Chicago Press.

_____, ed. 1975. *Folktales Told Around the World*. Chicago: University of Chicago Press.

Dundes, Alan. 1972. *The Study of Folklore*. Englewood Cliffs, N.J.: Prentice-Hall.

_____. 1980. *Interpreting Folklore*. Bloomington: Indiana University Press.

_____. 1980. "Projection in Folklore: A Plea for Psychoanalytic Semiotics." In Dundes, *Interpreting Folklore*, pp. 33-61.

_____, and Alessandro Falassi. 1975. *La Terra in Piazza*. Berkeley: University of California Press.

Elley, Derek. 1984. *The Epic Film: Myth and History*. London: Routledge & Kegan Paul.

Entwistle, William. 1939. *European Balladry*. Oxford: Clarendon Press.

The Epic of Gilgamesh. 1972. Trans. and ed. N. K. Sandars, N. New York: Penguin.

Farb, Peter. 1974. *Word Play: What Happens When People Talk*. New York: Bantam.

Fenik, Bernard. 1986. *Homer and the Nibelungenlied: Comparative Studies in Epic Style*. Cambridge: Harvard University Press.

Fowler, Alastair. 1982. *Kinds of Literature: An Introduction to the Theory of Genres and Modes*. Cambridge: Harvard University Press.

Fowler, David. 1968. *A Literary History of the Popular Ballad*. Durham, N. C.: Duke University Press.

Freeman, Derek. 1983. *Margaret Mead and Samoa: The Making and Unmaking of an Anthropological Myth*. Cambridge: Harvard University Press.

Friedman, Albert B. 1956. *Folk Ballads of the English-Speaking World*. New York: Viking Press.

Gerould, Gordon H. 1932. *The Ballad of Tradition*. Oxford: Oxford University Press.

Greverus, Ina-Maria. 1980. *Forschendes Lernen und der Studentberg: Aus dem Alltag eines Uni-Instituts*. Frankfurt am Main, Institut for Kulturanthropologie.

Gilgamesh. In Pritchard, 1969:72-99.

Griaule, Marcel. 1965. *Conversations with Ogotemmêli*. London: Oxford University Press.

Grider, Sylvia A. 1973. "Dormitory Legend-Telling in Progress: Fall 1971-Winter 1973." *Indiana Folklore* 6:1-32.

_____. 1976. "The Supernatural Narratives of Children." Ph.D. diss. Indiana University, Bloomington.

Grimm, Jakob and Wilhelm. 1980. *The Grimms' German Folktales*. Trans. Francis P. Magoun, Jr., and Alexander H. Krappe. Carbondale: Southern Illinois University Press.

Grundtvig, Svend, Axel Olrik, H. Grüner-Nielsen, Erik Dal, et.al. 1853-1976. *Danmarks gamle Folkeviser*. 12 vol. and supplements. Copenhagen: Den Danske Literaturs Fremme, J. H. Schultz, et. al. Reprint with English-language introductions by Erik Dal, Universitets Jubilæets danske Samfund, 1966-1976 (volumes XI and XII comprising the music and indices are found only in this edition).

Gummere Francis B. 1897. *Old English Ballads*. Boston: Ginn and Company, Athenaeum Press Series. (This is a collection based on Child; it is important only for its introduction.)

______. 1907. *The Popular Ballad*. Boston: Houghton Mifflin.

______. 1901. *The Beginnings of Poetry*. New York: Macmillan.

Hall, Gary. 1973. "The Big Tunnel: Legends and Legend-Telling." *Indiana Folklore* 6:139-173.

Hand, Wayland D. 1961. "Abergläubische Grundelemente in der amerikanischen Volkserzählung." In *International Kongress der Volkserzählungsforscher in Kiel und Kopenhagen*, pp. 105-112. Berlin: Walter der Gruyter.

______, ed. 1961, 1964. *Popular Beliefs and Superstitions from North Carolina*. The Frank C. Brown Collection of North Carolina Folklore, vols. 6 and 7. Durham, N.C.: Duke University Press.

______. 1963. "Ein Katalog der americanischen Sagen." In *Tagung der "International Society for Folk-Narrative Research" in Antwerp*, pp. 43-48. Antwerpen: Centrum voor Studie en Documentatie.

______. 1965. "Status of European and American Legend Study." *Current Anthropology* 6:439-466.

Hansen, Wm. F. 1978. "The Homeric Epics and Oral Poetry." In Oinas, 1978, 7-26.

Hart, W. M. 1907. *Ballad and Epic*. Boston: Harvard Studies and Notes in Philology.

Heidel, Alexander. 1965. *The Babylonian Genesis*. 2nd ed. University of Chicago Press.

Hemenway, Robert E. 1978. *Zora Neale Hurston*. Urbana: University of Illinois Press.

Herskovits, Melville J. 1956. *Man and His Works*. New York: Knopf.

Hodgart, M. J. C. 1950. *The Ballads*. London: Hutchinson's University Library.

Homer. 1951. *The Iliad*. Trans. Richmond Lattimore. Chicago: University of Chicago Press, 1951.

______. 1963. *The Odyssey*. Trans. Robert Fitzgerald. Garden City: Anchor.

Hurston, Zora Neale. 1978 [1935]. *Mules and Men*. Bloomington: Indiana University Press.

______. 1981 [1938]. *Tell My Horse*. Berkeley: Turtle Island.

Hustvedt, S. B. 1930. *Ballad Books and Ballad Men*. Cambridge: Harvard University Press.

Hymes, Dell. 1975. "Breakthrough into Performance." In Dan Ben-Amos and Kenneth S. Goldstein, eds., *Folklore: Performance and Communication*, pp. 11-74. The Hague: Mouton.

Jackson, Bruce. 1987. *Fieldwork*. Urbana: University of Illinois Press.

______. 1988. "What People Like Us Are Saying When We Say We're Saying the Truth." *Journal of American Folklore* 101:276-292.

Jansen, William Hugh. 1965. "The Esoteric-Exoteric Factor in Folklore." In Dundes, *The Study of Folklore*, pp. 43-51.

Kaplan, Abraham. *The Conduct of Inquiry: Methodology for Behavioral Science*. San Francisco: Chandler Publishing Co. 1964.

Kaufman, Gloria and Mary Kay Blakely. 1980. *Pulling Our Own Strings: Feminist Humor & Satire*. Bloomington: Indiana University Press.

Kesey, Ken. 1962. *One Flew Over the Cuckoo's Nest*. New York: New American Library.

Kirshenblatt-Gimblett, Barbara. 1974. "A Parable in Context: A Social Interactional Analysis of Storytelling Performance." In Dan Ben-Amos and Kenneth S.

Goldstein, eds., *Folklore: Performance and Communication.* The Hague: Mouton, pp. 105-30.

Knapp, Mary and Herbert. 1976. *One Potato, Two Potato.* New York: Norton.

Kosko, Maria. 1966. *Le fils assassiné (At 939A): Étude d'un theme legendaire.* Helsinki. Kottak, Conrad Phillip, ed. 1982. *Researching American Culture.* Ann Arbor: University of Michigan Press.

Langlois, Janet. 1977. "Belle Gunness, The Lady Bluebeard: Community Legend as Metaphor." Ph.D. diss. Indiana University, Bloomington.

_____. 1978. "Mary Whales I Believe in You: Myth and Ritual Subdued." *Indiana Folklore* 11:5-34.

Laubach, David C. 1980. *Introduction to Folklore.* Rochelle Park, N.J.: Hayden Book Company.

Leach, MacEdward. 1955. *The Ballad Book.* New York: Harper and Brothers.

Lenihan, John H. 1980. *Showdown: Confronting Modern America in the Western Film.* Urbana: University of Illinois Press.

Liestøl, Knut. 1946. "Scottish and Norwegian Ballads." *Studia Norvegica* (Oslo): 3-16.

Lord, Albert B. 1960. *The Singer of Tales.* Cambridge: Harvard University Press.

Lomax, John A. 1947. *Adventures of a Ballad Hunter.* New York: Macmillan.

Lüthi, Max. 1976. *Once Upon a Time: On the Nature of Fairy Tales.* Trans. Lee Chadeyane and Paul Gottwald. Bloomington: Indiana University Press.

Mailer, Norman. 1979. *The Executioner's Song.* Boston: Houghton-Mifflin.

Malaurie, Jean. 1982. *The Last Kings of Thule.* Trans. Adrienne Foulke. New York: Dutton.

Masumoto, D. Mas. 1983. "Brown Rice Sushi." *Western Folklore* 42:140-144.

McClatchy, J.D. 1978. *Anne Sexton: The Artist and Her Critics.* Bloomington: Indiana University Press.

Mayhew, Henry. 1968 [1861-1862]. *London Labour and the London Poor.* 4 vols. New York: Dover.

Mitchell, W. J. T. 1978. *Blake's Composite Art: A Study of the Illuminated Poetry.* Princeton: Princeton University Press.

Montell, William Lynwood. 1976. *Ghosts along the Cumberland: Deathlore in the Kentucky Foothills.* Knoxville: University of Tennessee Press.

Moore, Willard Burgess 1973. *Molokan Oral Tradition: Legends and Memorates of an Ethnic Sect.* Berkeley: University of California Press.

Mullen, Patrick B. 1978. *I Heard the Old Fishermen Say.* Austin: University of Texas Press.

Oinas, Felix, ed. 1978. *Heroic Epic and Saga.* Bloomington: Indiana University Press.

Okpewho, Isidore. 1979. *The Epic in Africa: Toward a Poetics of the Oral Performance.* New York: Columbia University Press.

Olrik, Axel. 1939. *A Book of Danish Ballads.* Trans. E.M. Smith-Dampier. Princeton, New Jersey: Princeton University Press for The American-Scandinavian Foundation.

_____. 1965. "Epic Laws of Folk Narrative." In Dundes, *The Study of Folklore,* pp. 129-141.

Ondaatje, Michael. 1970. Collected Works of Billy the Kid. Toronto: University of Toronto Press.

Ong, Walter J. 1982. *Orality and Literacy: The Technologizing of the Word.* London: Methuen.

Oring, Elliott. 1981. *Israeli Humor: The Content and Structure of the Chizbat of the Palmah.* Albany: State University of New York Press.

Page, Denys. 1959. *History and the Homeric Iliad*. Berkeley: University of California Press.

Pound, Ezra. n.d. [1960] *ABC of Reading*. Norfolk, CT: New Directions.

Pritchard James B., ed. 1969. *Ancient Near Eastern Texts Relating to the Old Testament*. 3rd ed. Princeton: Princeton University Press.

Propp, Vladimir. 1979. *The Morphology of the Folktale*. Trans. by Laurence Scott. Austin: University of Texas Press.

Radin, Paul. 1973. *The Trickster: A Study in American Indian Mythology*. New York: Schocken Books.

Randolph, Vance. 1976. *Pissing in the Snow and Other Ozark Folktales*. Urbana: University of Illinois Press.

Redfield, James M. 1975. *Nature and Culture in the Iliad*. Chicago: University of Chicago Press. 1975

Richmond, W. Edson. 1963. "'Den utrue egetemann': A Norwegian Ballad and Formulaic Composition." *Norveg 10* (Oslo: Universitetsforlaget):59-88.

_____. 1972. "Narrative Folk Poetry." In Dorson, *Folklore and Folklife: An Introduction*, 85-98.

Rose, Dan. 1987. *Black American Street Life: South Philadelphia, 1969-1971*. Philadephia: University of Pennsylvania Press.

Russell, Louise B. 1978. "Legendary Narratives Inherited by Children of Mexican-American Ancestry: Cultural Pluralism and the Persistence of Tradition." Ph.D. diss. Indiana University, Bloomington.

Sargent, Helen Child, and George Lyman Kittredge. 1914. *English and Scottish Popular Ballads*. Boston: Houghton Mifflin (Student's Cambridge Edition. 1904.)

Sebeok, Thomas A., ed. 1968. *Myth: A Symposium*. Bloomington: Indiana University Press.

Seitel, Peter. 1980. *See So That We May See: Performances and Interpretations of Traditional Tales from Tanzania*. Bloomington: Indiana University Press.

Seki, Keigo. 1963. *Folktales of Japan*. Chicago: University of Chicago Press.

Sexton, Anne. 1971. *Transformations*. Boston: Houghton Mifflin.

Sexton, Linda Gray, and Lois Ames. 1977. *Anne Sexton: A Self-Portrait in Letters*. Boston: Houghton Mifflin.

Siringo, Charles. 1979 [1886]. *A Texas Cow Boy: or, Fifteen Years on the Hurricane Deck of a Spanish Pony*. Lincoln: University of Nebraska Press.

Sliney, Deanna. 1974. "Haunted Sites in Indiana: A Preliminary Survey." *Indiana Folklore* 7:27-52.

Snell, Bruno. 1953. *The Discovery of the Mind: The Greek Origins of European Thought*. Trans. T.G. Rosenmeyer. Cambridge: Harvard University Press.

Sproul, Barbara C. 1979. *Primal Myths: Creating the World*. San Francisco: Harper and Row.

Stone, Kay Stone. 1981. "Märchen to Fairy Tale: An Unmagical Transformation." *Western Folklore*, pp. 232-244.

Tallman, Richard, and Laurna Tallman. 1978. *Country Folks: A Handbook for Student Folklore Collectors*. Batesville: Arkansas College Folklore Archives Publications, 1978.

"Tagung der Sagencommission der International Society for Folk-Narrative Research." 1964. *Acta Ethnogrpahica* 13:129-131.

Taylor, Archer. 1951. *English Riddles from Oral Tradition*. Berkeley and Los Angeles: University of California Press.

Tedlock, Dennis. 1983. *The Spoken Word and the Work of Interpretation.* Philadelphia: University of Pennsylvania Press.

Thigpen, Kenneth A. 171. "Adolescent Legends in Brown County: A Survey." *Indiana Folklore* 4:141-215.

Thompson, Stith. 1955-58. *Motif-Index of Folk-Literature.* 6 vol. Rev. and Enlarged. Bloomington, Indiana: Indiana University Press; Copenhagen: Rosenkilde and Bagger.

______. 1956. *Folklorist's Progress.* Unpublished manuscript.

Thoms, William. "Folklore." In Dundes, *The Study of Folklore,* pp. 4-6.

Jeffrey H. Tigay. 1982. *The Evolution of the Gilgamesh Epic.* Philadelphia: University of Pennsylvania Press.

______. *Empirical Models for Biblical Criticism.* Philadelphia: University of Pennsylvania Press.

Toelken, Barre. 1979. *The Dynamics of Folklore,* and *Instructor's Manual: The Dynamics of Folklore,* Boston: Houghton Mifflin Co.

______. "Preface and Introduction: Into Folkloristics with Gun and Camera." In Toelken, *The Dynamics of Folklore,* pp. ix-21.

Tucker, Elizabeth G. 1977. "Tradition and Creativity in the Story Telling of Pre-Adolescent Girls." Ph.D. diss. Indiana University, Bloomington.

Wells, Evelyn Kendrick. 1950. *The Ballad Tree.* New York: Ronald Press.

Whitehead, Tony Larry, and Mary Ellen Conaway, eds. 1986. *Self, Sex, and Gender in Cross-Cultural Fieldwork.* Urbana: University of Illinois Press.

Wilgus, D. K. 1959. *Anglo-American Folksong Scholarship since 1898.* New Brunswick, New Jersey: Rutgers University Press.

Wilson, William A. 1981. *On Being Human: The Folklore of Mormon Missionaries.* Logan: Utah State University Press. Reprinted in *New York Folklore* 8:3-4 (1982), 5-27.

Wimberly, L. C. 1928. *Folklore in the English and Scottish Popular Ballads.* Chicago: University of Chicago Press. (Reprint: New York: Dover, 1965.)

Winkless, Terence H. 1971. *Foster's Release.* Color, 16mm., 14 min.

Wister, Owen. 1979. [1902]. *The Virginian.* New York: Signet.

Zeitlin, Steven J., Amy J. Kotkin, and Holly Cutting Baker. 1982. *A Celebration of American Family Folklore.* New York: Pantheon Books.

Contributors

BRUCE A. BEATIE earned his Ph.D. in Comparative Literature at Harvard University after earlier studies at the University of Colorado and the University of California at Berkeley. He is now Professor of German and Comparative Literature at Cleveland State University, where he chaired the Department of Modern Languages from 1970 until 1977. Originally a medievalist specializing in lyric poetry, he has broadened his teaching and research interests into folklore, the humanities, language-teaching methodology, and the opera. He is the author of more than fifty publications dealing with all these areas. He is now working on three books: one on the morphology of Arthurian narrative, another on best-seller lists, and a third on developing second-language reading skills.

ROBERT H. BYINGTON received his Ph.D. in English from the University of Pennsylvania in 1959, and for the next fourteen years taught English and Folklore, respectively, at Lycoming College, Williamsport, Pa., where he was chairman of the English Department, and at various institutions in Pittsburgh under the auspices of the Pittsburgh Council on Higher Education (the consortium of Pittsburgh colleges and universities). During most of that time (1960-1973) he was Executive Secretary of the Pennsylvania Folklore Society, and also served as chairman of several important American Folklore Society committees, including the Committee on Applied Folklore. From 1972-1974 he was second vice president of the AFS. He joined the staff of the Smithsonian Institution in 1974 as deputy director of the Festival of American Folklife, and was deputy director of Folklife Programs there when he resigned his position in 1978. He is currently chairman of the Department of English at the University of North Carolina at Wilmington.

LARRY DANIELSON, an associate professor in the English Department of the University of Illinois at Urbana-Champaign, teaches courses in folklore and film. He often presents papers and informal lectures on folklore topics to academic and non-academic groups. His research interests include the uses of ethnic folk tradition in contemporary American life, oral and popular print narratives about the paranormal, folk history, and film/folklore relationships. He is editor of the *Publications of the American Folklore Society*, and has served as film review editor for *Western Folklore*, edited *Studies in Folklore and Ethnicity* (1978), and contributed articles to such journals as *Journal of the Folklore Institute*, *Western Folklore*, *Indiana Folklore*, and the *Oral History Review*, and to *Folklore On Two Continents: Essays in Honor of Linda Dégh* (1980) and *The Occult in America: New Historical Perspectives* (1983).

LINDA DÉGH is distinguished professor of Folklore at the Folklore Institute, and member of the faculty of the Russian and East European Institute and the West European Studies Program of Indiana University. She received her Ph.D. at the Eötvos Lorand University of Budapest, Hungary, and joined the faculty of Indiana University in 1965. She has published 22 books and more than 100 articles, mostly in the fields of folk narrative, the sociology of story telling, folklore in urban and rural ethnic contexts in Europe and North America. She is founder and editor of

Indiana Folklore (1965—). She was awarded the Guiseppe Pitre Prize (1963) and a Guggenheim Fellowship (1971). She is a member of the Joint Commission of the American Council of Learned Societies and the Hungarian Academy of Sciences representing anthropology and folklore. She served the American Folklore Society as president (1981), as president of the Fellows (1972), and as member of the editorial board of *Journal of American Folklore*. She was director and chair of the Folklore Institute from 1981 until 1984.

LYDIA FISH received her B.A. (1960) and M.A. (1962) degrees in history from the University of North Carolina (her M.A. thesis was on James I and witchcraft). She spent the next two years teaching history in the English government school system and performing in folksong clubs in London. After her return to the United States in 1964, she sang professionally, then taught history at the University of North Carolina extension division at Fort Bragg for a year. Her students were members of the 82nd Airborne and the Fifth Special Forces, on their way back from or to Vietnam. In 1965 she entered the Folklore Program at Indiana University. Her dissertation was on occupational folklore of coal miners in the north of England. Since 1967 she has been on the faculty of State University College at Buffalo. She has done fieldwork in several Buffalo ethnic communities, mostly in the area of religious and calendar custom. For the past few years, she has been most concerned with the pilgrimage and has done fieldwork at the shrine of St. Anne at Beaupré in Quebec and at the Vietnam veterans' memorial in Washington. She has published articles on all these subjects, as well as on urban religious legends.

THOMAS A. GREEN is associate professor of English at Texas A&M University where he teaches literature and an undergraduate introduction to folklore. While serving on the faculties of the University of Texas at Austin, the University of Texas at El Paso, Idaho State University, and the University of Delaware, he taught a variety of courses in folklore, literature, anthropology, and linguistics. His published work includes articles on American Indian folklore, riddles, cultural revitalization movements, and folk drama, as well as *The Language of Riddles: New Perspectives* (1984), co-authored with William J. Pepicello. Green currently serves as film review editor of the *Journal of American Folklore*.

ROBERT A. GEORGES is Professor of English and Folklore at the University of California, Los Angeles, where he has taught since 1966, following earlier academic appointment in the Department of English at the University of Kansas (1963-1966). He holds an M.A. in English and American Literature from the University of Pennsylvania and a Ph.D. in Folklore from Indiana University (1964). From 1966-1982 he served as vice-chairman, and since 1982 he has been chairman, of the UCLA Folklore and Mythology Program. Georges's principal areas of teaching and research are traditional narrating and narrative, folk speech, American immigrant folklore, methodology, and the history of folklore studies. His major publications include *Studies on Mythology* (1968); *People Studying People: The Human Element in Fieldwork*, co-authored with Michael Owen Jones (1980); *Greek-American Folk Beliefs and Narratives* (1980); and *American Immigrant and Ethnic Folklore: An Annotated Bibliography*, co-compiled with Stephen Stern (1982). He has held offices in Kansas, California, and American folklore societies; and he has been the recipient of a Guggenheim fellowship and grants from the Ford Foundation and other private and public foundations and agencies.

EDWARD D. IVES was born in White Plains, New York, in 1925. After a three-year stretch in the Marines, he received his B.A. from Hamilton College (1948), his M.A. in Medieval Literature from Columbia University (1950), and his Ph. D. in Folklore from Indiana University (1962). He first taught at Illinois College (Jacksonville, Illinois) from 1950 through 1953, then at CCNY from 1953 to 1954; since 1955 he has been on the faculty of the University of Maine at Orono, first in the English Department and since 1967 in the Anthropology Department (he now serves as chairman of that department). In 1958, together with Bacil Kirtley, he founded the Northeast Folklore Society, and since 1961 he has been editor of the Society's journal (more nearly a monograph series), *Northeast Folklore*. He is director of the Northeast Archives of Folklore and Oral History, which he founded. He has been a Guggenheim Fellow (1965) and a member of the National Endowment for the Arts Folk Arts Panel (1977-1980); he was elected a Fellow of the American Folklore Society in 1980. He likes to trout fish, and while he will sit at the same table with a worm fisherman, he will not pass him anything. His publications include *Larry Gorman: The Man Who Made the Songs* (1964), *Lawrence Doyle: The Farmer-poet of Prince Edward Island* (1971), *Joe Scott: The Woodsman-songmaker* (1978) and *The Tape-recorded Interview* (1980).

BRUCE JACKSON is director of the Center for Studies in American Culture and professor of English and Comparative Literature, State University of New York at Buffalo; he directs the English Department's Ph.D. Program in Folklore, Mythology, and Film Studies. Jackson is the author or editor of twenty books and director of five documentary films. Before joining the SUNY/Buffalo faculty in 1967, Jackson was a Junior Fellow in the Harvard Society of Fellows. His research and filmwork have been supported by grants from the Guggenheim Foundation, NEA, NEH, Wenner-Gren Foundation, ACLS, Playboy Foundation and other foundations and agencies. He has been president of the American Folklore Society and chairman of the board of trustees of the American Folklife Center in the Library of Congress. He is the editor of *Journal of American Folklore*. His most recent folklore books are *Fieldwork* (1987) and *The Centennial Index* (1988, co-edited with Michael Taft and Harvey S. Axlerod).

W. F. H. NICOLAISEN is Professor of English and Folklore at the State University of New York at Binghamton. Before moving to Binghamton in 1969, he had been on the staff of the School of Scottic Studies in the University of Edinburgh (1956-1969) and had also taught at the University of Glasgow, University College of Dublin, and Ohio State University. He is a former president of the New York Folklore Society (1971-73, 1973-75, and 1981-83), the American Name Society (1977), the Fourteenth International Congress of Onomastic Sciences (1981), and the American Folklore Society (1982-83).

W. EDSON RICHMOND received his Ph.D. in Medieval Literature from Ohio State University in 1947. He joined the faculty of Indiana University in 1945 and has served as acting chairman of the Folklore Program (1952-1954) and acting director of the Folklore Institute (1981-1982); he is presently professor of English, Comparative Literature, and Folklore. Richmond has been editor of *Hoosier Folklore*, *Midwest Folklore*, and, since June 1981, of the *Journal of Folklore Research* (formerly the *Journal of the Folklore Institute*). He has been book review and acting editor of the *Journal of American Folklore*. He was for fifteen years the bibliographer of the

American Folklore Society; he also served as that organization's parliamentarian and vice-president. He was elected to the AFS Society of Fellows in its second year and has served as its secretary, vice-president and president. Since 1980 he has been the AFS delegate to the American Council of Learned Societies. Richmond visited the Universities of Helsinki and Oslo as a Fulbright fellow and was three times visiting professor at the University of Oslo. His publications of significance have all had to do with traditional ballads. In 1977 Richmond was elected to the Norwegian Academy of Sciences.

NEIL V. ROSENBERG was born in Seattle, Washington. His training includes a B.A. in history from Oberlin College and the M.A. and Ph.D. in folklore from Indiana University. He presently teaches in the Folklore Department at Memorial University of Newfoundland, where he is director of the Memorial University of Newfoundland Folklore and Language Archive. He is a former president of the Folklore Studies Association of Canada, has served on the editorial board and council of the Society for Ethnomusicology, and was a member of the executive board of the American Folklore Society.

ELLEN J. STEKERT is professor of English at the University of Minnesota. At Cornell, she majored in philosophy and for three years assisted Harold W. Thompson teaching folklore courses in the Department of English. Inspired by Ben Botkin to continue her graduate work in folklore, she attended Indiana University for four years, finishing her M.A. and most of her Ph.D. work there. To write her dissertation (on creativity in folksinging) she transferred to the University of Pennsylvania to work with MacEdward Leach, Tristram Coffin and other ballad scholars. During her nine years at Wayne State University she reorganized and developed the current Wayne State University Folklore Archive. After a year as visiting professor in anthropology at the University of California, she joined the faculty of the University of Minnesota. In 1976 she drafted and helped pass into law the Minnesota legislation which established a Center for the Study of Minnesota Folklife to be housed in the Minnesota Historical Society. She spent four years directing this Center while teaching full time. During this period she also served on the executive board of the American Folklore Society and was elected president in 1977. Since then she has been teaching, consulting, and serving on the American Folklore Society's Centennial Coordinating Council. Her current major research project is a biography of Malvina Reynolds, the songwriter, political activist and performer who died in 1978.

ZORA DEVRNJA ZIMMERMAN was born in Marienbad, Czechoslovakia in 1945. After completing the Ph.D. in Comparative Literature at the State University of New York at Buffalo in 1974, she began teaching at Iowa State University in Ames. An associate professor of English, she teaches courses in folklore, the ancient classics, the Romantic period, and the Bible as literature. She has published essays and review articles on Serbian folk customs and traditional poetry, current Yugoslav literature, and contemporary American poetry. Her forthcoming book, Serbian *Folk Poetry: The Oldest Epics*, combines original translations with analytical essays.

(Notes on contributors other than the editor are from the 1984 edition.)